Mobs and
Demagogues

Studies in
American History and Culture, No. 3

Other Titles in This Series

Mobs and Demagogues

The New York Response to Collective Violence
in the Early Nineteenth Century

by
Paul O. Weinbaum

umi
RESEARCH PRESS

Library of Congress Cataloging in Publication Data

Weinbaum, Paul Owen, 1945-
    Mobs and demagogues.

    (Studies in American history and culture ; no. 3)
    Bibliography: p.
    Includes index.
    1. Riots—New York (City)—History. 2. Riot control—
New York (City)—History. 3. Violence—New York (City)—
History. I. Title. II. Series.

HV6483.N7W44 1978   363.3'2'097471   78-27662
ISBN 0-8357-0978-7
ISBN 0-8357-0979-5 pbk.

CONTENTS

TABLES

CONTENTS

FIGURES

CHAPTER ONE

RIOTING BEGINS: THE ELECTION OF 1834

I

Mob violence moved to the forefront of the American consciousness during 1834—and for good reason. That year, anti-Catholic rioters burnt the Ursuline Convent in Charlestown, Massachusetts and New York City rioters attacked the homes and churches of Negroes and abolitionists. In less well-known incidents, Philadelphia was the scene of a major race riot in August and a major election riot in October; and railroad laborers rioted outside Baltimore in June and again in November. In the course of the year, one New York newspaper reported smaller scale mob violence in an additional twelve places[1]—Utica; Portsmouth, New Hampshire; New Orleans; Newark; Buffalo; Lockport, NewYork; New Britain; Plainfield, New Jersey; Richmond; and Troy; and among canal laborers in Maryland and railroad laborers in Massachusetts.

New Yorkers read of these repeated unleashings of popular fury with mounting concern, and as the rioting in the nation continued, they gradually came to consider one riot—the riot during their own charter, or municipal, election of April—as the start of this violence. Although anti-abolitionist and anti-Negro feeling was central to the mid 1830s riots, as Leonard Richards pursuasively argues,[2] a balanced discussion of New York City mob violence during this period must begin with the election riot, an event that contemporaries considered especially significant.

At the core of the election riot was the matter of where power in the nation should lie and what was the proper style of political leadership. President Andrew Jackson was allegedly usurping power at the expense of Congress and local leaders, and he was organizing a political party to carry out this policy.[3] The particular point at issue was the President's decision to destroy the Bank of the United States.[4] With Congress, in the spring of 1834, debating the removal of the deposits from the Bank, New York's municipal election was turned into a momentous test of strength between Jackson and his opponents. According to the anti-Jacksonians, the election could determine the future of the Republic. A victory in New York, assuming national importance, became unusually urgent. Panic which lay just beneath the surface, readily turned the election into a riot.

The best evidence for this outlook, buttressing the public pronouncements of the party press, is found in the private correspondence of Gulian C. Verplanck, the Whig mayoral candidate. In the weeks preceding the election, Verplanck exchanged letters with his liaison in Congress, R. H. Wilde.[5] The two men discussed campaign strategy and the role that national political leaders could play in New York's municipal election, but this concern with tactics did not obfuscate what they saw as the larger issue—the fate of the republic. The Democratic party had to be defeated.

Wilde and his Washington, D. C. political friends had urged Verplanck to run before he was nominated. They believed the New York City election was crucial to their cause. On the result of this election and the Virginia election hung "everything."[6] These contests alone were "standing between us and the dictatorship."[7] Wilde feared that "if we are defeated in both quarters I consider there is nothing left to struggle for, the Republic exists no longer."[8]

Once nominated, Verplanck did not hesitate to remind the Wilde group of its responsibility for his decision. Verplanck reminded Wilde that "my friends at Washington have aided to force me into the field and must help me to come off triumphantly." He asked Wilde to use his influence with politicians and others who might have an effect on the vote in New York.[9] From Washington there came a positive reply: "everything shall be done, that can be done." Wilde had convened a meeting to discuss Irish Catholic support. Daniel Webster was present, and, when told of the campaign's importance, offered his help. Wilde assured Verplanck that he would keep all in Washington awake "to the importance of doing every thing for you."[10]

Philip Hone's diary provides additional evidence of the importance the anti-Jacksonians attached to the Charter election. Hone represented a wing of the coalition which had played no role in the Verplanck nomination, yet his diary echoes the themes of the Verplanck-Wilde correspondence. Although he thought Verplanck an impractical man, and, in an allusion to his recent conversion to the cause, "politically unstable," Hone still supported the party's candidate: "The salvation of the Country depends in a great measure upon the defeat of the Jackson Party in the Struggle which will come on next month, and personal predilictions must give way to the public good."[11] In Washington in early March, Hone found the Congressional leaders already keenly interested in the municipal election. Well before the nominees had been named and the campaign begun, Henry Clay told him the New York State and Pennsylvania elections were their "only hope;"[12] and John Quincy Adams went further and singled out the city's Charter election as of particular significance.[13] In early April, Webster repeated to the leaders of the city's anti-Jackson coalition what he had said to Hone the month before. "The Hopes of our Friends there (in Washington) to bring about a favorable change in the affairs of the Country rely mainly upon the success of the great struggle which is to take place in New York."[14]

It is clear, then, that important politicians saw the election as a crucial one. The general atmosphere in which it was conducted was highly charged. Moreover, in the context of 1834, partisan politics was a species of warfare. When Congress debated the removal of the deposits, a number of Congressmen spoke belligerently. Some of the rhetoric was laden with literary conceits intended merely to score debating points. Representative George McDuffie of South Carolina, for example, called his opening remarks "a skirmishing attack on the outposts of the enemy in his front, in order to compel them to come out from behind their intrenchments, expose their position, and take their line of battle in open field."[15] He used such words as "generalship," "reenforcements," and "retreat." Representative John Y. Mason, in reply, borrowed from McDuffie's metaphor and labeled the Jacksonian attempt to limit debate as the "stern order of 'charge bayonet,'" aimed at bringing "a maneuvering adversary to decisive action."[16]

Congressional rhetoric would, at times, relate more closely to a violent reality. When an anti-Jacksonian Philadelphia voter was beaten to death, Wilde, Verplanck's friend, eulogized "the patriot"—"our gallant and noble comrade" who "fell, as he had ever stood, in the front rank warring for the Constitution. Here, as in battle, in our companions fall, we close ranks and hurry on."[17] Senator William Campbell Preston spoke more plainly. "It may well be said that we were in a revolution, hitherto bloodless, but it was not so now. Murder had been committed; blood had been spilt; the life of an individual had been sacrificed, in performing a duty secured to him by the Constitution."[18]

In New York City, the most belligerent anti-Jackson politician of influence was James Watson Webb, the editor of the *Morning Courier and New-York Enquirer*. A youthful thirty-two in 1834, Webb had been a professional soldier who had volunteered for duty on the frontier. In 1827, he resigned his commission after a dispute with his commanding officer had led him to the brink of a duel. When he came to New York soon after to begin his journalistic career, he supported Andrew Jackson, a man whose military exploits he admired. Webb continued to support Jackson until the summer of 1832. In an age noted for vitriolic personal journalism, Webb stood out; his feuds were infamous. In May 1830, he went so far as to travel to Washington to personally confront Duff Green, the Calhoun supporter who edited the *United States Telegraph*. Green, afraid for his life, met him with a gun, but Webb, in a show of bravado, dared Green to fight without weapons. Webb switched political sides, as did so many anti-Jacksonians, over the bank; and, in 1834, the tense local election made Webb, with his militaristic outlook, the man of the hour.[19]

Webb abandoned moderate political rhetoric beginning with the election of 1830. He excoriated the Anti-Masons, calling them a "bitter and persecuting party," which "pursues every citizen with fire and sword." Every freeman had to "buckle his armour, and put it down." Webb warned that "the flames of the Inquisition and of the *Auto da foi* [fe] and the rack, and other tortures" would follow Anti-Masonry's triumph. In the purely local elections of 1831 and 1832, Webb's frame of reference was the same, if the level of invective was lower. The opposition remained the "enemy."[20] In his language, Webb differed sharply from William Cullen Bryant, the poet, and editor of the other leading Jackson paper, the *Evening Post*.

In April 1834, Webb's was only one Whig voice countenancing forceful defensive measures. The day before the election, Whig leaders considered closing their businesses at noon on the three polling days. Webb supported the proposal. He spoke of the need to protect workers against the Jacksonian "bullies." "Thousands of mechanics, merchants, traders, and clerks" would become available for quieting the "hired disturbers of the peace."[21]

The first day of the election, Webb's paper charged, two "Tory bullies" had attacked a Whig newspaper carrier; the incident, the paper claimed, showed that a Reign of Terror would follow a Jacksonian victory. The Jacksonians, furthermore, had threatened to tear off the clothes of any clerk who voted and had even boasted the support of enough office-holders and bullies to carry out such acts. Webb dared the Jacksonians to act as he predicted they would.[22]

Webb's strident attacks aside, it was obvious that intense excitement gripped the city. With the two parties of equal strength, the outcome of the mayoralty election and control of the Common Council remained in doubt. Every vote counted.[23] The party faithful was warned by several Whig papers to guard against voting irregularities. The Jacksonians were printing "Whig" ballots that would be disqualified if used; the Jacksonians were attempting to have unqualified persons vote.[24]

Nor was this all. The Whigs took the offensive with a direct appeal to the electorate. They organized a procession which was headed by a model frigate manned by seamen. Two bands of music and some five hundred additional seamen followed the ship the Whigs named the "Constitution." About one thousand other persons, joining along the way, brought up the rear. The procession wound its way through Broadway,

Greenwich Street, and the Bowery on its way to Wall and Broad streets, a major commercial intersection; it then went along the wharves, stopping all the while at the houses of Whig citizens.[25]

Serious violence began on Tuesday, the afternoon of the first day.[26] According to the Whigs, between 100 and 200 Jacksonians entered their sixth ward committee room, tore down the banners, destroyed the Whig ballots, and assaulted the twenty or so Whigs present in the room. Several of the Whigs were beaten into insensibility, and the high constable, on intervening, was also beaten severely. According to some reports, an ex-alderman led the invading Jacksonians.

In general, the Whig press reacted with great indignation, but the newspaper editors who had earlier sought to make violence into an issue, showed consistency, and published the most inflammatory accounts. William Leete Stone's *Commercial Advertiser* charged: the gang of "infuriated wretches" had delineated the "true spirit of Jacksonism"—"in characters of blood." According to that paper's account of the attack, the rioters, some armed with knives, had held up a Whig they had presumably beaten to death "in triumph to the exulting mob by the hair of his head."[27]

Webb's *Courier and Enquirer* published an even more provocative account. A "REIGN OF TERROR" had begun. "The blood of Freemen had been shed." "The very foundation of our social system" had been "uprooted and cast to the four winds of Heaven!!" Web claimed that after the Jacksonians attacked the Whig committee room, they had followed even the wounded and disabled "from house to house with a bloodthirsty spirit which would have disgraced Paris in its most revolutionary days." He reported that one man, pronounced dead and carried off, was "even then pursued by these fiends in human shape to get possession of his body!!!"[28]

The Whig reports, especially those of Webb and Stone, provided a distorted account of what actually had occured. No Whigs had been mortally wounded, and, in fact, the Whigs (though not necessarily deserving the beating they endured) had provoked the disturbance. The *Evening Post*, a Jacksonian paper which neither approved nor justified the violence, told a different story, and its account, at least its crucial part, was corroborated by the *Journal of Commerce*, a Whig paper, and the *New-Yorker*, a Whig-leaning paper. The *Post* reported that the Whigs had sent twenty young men from the first and second wards to observe the sixth Ward election. One of them read a scurrilous article from the *Courier and Enquirer*, interspersing his reading with irritating comments. After he remarked "we should get along well enough if it were not for the low Irish," the sixth ward Irish had had enough and the disturbance began. At first, the crowd only pushed the Whig outsiders but it did not take long for fighting to begin. The outsiders were roughly handled and forced to flee. The *Post* claimed that no serious injuries resulted.[29]

The Whig faithful adhered to their version of events and reacted bellingerently. Meeting at Masonic Hall Tuesday night, they listened to the sixth ward Whig Committee's appeal for protection and they appointed a committee to demand of the mayor protection at the polls. The mayor refused this demand. He claimed that the regular police could not be spared. Instead, he offered to appoint special constables drawn from citizen volunteers. The offer was distrusted. The Whigs resolved to meet at Masonic Hall at 7:30 a.m. the next morning and proceed as a body to the sixth ward poll to guard it until the Mayor appointed a "sufficient number" of special constables.

A Tammany mayor held office, so the Whig action was understandable; but it also reflected an unreasonable fear. The Whigs were reacting to a situation that did not exist. From the Masonic Hall meeting came the statement that "the authority of the POLICE of the City has been set at defiance by a band of *hirelings*, *mercenaries*, and *bullies* in the 6th ward and the LIVES of our fellow citizens put in jeopardy and. . .it is evident that we are in a state of ANARCHY which requires the prompt and efficient interposition of every friend of good order who is disposed to sustain the Constitution and the Laws."[30]

Tuesday night saw at least one ward Whig meeting in addition to the Masonic Hall general meeting. Ninth ward party leaders took a position in advance of the party line and nearly likened the Whig situation to a nation at war. The meeting sketched out something of a battle plan: "That a Committee of One Hundred citizens from the 9th ward be tendered to the General Committee of the city, who, with a like committee of one hundred from each of the other fourteen wards, will form a phalanx of 1500 freemen in aid of the civil authorities, to move at a moment's notice to the poll of any ward where ruffians may attack the peaceable citizens while exercising the SACRED RIGHT OF SUFFRAGE."[31]

Mayor Gideon Lee took action on Wednesday in response to the Whig threat—or perhaps out of a sense of duty to his office. He returned the Whigs to their committee room and posted a guard at the entrance to the sixth ward poll. In taking this action, he accompanied the district attorney, the sheriff, and a posse comitatus of twenty specially appointed deputy sheriffs. Several Whig papers conceded the mayor's good intentions.[32]

James Watson Webb, however, was not conciliated. He ignored Mayor Lee, and, in accordance with the Masonic Hall resolution, repaired on Wednesday morning to the sixth ward poll with a force of

200 citizens, fulfilling both the prophecy and the promise he was simultaneously making in that day's edition of the *Courier and Enquirer.* There he reported "that we are in the midst of a REVOLUTION, and that if we would protect our *persons,* our *property,* or our LIBERTIES, we must prove ourselves to be worthy of the rich inheritance we enjoy."[33]

Once at the sixth ward poll, the Whigs stayed on one side of the street and Jacksonians on the other. At ten o'clock, the passage of the "Constitution," the Whigs' model frigate, provoked the second major election incident. The crowd greeted the arrival of the frigate with a deafening roar, and between 200 and 300 partisans from each side of the street—armed with clubs, stones, and brickbats—joined in a general melee. However, despite the scale of the disturbance, the mayor's force quickly restored order with help from private citizens at the scene. Twenty to thirty persons were arrested.

In the day that followed, events surpassed Webb—he was no longer needed to incite violence. Wednesday's second disturbance erupted shortly before noon. The mayor's force again intervened and arrested the ringleaders. Presumably all or most were Jacksonians. A crowd of several thousand persons, both Whigs and Jacksonians, followed the arrested men to the City Hall Park police office, and the Whigs claimed credit for preventing the Jacksonians from rescuing the prisoners. The uninvolved observer, however, would have found it difficult to apportion blame or credit for what had occurred. Even if most of those arrested were Jacksonians, the Whigs, in ostensibly aiding the police, had become a vigilante group. They were reacting not to a real threat, but out of fear. Both sides were "mobs"—both sides engaged in lawless violence.

After the poll incident, rumors of Jacksonian violence spread amongst the city's Whigs. Although several severe beatings and a broken arm were the full extent of injuries, rumors spread that the rioting led to the death of as many as ten persons.[34] Whig merchants who had kept their shops and stores open on Tuesday despite the party's call, closed them on Wednesday because they had come to believe that violence would continue. Michael Floy, Jr., a Jacksonian taking no active role in the campaign, visited downtown and after returning to his uptown home wrote in his diary that the city was "all in a commotion," that almost all the stores were shut up and that groups of men could be seen talking at every corner.[35]

The Masonic Hall Whigs, warming to the general excitement, met in continuous session to aid the authorities (who had neither requested nor required their services). Serious violence did not occur. In the evening, however, the Whigs received a note threatening a serious riot in the sixth ward and they issued a call for a meeting of the General Committee the next morning at 8:00 a.m.[36] They also appointed a delegation to call upon the mayor who took precautionary steps against a renewal of the rioting, whether or not he was influenced by the Whig appeal. The mayor ordered 300 watchmen to remain in the Watch House in case trouble erupted, and at seven o'clock the next morning, he led a number of officers to the sixth ward poll.[37] The mayor showed none of the reluctance to act manifest twenty-four hours earlier.

Despite the mayor's attempt to control the situation, the city was in an uproar on Thursday. By mid-morning, crowds thronged the streets, and the "Constitution" provoked disturbances when it passed Reed and Cross streets and Duane and Augustus streets. As he had the day before, the mayor led a force in attempting to restore order. The police made a number of arrests, including a man who struck the mayor on the head with a stick. Although Mayor Lee was not seriously injured, the attack on his person hardly served to calm the city's mood. Outsiders in large numbers entered the sixth ward and crowded the streets in the polling area "to excess."[38]

At about noon, the "Constitution" sparked still another incident. As it passed Masonic Hall, on Broadway between Duane and Pearl streets, the Whigs in the area cheered the ship; and the Jacksonians raised a cheer for Lawrence. The Jacksonians hissed the ship, and, according to the Whig reports, threatened to destroy it. One account had the Jacksonians throwing stones, but what happened was probably nothing more than a noisy shouting match. The General Committee, in session in Masonic Hall, however, overheard the shouting and immediately assumed that its services were required. Without further inquiry, about 200 committee members joined with the Whigs already in the street to drive the handful of Jacksonians away from the Masonic Hall area. This time, the shoe was on the other foot. The Whig press mentioned no injuries. The Jacksonian papers claimed that from one to four Democrats were severely beaten.

The Jacksonians went to the sixth ward poll for reinforcements only after the Whigs had attacked and pursued them; but when they returned, they came rushing up Duane Street, armed with clubs and stones and "howling and screaming in a savage manner."[39] On reaching Broadway, they began an indiscriminate attack; the melee resulting involved hundreds on each side.

The mayor sent police officers, constables, and about forty watchmen to restore order. But, for the first time, the violence had gotten out of hand. The mob overwhelmed the police. A watchman died. At least twenty persons were injured, including a watch captain who was badly beaten. Eight watchmen were taken to the hospital. The aggressiveness of the Jacksonian mob could not be refuted; the party press only offered varying excuses. One newspaper claimed that the police did not appear in their usual outfit, another that the watch had sided with the Whigs.[40]

The disturbance naturally provoked rumors of further property damage, injury, and death.[41] It was said that the Jacksonians intended marching on the arsenal (located at Elm and Franklin streets). Whigs, taking this rumor seriously, went there themselves expecting to fend off the Jacksonian mob. When the arsenal's caretaker refused them entry, more than 500 Whigs, most young men and many still in their teens,[42] broke in and began to arm themselves. As word of the takeover spread, both Jacksonians and Whigs rushed to the site. The press estimated the crowd in the thousand, as high as 20,000. Duane, Elm, Pearl, Cross, Augustus, and Chatham streets were filled with men from all walks of life—merchants, mechanics, carmen, porters, and laborers. The shops in the area closed down. As the sensationalist *Sun* reported it, "we were indeed in the midst of a revolution."[43]

Mayor Lee arrived with posse comitatus and called on the Whigs to cease and desist. According to the *Sun*, (perhaps paraphrasing rather than quoting him) the mayor told the Whigs that if they disarmed and dispersed they could escape "the awful vortex of revolution! But if they persisted in this headstrong course[,] before tomorrow's sun the torch of civil war would blaze up in the midst of comparative peace and happiness." The mayor colored his appeal with visions of apocalypse: "'You are rash—you know not what you do—you think not of the consequences of this headstrong step! Do not cause the streets of our city to be dyed in blood! Do not call down upon your heads the curses of the widow and homeless orphan which such movements are calculated to make.'"[44]

After some hesitation, the Whigs acceded to this lachrymose rhetoric and a guard was placed atop the wall. Soon, the militia appeared not only at the aresenal, but also at City Hall, the Merchants' Exchange, and at the local branch of the Bank of the United States. In all, some 1,200 troops turned out for duty. At 2:00 p.m., two hours after the initial Masonic Hall riot, the mayor officially proclaimed the day's disturbances at an end. Although other incidents did occur later on Thursday, none were of a very serious nature. There was no bloodbath, no revolution; the doom sayers were proven wrong.[45]

From our present distant perspective, it is easy to dismiss the election incidents as trivial—which in the context of the 1830s they assuredly were not. Yet it is also undisputably true that the seriousness of the disturbances was exaggerated by the press (especially Webb's

Courier and Enquirer), the politicians, and the politically active citizenry. In fact, it was only the wildly inaccurate rumors which made the situation potentially explosive. The violence itself never amounted to much.[46]

Except for the riot outside Masonic Hall, none of the individual violent episodes lived up to the Whigs' predictions. Except for Tuesday night's invasion of the committee room and the Masonic Hall incident, all of the disturbance were quieted within minutes. None, including the assault on the arsenal, involved more than 500 active participants compared to the election's 35,000 voters. Property destroyed was restricted to political banners, the American flag, Whig ballots, and windows in Masonic Hall. All of the action, excepting minor scuffles, occurred in the sixth ward; citizens in other parts of the city went about their business and voted in peace.[47]

For Thursday's rioting, which convulsed the city for the two hours between noon and 2:00 p.m., the Whigs were responsible by and large. They were the ones who began the Masonic Hall disturbance; they were the ones who charged the arsenal. The Whigs claimed initially that their action prevented a Jacksonian seizure of the arsenal, but they seldom, if ever, repeated the allegation after the election since it had so little basis in fact.[48]

Indeed, by Thursday afternoon, the Whigs were so aroused that they no longer even sought official cooperation. Mayor Lee, from Wednesday morning on, had shown himself willing to suppress disorder to the point of personally leading the riot force. The Whigs, however, doubted the government's ability to control the Jacksonians. The Whigs' opinion of the city administration was so low—their panic so great—that during the arsenal incident, some Whigs took it upon themselves to obtain *federal* troops to deal with the crisis. They first sent a message to the United States Navy Yard in Brooklyn for a detachment of marines. When the commanding colonel refused this highly irregular request, explaining that he had just sent the marines aboard two ships where he could no longer give them orders, the Whigs persisted, turning to the commanders of Fort Columbus (on Governors Island) and another fort which protected New York's harbor.[49] Both commanders refused, saying they had no authority to intervene; but before the Whigs had received this reply, the militia had assembled and the Whigs had to issue a hurried counterrequest, thus revealing their firm conviction that the mayor would not act.[50]

II

If 1834 had been the first year of election rioting, the Whigs' overreaction could be accepted as the panic of men confronted with an unfamiliar and threatening situation. Election turmoil, however, was not a new phenomenon, and given past experience, the Whigs might have been expected to accept a certain amount of trouble as predictable and unavoidable and altogether *tolerable*.

Serious electoral violence did not occur between the end of the War of 1812 and 1834, but what violence there was, was reported by the press only in passing.[51] Prior to 1825, the papers made only occasional oblique references to disorder. In 1822, a complaint was registered that rude and uncivil conduct could lead to "brawls, and disturbances of the most serious nature."[52] Another paper, the following year, casually noted the "in most of the wards the contest was spirited, but conducted with much good order and more good nature than we have generally witnessed on such occasions."[53]

After 1825, mild concern replaced the previously cavalier attitude towards election violence. Andrew Jackson was a presidential candidate and then president; New York State had adopted universal suffrage; and Tammany Hall was beginning to court Irish voters.[54] In 1827, the *American* linked Andrew Jackson, the "Military Chieftain," with "the lovers of tumult and discord, the brawlers, and rioters;" and it declared, the "friends of virtue, peace, and good order" supported the administration of John Quicy Adams. A second paper however, in describing the same election, offhandedly referred to "broken heads, bloody noses and outrages of different descriptions."[55]

While election rioting received more attention after the mid 1830s, it does not necessarily follow that violence itself increased. In October 1834, in the midst of a heated debate on who was to blame for the charter election riot, the *Commercial Advertiser* charged that rioting had occurred at almost every election for the previous ten years; that "a set of bullies," most of them nonvoters (presumably because they were underage or noncitizens) had habitually "surrounded as many of the polls as they dared;" that "they insulted by noise and threats of violence every decent man who opposed them publicly at the polls." They had blocked the entrances to the polls "and [with] the various other annoyances that low profligates can employ," they deterred large numbers "of respectable classes" from voting.[56]

In the 1820s no newspaper reported election violence in such explicit terms, although later—in 1834—it was alleged to have occurred. No newspaper in 1820 alleged that "tumult and outrage" in the upper wards accompanied the gubernatorial election. In 1834, the *Commercial Advertiser* charged that Tammany's "hired bravadoes" drove De Witt Clinton's committees from some of the wards, in 1820, and that "by their violence, actually compelled them to rush into the houses of strangers for protection." In 1828, at the time of the presidential election, several papers reported that the polls were "orderly and quiet" and the electors voted "without interruption and without turbulence."[57] Later, the paper alleged that for hours on the election's second day the Jacksonians prevented Adams' supporters from voting. They also removed the ballot boxes from the inspection of the inspectors. Those National Republicans who challenged the right of certain Jacksonians to vote "were knocked down and dragged out."[58]

The offhand attitude towards election rioting prevailed as late as November 1832 when New Yorkers voted for both national and state officials. Although the Bank had emerged as a divisive political issue (both Webb and Verplanck had already left the Jacksonian fold), the election could have passed as a calm one. Only three of nine papers examined (two favoring Jackson, six opposed) even so much as mentioned any rioting.[59] Yet those three reported threats, mob violence, and small scale fighting which together with widespread fraudulent voting marred the election in nearly all the wards. On the first day, the landlord of the Fifth Ward National Republican Committee entered the committee room and with the help of bullies threw out his unfortunate tenants, the committeemen. One man had his coat torn.[60] On the third election day, serious fighting erupted in the seventh and fourteenth wards. Accounts vary so widely, that the sequence of events are probably beyond reconstruction. It is indisputable, however, that several people, including "respectable citizens," were injured in each of the two wards when about fifty toughs, both National Republican and Jacksonian, tangled. The *Evening Post*, a Jackson paper, described the incident as "of so unpardonable a character" that it hoped special efforts would be made to apprehend all persons connected; the *Commercial Advertiser* said that charges should be brought against the Jacksonians involved in the "shameless fraud and brutal violence."[61]

These two newspapers were atypical, however. In general, the press dismissed the minor turmoil occurring as insignificant. Hence, reports such as these: there was "more civil deportment at the polls than was anticipated;"[62] "the election was conducted yesterday with extraordinary spirit, though, as far as we could learn, without violence or disorder, except in one or two instances;"[63] "apparent good temper prevailed;"[64] "this [second] day has terminated as quietly perhaps as could have been expected; numerous fights have occurred at many of the wards, but the result has been nothing more serious than a black eye."[65]

Webb's paper, the *Courier and Enquirer*, reported the election turmoil—but in passing. Several days after the polls closed, the paper noted that an unusual number of "complaints and prosecutions for assaults and batteries" had been provoked by the election, but some of the defendants charged with rioting "appeared to have had the worse of the battle."[66] So Webb too did not take the rioting seriously. It is unquestionable that the National Republican-Whig press assumed an attitude towards the mob in the spring of 1834 which reflected a concern entirely out of keeping with its previously expressed attitude. Barring evidence to the contrary, it can be presumed to have mirrored the attitude of the public at large.

III

Jacksonian observers did not fail to recognize and to condemn the Whigs' overreaction in 1834. The *Evening Post* claimed that "disturbances may take place at elections without previous design," but that the Whigs had brought about the rioting during the 1834 charter election by their own actions. The *Post* charged that when the Whigs met in Masonic Hall Tuesday night they made "a deliberate premeditated plan for arraying a whole party for deeds of bloodshed; followed by an exhortation to be 'PREPARED,' with weapons of course, 'TO STRIKE A BLOW FOR LIBERTY.'" The paper called the Whig merchants' decision to close their stores a "mad and unwarrantable act" which served only to exasperate the situation.[67]

Although there is no evidence for the *Post* charge of Whig premeditation, rioting after the 1834 election was not treated casually. Both the Whig and Democratic press disapproved of rioting and condemned it wholeheartedly. Moreover, both parties pointed to the charter election riot as the beginning of the riot period (1834-1837) in New York and each party blamed the other for that riot.

What the Whigs feared in April 1834 was a mob they could not control. This was a new fear. Until the 1820s, the ability of respectable citizens to control mobs was generally not questioned, but the city had grown to a quarter million disharmonious people. The election riot set off an unacknowledged unease. Years of adjustment followed.

Mayor Lee's vigorous attempt to suppress the election rioting suggests that the Jacksonians in 1834 also feared the Jackson "mob" but that they were loath to say so. Several Democratic papers euphemistically described the Irish as "easily excited."[68] The *Evening Post*, the paper most famed for its alliance with the Radical wing of the

Democratic party, stated clearly why fear of the mob was not a respecter of party lines. New Yorkers were of a different cast now:

> Everybody knows the peculiarities of the Irish character. Quick, irritable, and generous, with a clash of strong nationality, and particular disinclination to a row, it combines with all these qualities an impatience of insult and concern derived from a long experience with despotic power, . . .No rational, or prudent man, would go to work deliberately to light a fire among such combustible materials.

Second, the city was big and unmanageable:

> In a city like this swarming with countless multitudes of people easily excited, and difficult to be restrained, dissention [*sic*] runs like wild fire, and impulses leap from man to man like flashes of lightning. Once set infuriated mobs by the ears, and nothing but blood will cool them. Armed soldiers must supercede the civil power, . . .and no one can tell where, or when the flood of popular fury will subside.[69]

NOTES

[1]The *New-York Commercial Advertiser* reported rioting in Utica, January 29, 30; Portsmouth, April 23; New Orleans, May 2 and December 27; Newark, July 12; Buffalo, July 25; Lockport, August 1; New Britain, August 1; Plainfield, August 7; Richmond, September 26; and Troy, October 31. Rioting was also reported among canal laborers in Maryland, January 24; and among railroad laborers in Massachusetts, April 25. On the Charleston riot, see Oscar Handlin, *Boston's Immigrants: A Study in Acculturation,* rev. and enl. ed., (New York, 1968), pp. 187-89.

[2]Leonard L. Richards, *"Gentlemen of Property and Standing:" Anti-Abolition Riots in America in the 1830's* (New York, 1969), pp. 15-19.

[3]Arthur M. Schlesinger, Jr., *The Age of Jackson* (Boston, 1945), pp. 45-47; Lynn L. Marshall, "The Strange Stillbirth of the Whig Party," *American Historical Review* 72 (January 1967): 445-68.

[4]Schlesinger, *The Age of Jackson,* pp. 74-114, passim; Edward Pessen, *Jacksonian America: Society, Personality, and Politics* (Homeward, Ill., 1969), pp. 328-36.

[5]Robert W. July, *The Essential New Yorker: Gulian Crommelian Verplanck* (Durham, N. C., 1951), pp. 170-79. For a biographical sketch of Wilde, see the *Dictionary of American Biography.*

[6]R. H. Wilde to Gulian C. Verplanck, March 17, 1834, Box 8, #113, Gulian C. Verplanck Papers, Manuscript Division, New-York Historical Society.

[7]Wilde to Verplanck, March 27, 1834, Box 8, #118, ibid.

[8]Wilde to Verplanck, April 1, 1834, Box 8, #137, ibid.

[9]Verplanck to Wilde, March 24, 1834, Miscellaneous Mss. V, Manuscript Division, New-York Historical Society.

[10]Wilde to Verplanck, March 27, 1834, Box 8, #118, Verplanck Papers.

[11]Philip Hone, MS Diary, March 19, 1834, Manuscript Division, New-York Historical Society.

[12]Philip Hone, *The Diary of Philip Hone, 1828-1851,* ed. Allan Nevins, new and enl. ed. (New York, 1936), p. 116 (March 4, 1834).

[13]Ibid., p. 117 (March 6, 1834).

[14]Philip Hone, MS Diary, April 2, 1834.

[15]*The Congressional Globe,* April 3, 1834, p. 288.

[16]Ibid., April 4, 1834, p. 291.

[17]Ibid., March 18, 1834, p. 250.

[18]Ibid., March 26, 1834, p. 266.

[19]The biographical sketch has been drawn from James L. Grouthamel, *James Watson Webb: A Biography* (Middletown, Conn., 1969), pp. 3-30, passim.

[20]*Morning Courier and New-York Enquirer*, November 2, 1830; April 15, 1831; April 1832.

[21]Ibid., April 7, 1834.

[22]Ibid., April 8, 1834.

[23]Verplanck to Wilde, March 24, 1834, Miscellaneous Mss. V.; Gideon Lee, Mayor of New York in April 1834, commented on the balance betwwen the two parties as a cause of the rioting in a letter to Aaron Clark, January 8, 1839, in New York (City), Board of Aldermen, Doc. 2 annexed to *Communication from His Honor the Mayor in Relation to the Precautionary Measures Adopted by Him to Secure the Public Peace at the Recent Election in This City, with Documents and a Report from the Comptroller Relative to the Expenses Incurred during Said Election*, Doc. No. 29, Vol. V (1839).

[24]*Commercial Advertiser*, April 9, 1834; *New-York American*, April 8, 12, 1834.

[25]*New-York Daily Advertiser*, April 8, 1834; *The Evening Star* (New York), April 8, 1834. Tammany answered the Whig show of strength with a model frigate of its own, the "Veto;" but the turnout was so disappointing that the Jackson papers failed to report the effort. The Whig press trumpeted the debacle as an omen of victory for themselves.

[26]The account of the election which follows has been reconstructed from the reports of the following newspapers: *New-York Daily Advertiser, American, Commercial Advertiser, Morning Courier and New-York Enquirer, New-York Gazette and General Advertiser, Man* (New York), *New-Yorker, Evening Post* (New York), *New York Standard, Evening Star* (New York), *Sun* (New York), *Truth Teller* (New York), *New York Journal of Commerce*. The election began April 8 and ended April 10. Where particular reports have helped ascertain the sequence of events, they are individually cited, as are reports sustaining the argument of the thesis.

[27]*Commercial Advertiser*, April 9, 1834.

[28]*Courier and Enquirer*, April 9, 1834.

[29]*Post*, April 9, 1834; *Journal of Commerce*, April 9, 1834; *New-Yorker*, April 12, 1834.

[30]*Courier and Enquirer*, April 9, 1834, for the publication of the resolution and its preamble.

[31]*Commercial Advertiser*, April 9, 1834.

[32]Ibid.; *Star*, April 9, 1834.

[33]*Courier and Enquirer*, April 10, 1834, reported that the sherff agreed to appoint the Whig citizens special constables after the mayor refused to.

[34]*Daily Advertiser*, April 10, 1834; *Journal of Commerce*, April 10, 1834; *Post*, April 9, 1834.

[35]Hone, *Diary*, p. 121 (April 8, 1834). *The Standard*, April 10, 1834, alleged that only a fifth of the merchants had closed their shops. Michael Floy, Jr., *The Diary of Michael Floy Jr.: Bowery Village 1833-1837*, ed. Richard A. E. Brooks (New Haven, Conn., 1941), p. 77 (April 10, 1834).

[36]*Courier and Enquirer*, April 12, 1834.

[37]*Sun*, April 11, 1834.

[38]This phrase was used by the *Courier and Enquirer*, April 12, 1834.

[39]The *Commercial Advertiser* included this report of the Jacksonian mob in a 1:00 p.m. postscript of its April 10, 1834 edition.

[40]*Standard*, April 11, 1834; *Man*, April 11, 1834.

[41]*Daily Advertiser*, April 11, 1834; *Man*, April 11, 1834; *Sun*, April 11, 1834; New York (State), Assembly, *Report of The Commissary-General to the Committee on the Militia and the Public Defence, in Relation to the Arsenal in the City of New York*, Doc. 389, 57th sess., 1834, p. 8.

[42]*Man*, April 11, 1834. New York (State), Assembly, *Report of the Commissary-General*, p. 7.

[43]*Daily Advertiser*, April 11, 1834; *Courier and Enquirer*, April 11, 1834; *Sun*, April 11, 1834.

[44]*Sun*, April 11 1834; see also New York (State), Assembly, *Report of the Commissary-General*, p. 11.

[45]Ibid.; Hone, *Diary*, p. 123 (April 10, 1834).

[46]For measuring the magnitude of rioting, see Charles Tilly and James Rule, *Measuring Political Upheaval*, Center of International Studies, Princeton University, research monograph no. 19 (Princeton, N. J., 1965) pp. 74-80.

[47]Michael Floy, Jr., living uptown at Broadway and Eleventh Street, reacted to the rioting as an outsider. *Diary*, p. 77 (April 10, 1834).

[48]New York (State), Assembly, *Report of the Commissary-General*, p. 12.

[49]Contemporaries called the second fort the "Station," but did not name or locate it. Any one of at least six United States forts in new York harbor, Brooklyn, or Staten Island could have supplied troops.

[50]For the episode involving federal troops, see the *Courier and Enquirer*, April 12, 1834; *Journal of Commerce*, April 11, 1834; *Sun*, April 11, 1834. The exact time the mayor called out the militia cannot be pinned down. Several Whig papers (*Daily Advertiser*, April 11, 1834; *Courier and Enquirer*, April 12, 1834), perhaps sensitive to the charge

that a Whig "mob" had assaulted the arsenal, claimed that the mayor ordered out the militia after the Masonic Hall disturbance, a riot for which the Jacksonians could more readily be blamed; but several more authoritative accounts exist which contradict this claim. Unfortunately, however, they do not agree with each other. On April 11, 1834, the *Journal of Commerce* reported a conversation between its editor and Major-General Jacob Morton in which the latter claimed, according to the newspaper, that he ordered out the division under his command at 11:00 a.m. before even the Masonic Hall disturbance and that the troops had nearly all assembled by 2:00 p.m. at the arsenal where they had *coincidentally* been ordered to report. If this account is true, it only confirms Mayor Lee's eagerness to take preventive measures and the unjustified nature of the Whig hysteria. (It also warns us against judging the seriousness of a riot by the counter force used by the legal authorities.) However, Henry Arcularius, the Democratic Commissary-General of the arsenal, in his report to the New York State Assembly militia committee, p. 12, claimed that he met with the mayor during the assault, and that the mayor "asked whether the whole of General Morton's division should not be ordered out at the arsenal. I assented, and the corps was accordingly assembled under arms at the arsenal yard during the latter part of the afternoon." The order to appear at the arsenal is reprinted in Emmons Clark, *History of the Seventh Regiment of New York 1806-1889*, 2 Vols. (New York, 1890), 1:215, but it gives only the date and not the hour of the order. The primary sources are of no help because they too do not provide the hour of the order. New York (State), 27th Regiment Artillery, Fourth Company, MS Orderly Book 1828-39, April 10, 1834 and idem. Second Company, MS Minute Book, 1826-39, April 10, 1834, Seventh Regiment Collection, New-York Historical Society.

[51]For this section, the *Commercial Advertiser*, the *Gazette and General Advertiser*, and the *Evening Post*, were scanned for the years 1816 to 1834; the *Daily Advertiser* for 1817 to 1834; and the *American* for 1819 to 1834.

[52]*Commercial Advertiser*, June 7, 1822.

[53]*Daily Advertiser*, November 6, 1823.

[54]Tammany Hall (the Republican party in New York City) began seeking foreign votes in the mid twenties, when the suffrage widened. The party favored reducing the five year naturalization period; by November 1827, alien support for the Jacksonians proved a major factor in the election. See Gustavus Myers, *The History of Tammany Hall*, 2d ed. rev. and enl. (New York, 1917), pp. 73-74, 128.

[55]*American*, November 6, 1827; *Commercial Advertiser*, November 10, 1827.

[56]Ibid., October 1, 1834.

[57]*American*, November 6, 1828 (the administration paper); *Evening Post*, November 7, 1828 (the Jackson paper).

[58]*Commercial Advertiser*, October 1, 1834.

[59]The newspapers examined include: *Daily Advertiser, American, Commercial Advertiser, Courier and Enquirer, Gazette and General Advertiser, Journal of Commerce, Evening Post*, and the *Standard*. The last two papers supported Jackson; the others opposed him.

[60]*Commercial Advertiser*, November 6, 1832.

[61]*Daily Advertiser*, November 8, 1832; *Commercial Advertiser*, November 8-9, 1832; *Evening Post*, November 8, 1832. Of the three papers that did report rioting, the *Post* commented only on the third day's disturbances, and the *Daily Advertiser* seemed resigned to the situtation. Even the *Commercial Advertiser*, which alone reported election rioting at length and criticized it harshly, did not make this issue its preeminent concern.

[62]*Gazette and General Advertiser*, November 6, 1832.

[63]*American*, November 6, 1832.

[64]*Journal of Commerce*, November 6, 1832.

[65]*Daily Advertiser*, November 7, 1832.

[66]*Courier and Enquirer*, November 10, 1832.

[67]*Evening Post*, April 11, 1834.

[68]*Man*, April 11, 1834; *Standard*, April 11, 1834. The citation is from the *Standard*.

[69]*Evening Post*, April 12, 1834.

CHAPTER TWO

RIOTING CONTINUES: THE ANTI-ABOLITIONISTS

I

In rioting that began on July 4, 1834, and for more than a week thereafter, mobs—sometimes several thousand strong—broke up the meetings of abolitionists and attacked them and the city's Negroes in their homes and churches. From day to day, the tempo of violence increased steadily, with the rioters resisting the attempts of the civil authorities to restore order. Rioting ended only after the mayor called upon citizen volunteers, as well as the military, and threatened to use deadly force.

At the beginning, mobs only disrupted public gatherings, but from the evening of July 9 through July 11, rioters attacked the homes and churches of abolitionists and Negroes.[1] Mobs destroyed black property indiscriminately and victimized three abolitionists: Lewis Tappan, Samuel H. Cox, and Henry G. Ludlow. On Wednesday night, the ninth, in the first assault on private property, a mob marched on Lewis Tappan's house, smashed the windows, broke in the doors, and piled in the street and burned about $300 worth of bedding and furniture. At sunset the next night, a crowd again began to gather at the Tappan house. However, they went elsewhere when confronted by a force of watchmen anticipating trouble. On Friday night, the eleventh, the anti-abolitionists shifted their attention slightly, moving on to the Arthur Tappan & Co. store. (Arthur was Lewis' brother and business partner.) The rioters stoned the windows, chased the fifteen or twenty watchmen assigned to the building away, and continued the barrage for about two hours until 100 reenforcements arrived.

The attack on Cox began on Thursday night; about 150 to 200 rioters threw stones and brickbats at the windows of his church. The presence of the watch limited damage, and the rioters shifted the attack to the minister's house, eight blocks away. Here they smashed more windows and broke in the door. The arrival of the watch, several magistrates, and the mayor at the head of two companies of militia again successfully thwarted an assault—although it was not for a want of trying. The mob erected a barricade and attempted to outflank the troops by going around the block to the rear of the building. The assault on the house lasted for more than three hours. On Friday afternoon, about fifty boys followed Cox home, hissing him; and he was forced to take refuge in a parishioner's home. In the evening, both the church and the house were again mobbed. With the watch present, the rioters only managed the smashing of more windows and the break in of the church door.

Rev. Henry G. Ludlow's church became a target on Friday after the watch had stopped the mob at Cox's church. The rioters smashed the windows and broke in the doors. Once inside, they destroyed what they could, and then went on to the adjoining session house. When the militia arrived to disperse them, the rioters erected a barricade and threw stones at the troops.

There is no doubt why these particular abolitionists were targeted. The press had reported that all three actively promoted amalgamation. Rev. Ludlow had allegedly officiated at a marriage between a white and a black. (After the rioting ended, Ludlow denied the charge and asked the newspapers which had circulated the story to publish a retraction.)[2] Lewis Tappan was the brother of Arthur, the American Anti-Slavery Society's president and executive committee chairman, as well as its leading financial backer.[3] And Lewis himself had taken an active and public part in the society in the months preceding the rioting. In early May, he had conducted a public interrogation of a Negro recently returned from Liberia whose testimony created an uproar—the colony's governor had allegedly fathered a mulatto child and intemperance was said to mark life there. The scandalized colonizationists, who attended the meeting in force, refused to allow Tappan to complete his interrogation. They insisted noisily on the right to cross-examine the witness. Eventually they took over the meeting and appointed the secretary of the colonization society to the chair. The press reported the incident in detail using the occasion to condemn the abolitionists.[4]

Rev. Samuel H. Cox, who first chaired the meeting, was mentioned in the reports. A month later, on June 12, the minister delivered an "amalgamation" sermon that alerted the colonizationists to indignation. Cox characterized Christ as "colored"—that is, as having an Asiatic rather than a European complexion. An excited campaign against Cox and the abolitionists was thereupon initiated. This vilification of abolitionism by the press probably initially encouraged and then reenforced the amalgamation rumors that flourished in the city in the weeks preceding the riot.[5] Unquestionably, the newspapers' attack on Cox made him the mob's number one target.

The newspapers of the 1830s did not report sermons regularly and only the *Commercial Advertiser* took notice of it at first. William Leete Stone, the editor, was also the secretary of the colonization society. Apparently he hoped to hold up the abolitionists to public scorn by publishing Cox's extreme ideas. Stone misstated the minister's meaning. Cox, the newspaper claimed, had said Christ was a Negro. The

Commercial Advertiser, insisting that Semites were whites, argued that they had remained unamalgamated and that Christ was "uncommonly fair and comely." Questioning Cox's right to preach, the paper suggested to the Presbyterian Church that it inquire into the abolitionist opinions of its clergy.[6]

Cox defended himself in a letter "To The Public," printed in the *Journal of Commerce.* He took issue, first of all, with the publicizing of his sermon. He had intended it only for his congregation, not outsiders—he had said so at the time he delivered it. He therefore spoke on emancipation with greater freedom than ordinarily. On the issues themselves, Cox denied that majority opinion was necessarily right and reaffirmed his stand on Christ's color. He contended that on a color scale which included Asiatics as well as Negroes and whites, Christ could be considered a colored man. Furthermore, Cox asserted that since Europeans formed a minority of the world's population, their complexion should not be taken as the norm. Finally, Cox dismissed colonization as a useless remedy for slavery.[7]

This wide-ranging attack on white racial assumptions made the sermon, not at first a news item, into a source of continuing controversy. The *Commercial Advertiser* questioned Cox's mental faculties, even claiming that the anti-slavery issue had agitated him to a degree "bordering on hallucination." It criticized his letter point by point and repeated its assertion that Christ's complexion was not that of an Asian. The paper rejected Cox's notion of a spectrum of skin colors and claimed that only Negroes could be called colored men.[8]

The *Courier and Enquirer* joined the controversy. James Watson Webb's paper printed a series of vituperative articles in which it denounced Negro equality and abolitionism and Cox in particular. Webb denied that Christ was Negro and he charged that only "misled and deluded females" had listened to the sermon. Responding to abolitionist egalitarianism, Webb launched into a lengthy denial of Negro equality. Since slavery existed in Africa, he argued, the Negroes had benefited by their removal to the United States. When in a state of freedom, Negroes, the intellectual inferiors of whites, resorted to prostitution, debauchery, idleness, and crime. Because of their habits, they were also subject to premature disease and death.[9]

The *Courier and Enquirer* persisted in its attack after the first of the disturbances, the disruption of a July 4 anti-slavery meeting. Departing from the established segregationist pattern, Negroes had sat with whites, not in their own section. Webb was disgusted:

> Dr. Coxe[*sic*] particularly distinguished himself by his attention to the ladies, both ivory and ebony—seeming to be particularly alive to their accomodation even during prayers. Winking in this direction

and blinking in that—motioning dexter and gesticulating sinister whenever the fair sex, especially the mahogany portion of it, lacked the facilities of location.   Many a matronly wench will long have cause to remember the tender attentions of the Doctor upon this excellent anniversary.[10]

On Friday morning, July 11, after the mob had already attacked Cox's house and church, the *Courier and Enquirer* again cited Cox's sermon in denying that the abolitionists had a right to police protection:

When they vilify our religion by classing the redeemer of the world in the lowest grade of the human species, when they debase the noble race from which we spring, that race which called civilization into existence, and from which have proceeded all the great, the brave, and good, that have ever lived—and place it in the same scale as the most stupid, ferocious and cowardly of the divisions into which the Creator has divided mankind, then they place themselves beyond the pale of all law, for they violate every law divine and human.[11]

The *Commercial Advertiser* and the *Courier and Enquirer,* having incited the rioting, used it in an apparent attempt to silence the abolitionists.   On Monday night, July 7, Negroes, meeting in the Chatham Street Chapel to celebrate New York State's ending of slavery, fought with white members of the New York Sacred Music Society. The society normally met in the chapel on Monday evenings, but on this particular evening the room was sublet to the Negroes. Apparently, not all the music society's members were informed. Fighting broke out when some of the blacks refused to vacate the room.   The next day, the *Courier and Enquirer,* aroused by such Negro "impudence," virtually demanded that a mob put down the "amalgamationists" by violence. The paper demanded, "How much longer are we to submit?   In the name of the country, in the name of Heaven, how much more are we to bear from Arthur Tappan's mad impudence?"[12]   The *Commercial Advertiser* did not openly provoke the rioters to further violence, but it, too, goaded the mob by its lurid and probably fanciful description of events that followed the incident. The newspaper charged that gangs of blacks had congregated on street corners during the night and threatened to burn the city.   It claimed that these blacks had promised to turn out in sufficient numbers in any future confrontation to overcome the whites. The *Commercial Advertiser* said that the blacks had paraded the streets until after daylight "breathing violence and revenge."[13]

On Tuesday night, July 8, the all-white Moral Lyceum met at Clinton Hall to debate the feasibility of abolishing slavery. Although the Lyceum had previously debated this issue without criticism or comment and with both colonizationists and abolitionists invited to participate,[14] it was rumored that the debate scheduled for July 8 would be another abolitionist meeting. As a result, about fifty blacks appeared, and so did 100 whites bent on disruption. The whites made sufficient noise to prevent the meeting from getting under way; during the disruption, an anti-Negro mob gathered at the door.

On the morning of July 9, the *Courier and Enquirer* used the incident to warn Negroes to stay away from the Chatham Street Chapel where, it reported, the abolitionists planned to meet that evening. The newspaper charged that "no one who saw the temper which pervaded last night, can doubt, that if the blacks continue to allow themselves to be made the tools of a few blind zealots, the consequences to them will be most serious." The chapel had been the site of two of the previous three disruptions, and an expectant crowd appeared, estimated at between 300 and 3,000. No abolitionists showed up, but the building was broken into anyway. There, the crowd listened to a speech on the evil consequences of abolition in Santo Domingo and passed a resolution to adjourn until the next meeting of the anti-slavery society. Some lamps and benches were broken, but no concerted effort was made to damage the premises. After the meeting adjourned, most of the crowd dispersed, but some proceeded to the Bowery Theater and contributed to a riot in the making there, and later that night a portion of the Bowery mob went on to invade the house of Lewis Tappan.

The incident confirms Webb's ability as editor of the *Courier and Enquirer* to influence events. Webb alleged that when the paper reported that an abolitionist meeting would be held at the chapel and when it observed that mob violence might occur there, it only printed a rumor already circulating about the city.[15] If this is so, Webb certainly helped give the rumor credence by printing it; his newspaper had the largest circulation of any in the city.[16] Also, however—given the failure of any other newspaper to report the story as either rumor or fact—Webb could have created the rumor to suit his own purposes. Indeed, the *Journal of Commerce* (which favored colonization) credited Webb with originating the story in its assessment of the riot the following week.[17]

Several newspapers joined the *Commercial Advertiser* and the *Courier and Enquirer* in stridently attacking the abolitionists once rioting began. Both the *Mercantile Advertiser* and the *Evening Star* openly invited mobs to disrupt abolitionist gatherings following the Sacred Music Society disturbance of July 7. The *Advertiser* charged that "the leaders who have been the cause of this outrage" would have to answer to "many of our most respectable citizens" and "to the indignant community for the gross and daring insult."[18] The *Star* demanded:

> Will the citizens of this city longer submit to have their brethren attacked by the abetted mobs of Negroes: their ears harshly assailed with the vile and debased proposition of a general amalgamation of color? If they will not, let them fearesly assert their determination, and show, though slow to move, when once aroused, their wrath will come with redoubled force.[19]

The next day, after the Moral Lyceum incident, the *Times* spoke out. Confusing the incidents of July 7 and July 8, the paper castigated the Negroes' increasing "insolence"; obviously the blacks did not know their places. They had carried canes with bullet heads, and they had refused to relinquish their seats to the members of the debating society. Such actions might lead to the Negroes' refusing to "act in the capacity of servants, to determine that they will be hewers of wood and drawers of water to no men." The paper provocatively warned that the Negroes would suffer the fate of the abolitionists—there was a strong and growing antagonism against the Negroes which might lead to violence.[20]

Support for the mobs in the press continued even after the noisy disruption of meetings was largely replaced by the destruction of private property. The *Courier and Enquirer,* the *Commercial Advertiser,* and the *Times*—all denied that the abolitionists had a right to police protection.[21] As late as the morning of July 11, after the military had been called out, the *Times* defended violence, if not its excesses, and denied that the rioting was out of bounds. Although the rioters spent nearly four hours trying to gain entrance to Rev. Samuel Cox's house and church and had shown fear of neither the watch nor the militia, the *Times* claimed that the rioters could not be called a mob because they were governed "by a spirit of calmness." On that day too, the *Courier and Enquirer* hoped that rioting would stop—if only because the abolitionists had learned their lesson—but appealed to the mob demagogically all the same:

> When they endeavor to disseminate opinions, which if generally imbibed, must infallibly destroy our National Union, and produce scenes of blood and carnage horrid to think of; when they thus preach up treason and murder, the egis (!) of the law indignantly withdraws its shelter from them. When they vilify our religion by classing the redeemer of the world in the lowest grade of the human species, . . the most stupid, ferocious and cowardly of the divisions into which the Creator has divided mankind, then they place themselves beyond the pale of all law, for they violate every law divine and human.[22]

On July 12, another night of rioting at last convinced the newspapers which had supported the rioters to forgo their support. Now it was of paramount importance to end the violence. Even the ardent anti-abolitionists agreed it had gotten out of hand.

The newspapers probably played a lesser role in ending the violence than they had in creating it. The authorities had stiffened their attitude. The militia, with the citizenry, patrolled the streets, and the mayor gave the militia permission to use live ammunition. The threat was sufficient. There was no need to resort to this kind of violence to end violence. The rioting was easily suppressed.

Before this night, the rioters did not have to deal with an armed militia; but anti-abolitionist violence did end for another reason as well. The mayor probably would not have resorted to the threat of shooting if public opinion generally did not support him. Support from the previously pro-riot press justified the mayor's beliefs and sanctioned his actions. The loss of press support must also have discouraged the rioters from continuing in their actions.

II

Newspaper editors were probably New York's most important public opinion leaders. Their views, moreover, are known. Analyzing the press, therefore, may help us understand the attitude of the city's broader elite.

Five newspapers—*Daily Advertiser, American, Gazette and General Advertiser, Journal of Commerce, Evening Post*—did not agree with the four newspapers actively encouraging the mob. They condemned the abolitionists, but increasingly, they warned of the dangers inherent in allowing mob violence to continue.

The more moderate press considered the vocal disruption of the July 4 anti-slavery meeting a non-riot, but they became increasingly alarmed with successive incidents. Muted criticism of the rioters or not editorializing, after the July 7 Music Society incident, was followed by sharp criticism of both rioters and abolitionists after mobs, on July 8 and 9, disrupted the Moral Lyceum debate, broke into the Chatham Street Chapel, and stormed the Bowery Theater. After a mob, late on the night of July 9, invaded Tappan's house, the moderate press ceased to be even-handed. Editorialists demanded that the public support the authorities in suppressing the mob, should any more rioting occur.

The shift in the *American's* editorials illustrates the turnabout in the attitude of the more moderate press. After the July 7 disturbance, the paper merely expressed the hope that the incident would prove to be the last of the series in the Chatham Street Chapel.[23] Following the Moral Lyceum incident, the *American* became more anxious about the rising level of tension; it decided to speak out against the "fanatics," as they called the abolitionists, because their "guilty zeal" was "driving them so far as to prompt overt acts of violence." The paper condemned abolitionism as an illegitimate movement lacking numbers and led by men unknown in public service, inexperienced in affairs, and without the background of "quiet and veteran burghers." At the same time, however, the *American* hoped that a strong police would stand between the abolitionists and the exasperated community, and admonished the community to refrain from violence. Foreseeing the possibility of far worse rioting than had yet occurred, the paper warned that if the abolitionists should suffer death at the hands of the mob, they would only become martyrs.[24] Following the attack on Tappan's house, the *American* predicted that if rioters invaded the Tappan brothers' store, destroying the goods, "half of Pearl Street" would suffer. The paper acknowledged that the Chatham Street Chapel incident of July 9 had been conducted with moderation, but still it made for a "most dangerous" precedent. The *American* hoped therefore, that if violence erupted again, the law would "be supported with all energy."[25] On the following day, the paper, for the first time, did not sympathize with the rioters. After a long night of property assaults, the *American* claimed "this state of things *must* cease. . .however great the provocation. If the civil force be found insufficient, the military *must* be called in, and if called in, they must *act*." The *American* said the troops should fire if the rioters did not disperse.[26]

Why did New York's newspaper editors divide into two camps—one using and supporting mobs, the other keeping hands off? In 1834, only one daily newspaper editor, George W. Wisner, coeditor of the *Sun*, sympathized with the abolitionists.[27] The division, thus, was not based on anti-abolitionism.

According to Leonard Richards, anti-slavery societies threatened the social control exercised by traditional elites belonging to colonization societies.[28] Although Richards applies this thesis to Utica, Cincinnati, and Alton, but not New York City, where the elite themselves did not riot, we may attempt to apply the thesis to New York's editors. Did a threatened elite amongst New York's newspaper editors encourage the mob to riot against the abolitionists?

Certainly James Watson Webb's attitudes and family background entitle him to be called an elite traditionalist. His father, Brigadier General Samuel Webb, served as an aide to Washington during the war, and, afterwards, helped found the Society of Cincinnati. Webb himself married the daughter of wealthy merchant Alexander A. Stewart. Editing a newspaper at the time the penny press changed reporting, he refused to appeal to a mass audience: he viewed himself, more grandiosely, as the protector of New York's gentlemen merchants.[29]

William Leete Stone, the *Commercial Advertiser's* editor, also can be labeled an elite traditionalist. Although he grew up as the son of a poor frontier minister, he quickly rose to prominence when he assumed the editorship of the *Commercial Advertiser* in 1821, at the age of 29. As an editor, he immersed himself in charitable causes, and his paper circulated widely among the "more wealthy and benevolent classes." Furthermore, Stone, an active colonizationist, held various offices with the Colonization Society of the City of New-York.[30]

The class explanation, however, does not work for New York's other editors. First, the editors of New York's other leading colonization newspaper, the *Journal of Commerce, voiced early opposition to the anti-abolitionist rioting.* Gerard Hallock and David Hale defended the right of everyone, including the abolitionists, to meet and discuss all subjects. After the July 4 disruption, the *Journal of Commerce* charged that "public opinion needs reform in this city on this subject.[31] Just before the mob began destroying private property, the paper cautioned colonizationists and other opponents of the abolitionists against resorting to a "mob police."[32] Both Hallock and Hale were the sons of New England ministers. They became acquainted in Boston, editing religious newspapers. In 1826, Hallock became a part owner and editor of the *New York Observer,* a religious weekly. He joined the *Journal of Commerce* in 1828; Arthur Tappan had founded the paper the year before as a business-religious newspaper. Hallock had pronounced southern sympathies. Hale played an active role in religious and philanthropic activities. In 1840, he bought the building occupied by the Broadway Tabernacle, a Congregational Church. Under Hallock and Hale's joint editorship, the *Journal of Commerce* accepted neither theater nor lottery ads; and the paper boasted of conducting no business on Sunday, contrary to the practice of the rest of the morning press.[33]

Theodore Dwight, the editor of the *Daily Advertiser,* and Charles King, the editor of the *American,* did not support the mob either, although they had the highest status of any of New York's editors. Dwight's father was a well-to-do merchant, landowner, and office-holder in Northampton, Massachusetts; his grandfather, on his mother's side, was Jonathan Edwards; and Aaron Burr was a cousin. A resident of Hartford from 1791 until 1815, Dwight rose to prominence as an ultra-Federalist. Active as a party worker, a pamphleteer, and an editor, he also served a term in Congress, 1806-1807, and was the secretary of the

Hartford Convention of 1814. In 1817, at the age of 53 , he founded the *New York Daily Advertiser* and continued as its editor until 1836.[34]

Charles King's father was Rufus King, nominated by the Federalists for vice-president in 1804 and 1808, and for president in 1816. Charles went to England when President Adams appointed his father minister to that country in 1799. In England, he attended Harrow, where he remained after his father returned to the United States. He was a merchant from 1810 until 1823, when he took over the ownership and editorship of the *American*.[35]

Dwight was silent about the rioting until July 11, but King voiced early opposition. After King had called on the militia to use their weapons, if necessary,[36] an informant alleged that the mob "threatened most earnestly to tar and feather" him and that more than once during the evening of July 11, "they were on the point of proceeding to his house."[37]

Finally—aside from Stone and Webb of the *Commercial Advertiser* and the *Courier and Enquirer*—the editors of the three newspapers which encouraged rioting do not fit the elite traditionalist pattern. No biographical or genealogical information on William Holland 'and Edward Sanford, editors of the *Times*, the conservative Tammany organ, has been found. Mordecai M. Noah, editor of the *Evening Star*, was prominent in the Jewish community and had to contend with open anti-semitism when he ran for elective office. In 1828, Webb made a vigorous attempt to deny him the Tammany nomination for sheriff.[38] Redwood Fisher, editor of the *Mercantile Advertiser*, could trace his ancestry back to his great-great-grandfather who accompanied William Penn on his first voyage to Pennsylvania in 1682. Despite his ancestry, however, Fisher was not a conventional member of the elite. During most of his life, he was a religious doubter. As a young man, he left the counting house of his Quaker father and uncles and travelled to Europe and the Orient as a super-cargo. A privateer captured his ship in 1810 or 1811 and he had to spend two or three years in Copenhagen to obtain the ship's release, but he returned to the sea nonetheless.[39] Not succeeding as a merchant or achieving real economic security, Fisher obtained a political appointment by relying upon the help of a United States senator—a relative by marriage.

In sum, neither attitudes towards abolitionism nor elite status explain either the editorial support or the hesitant opposition of the press to the anti-abolitionist rioting.

NOTES

[1] The account of the anti-abolition rioting contained in this chapter has been reconstructed from the following newspapers: *New-York Daily Advertiser, New-York American, New-York Commercial Advertiser, Morning Courier and New-York Enquirer, New York Evangelist* (weekly), *New-York Gazette and General Advertiser, New York Journal of Commerce, Man* (New York), *Mercantile Advertiser and New-York Advocate, New-York Observor* (weekly), *Evening Post* (New York), *Evening Star* (New York), *Sun* (New York), *New-York Times, New-York Transcript.* All the papers are dailies except where noted. Newspapers are cited individually only where events were not generally reported and when reference is made to particular papers.

Also used have been the following sources: Cornelius Lawrence File on the Anti-Abolitionist Riots, New York City Miscellaneous Manuscripts, 1834, Manuscript Division, New-York Historical Society; New York (City), Board of Assistants, *Communication from His Honor, The Mayor, Relative to the Late Riots, Etc., Accompanied with Two Proclamations, Issued by the Mayor, on the 11th and 12th of July, 1834,* Doc. No. 11, Vol. I (1834); New York (City), Board of Aldermen, *Proceedings,* VII (1834), 157-58; Philip Hone, MS Diary, July 10, 12, 1834, Manuscript Division, New-York Historical Society; Philip Hone, *The Diary of Philip Hone, 1828-1851,* ed. Allan Nevins, new and enl. ed. (New York, 1936), p. 135 (July 12, 14, 1834); New York (State), 27th Regiment Artillery, Fourth Company, MS Orderly Book 1828-39, July 11-12,1834, Seventh Regiment Collection, New-York Historical Society; *Zip Coon* (New York, 1834).

Secondary accounts which have proved useful are: Leonard L. Richards, *"Gentlemen of Property and Standing",* Anti-Abolition Mobs in Jacksonian America (New York, 1970), pp. 113-22 and passim; Linda K. Kerber, "Abolitionists and Amalgamators: The New York City Race Riots of 1834," *New York History* 48 (January 1967): 28-39; Emmons Clark, *History of the Seventh Regiment of New York 1806-1889,* 2 vols. (New York, 1890): 221-24; Asher Taylor, *Recollections of the Early Days of the National Guard Comprising the Prominent Events in the History of the Famous Seventh Regiment, New York Militia, by an Ex-Orderly Sergeant* (New York, 1868), pp. 150-56; [Lewis Tappan], *The Life of Arthur Tappan* (New York, 1871), pp. 189-220 passim; Joel T. Headley, *The Great Riots of New York, 1712 to 1873* (New York, 1873), pp. 81-95.

[2] *Journal of Commerce,* July 25, 1834.

[3] Bertram Wyatt-Brown, *Lewis Tappan and the Evangelical War against Slavery* (Cleveland, 1969), pp. 111-13.

[4] *Commercial Advertiser,* May 10, 12, 1834; *Mercantile Advertiser,* May 10, 12, 1834; *Journal of Commerce,* May 17, 1834.

[5] *Emancipator, and Journal of Public Morals,* August 19, 1834.

[6] *Commercial Advertiser,* June 13, 1834.

[7] *Journal of Commerce,* June 19, 1834.

[8] *Commercial Advertiser,* June 21, 1834.

[9] *Courier and Enquirer,* June 23, 24, 26, 1834.

[10] Ibid., July 7, 1834.

[11] Ibid., July 11, 1834.

[12] Ibid., July 8, 1834.

[13] *Commercial Advertiser,* July 8, 1834.

[14] "We would remind our readers of the meeting of the New York Moral Lyceum THIS EVENING at Broadway Hall, 410 Broadway. Subjects for discussion:—Abolition and Colonization. Those who love spirited debate would do well to attend." Also see the *Emancipator,* July 29, 1834.

[15] *Courier and Enquirer,* July 10, 1834. The *Emancipator,* July 29, 1834, claimed that the rumor first surfaced at the Moral Lyceum disruption of July 8, but that Webb was responsible for giving it wide circulation.

[16] The *Courier and Enquirer* claimed a daily circulation of about 4,500, twice as much as any other paper and far greater than the average newspaper circulation of 1,000. Frank Luther Mott, *American Journalism. A History of Newspapers in the United States through 260 years: 1690 to 1950,* rev. ed. (New York, 1950), pp. 202-203.

[17] *Journal of Commerce,* July 16, 1834. Without specifying any incident, the *Evening Post,* July 25, 1834, credited the inflamed state of public opinion "chiefly, if not wholly, to the circulation of *lies,* lies which there is too much reason to believe were invented and published for the very purpose of breeding riots."

[18] *Mercantile Advertiser,* July 8, 1834.

[19] *Evening Star,* July 8, 1834.

[20] *Times,* July 9, 1834. No evidence is known which would verify the charge that the blacks carried canes with bullet heads.

[21] Ibid., July 11. 1834.

[22] *Courier and Enquirer,* July 11, 1834.

[23] *American,* July 8, 1834.

[24] Ibid., July 9, 1834.

[25] Ibid., July 10, 1834.

[26] Ibid., July 11, 1834.

[27] *Sun,* June 23, 1834; Frank M. O'Brien, *The Story of the Sun, New York: 1833-1928,* new ed. (New York, 1928), pp.20, 23.

[28] Richards, *"Gentlemen of Property and Standing,"* pp. 131-50, 155 and passim.

[29]Ibid., pp. 31-32; James L. Crouthamel, *James Watson Webb: A Biography* (Middletown, Conn., 1969), pp. 3, 10.

[30]William L. Stone, *The Life and Times of Sa-Go-Ye-Wat-IIa, or Red Jacket, by the late William L. Stone with a Memoir of the Author by His Son* (Albany, 1866), pp. 9-84 passim; Colonization Society of the City of New-York, *Fifth Annual Report with the Constitution of the Society* (New York, 1837) p. 30f.

[31]*Journal of Commerce*, July 7, 1834.

[32]Ibid., July 10, 1834.

[33]*Dictionary of American Biography.*

[34]Ibid.

[35]Ibid.

[36]*American*, July 11, 1834.

[37]C. F. Hoffman to Gen. Fleming, July 12, 1834, #52, New York City Miscellaneous Manuscripts, 1834, Manuscript Division, New-York Historical Society.

[38]Isaac Goldberg, *Major Noah: American-Jewish Pioneer* (New York, 1937), pp. 146-52; 189-215, 238-42, 247-48, 254-63 for Noah's role as a Jewish leader, pp. 155-60 for anti-semitism; *Morning Courier* (New York), October 30, 31, November 1, 3-5, 1828.

[39]Henry Simpson, *The Lives of Eminent Philadelphians, Now Deceased, Collected from Original and Authentic Sources* (Philadelphia, 1859), pp. 362-64; [William Logan Fisher, *An Account of the Fisher and Logan Families* (Wakefield, Penn., 1839), p. 2]; R[edwood] Fisher to Daniel Ullmann,, January 24, 1849, Ullmann Papers, Manuscript Division, New-York Historical Society.

CHAPTER THREE

A HISTORY FOR VIOLENCE

I

Attitudes towards the mob per se will need to be considered if we are to better understand the newspaper reaction to violence in 1834. As we have seen, almost the entire press did not at first condemn the anti-abolitionist rioting. Only when they had obviously lost control of the situation did they become truly alarmed.

This attitude was a manifestation of an historic toleration for some violence. The press condemned labor disturbances and mob violence that resulted in death and property damage,[1] but they tacitly sanctioned less threatening riots—such as the election riots we have discussed. The issue of abolitionism, moreover, was "moral" in tone, and issues of a "moral" character were particularly open to settlement by sanctioned violence and threats of violence. Disturbances greeted Frances Wright's first lecture series in New York City in 1829 (women did not speak in public);[2] and in 1831 a major brouhaha followed the New York Magdalene Society's charge that the city was home for 10,000 active prostitutes. (The threats of violence were directed against the society, not against the prostitutes.)[3]

Perhaps, the most intriguing parallel, however, occurred in 1821 when Sabbatarians attempted to prevent Sunday steamboat excursions. They circulated a petition whose signatories promised not to support those papers continuing to advertise the excursions. The clergy also requested that publishers withdraw the offensive ads. Several days later, a group of Sabbatarian clergy and laymen met and decided to expand their initially limited goal. Addressing the public through the press, they asserted that the divine obligation to keep the Sabbath was increasingly ignored in New York. They cited such flagrant violations as business as usual at the markets, pleasure gardens, houses of public entertainment, and livery stables. In addition, they mentioned active red light districts and Monday newspapers prepared on Sunday. Calling upon the friends of good order to do their duty, the Sabbatarians announced a public meeting at City Hall to consider measures to prevent the Sabbath's profanation.[4]

This attempt at enforcing Sabbatarianism, led by the Presbyterian minister, Gardiner Spring, met with massive and immediate community opposition. Some newspapers refused to print the Sabbatarians' address to the public. Several papers affirmed that New Yorkers respected the Sabbath and questioned the usefulness of rigorous enforcement. The

Evening Journal ascribed the decline of morals which the Sabbatarians observed to "an over-heated imagination."[5] The *American* considered the steamboat excursions "comparatively innocent."[6] The *Evening Post* justified Sunday markets on the grounds that the poor worked and were paid late on Saturday; and besides, fish, meats, and milk could not be kept in hot weather.[7] The *Mercantile Advertiser*, beneath the Sabbatarian notice, printed a notice asking anti-Sabbatarians to attend the Sabbatarian meeting:

PUBLIC MEETING

> The friends of Morality and Religion, who wish a proper and just regard for the Lords day, but who do not think it judicious or proper to unite Church and State, and to bind men down to certain limits, are respectfully invited to attend the meeting, this afternoon, at 4 o'clock, at the City Hall.[8]

The meeting at City Hall was attended by as many as 5,000 persons. As the overwhelming majority of the crowd was hostile to the Sabbatarian cause, they voted down the motion for Rev. Gardiner Spring to take the chair and chose an anti-Sabbatarian as chairman. The meeting then resolved "that the citizens of New York, deem it inexpedient, that the clergy should interfere with the local concerns of the City, or the Police thereof, and that such interference is highly improper."[9]

The anti-Sabbatarians reacted sharply. Contemporary press accounts are consistent with the minister's account of the incident as he recalled it in the 1860s. Implicit in the situation was the threat that the community would use force if the Sabbatarians did not abandon their campaign. When Spring and another minister pushed their way into the packed room at City Hall, they found themselves amidst an indignant assemblage. "We were marked men. The excited multitude looked daggers at us. They would not listen to us. Our persons were in danger."[10] Caricatures of ministers appeared in the print shops, and, about the city, abusive handbills and placards circulated.[11] The newspapers received a "flood" of anti-clergy letters. The clergy were portrayed as "bigots—living on the fat of the land; enjoying high salaries, and luxurious fare; and presuming upon their influence; . . .in short, of being everything but what they profess to be—*viz.* practical christians."[12] (Unfortunately for us, the press universally practiced restraint and no actual letters were published.) The editors, more moderate than their readers, did not attack the clergy's motives, but did argue that compulsory laws could not succeed where voluntarism had failed.[13]

Confronted with opposition that threatened violence, the Sabbatarians lapsed into silence. Most of his supporters, according to Spring, stayed away from the City Hall meeting out of fear: Mayor Stephen Allen, originally scheduled to preside over the meeting, was one such person. The *Commercial Advertiser*, the one New York paper which is known to have supported the Sabbatarians, did not print a word on the issue until the public clamor died down. When, finally, it did have something to say, the paper argued that the clergy had not tried to interfere in governmental matters, but had only sought to call public attention to the nonenforcement of an already existing law. The clergy, the paper said, had neither organized nor sanctioned the petitions promising to boycott the newspapers that published Sunday steamboat excursions.[14]

The press's role in the affair in ambiguous, as in so many other disturbances, but it did play some part. It is not known whether the call to the anti-Sabbatarians to attend the City Hall meeting first appeared in the *Mercantile Advertiser*, and the extent to which the press fanned the flames is a moot point. Spring, however, put the blame squarely on the newspapers. He charged that "even the most glaring Sabbath nuisances could not be abated, while the abettors of these efforts met a storm of protest from the press."[15]

Theater riots were another major type of disturbance that the press and the community tolerated and sometimes encouraged. As David Grimsted has shown, such incidents occurred regularly, and involved, throughout the half century preceding the Civil War, larger crowds than any other type of riot.[16] Sometimes, 5,000 persons or more would gather. At the height of the anti-abolitionist rioting in 1834, the rioters did not exceed half this number. In New York, disturbances occurred in 1825, 1831, and 1832 against English actors; in 1822 and 1825 against black actors; in 1827 after an actress failed to appear; in 1830 following a masquerade; and in 1833 for unascertainable reasons.[17]

The major riots involved English actors who allegedly insulted the American people.[18] The riots against Joshua R. Anderson are instances of how agitated a mob could become on this issue. Anderson had allegedly spoken against the United States and the American people in an argument with an American citizen, and word of the affront had spread widely through the city. When Anderson appeared on stage on Thursday night, October 13, 1831, a portion of the audience, refusing to listen to his attempted explanation, noisily reduced his performance to pantomime. The audience threw cents and oranges until the actor gave up and left the stage.   On Saturday night, October 15, with Anderson again scheduled to appear, the theater manager came on stage, apparently with the actor's written apology in his hand.   The audience refused to hear it, and the manager cancelled Anderson's appearance.

Victory, however, came too easily.   Anderson's opponents had come prepared for a disturbance, so during the second half of the performance, they threw onto the stage, cents, apples, oranges and eggs. After the curtain fell, they remained in the theater for about two hours. When 100 watchmen entered the theater to restore order, the rioters became enraged and began breaking some of the benches and destroying other property.   The watchmen were ordered withdrawn as a result.

Outside the building an immense crowd gathered which did not disperse until nearly dawn.   In the course of the night, the watch made forty arrests for assault and battery and for throwing stones.   The exterior of the theater sustained about $100 worth of damage.   On Sunday night, October 16, a crowd, about 1,000 strong, again gathered.   At 9 p.m., the rioters began a noisy attack on the theater, breaking many windows and battering the front doors.   The High Constable and the mayor, with a large body of watchmen, appeared, but the mob persevered until the management displayed the American flag, the American eagle, and the tri-color in front of the theater.   The violence ended with this gesture.[19]

In March 1832, Anderson made another appearance in New York.   Property owners in the vicinity of the theater brought an injunction against Anderson and against the owner of the theater where the actor had arranged to play, prohibiting him from appearing.   As a result, the theater owner came forward and asked the audience to decide whether Anderson should appear at some future time.   The vilified actor's supporters were in the majority although they could not agree on the date of the appearance.   A hostile crowd numbering about 5,000, however, had gathered outside the theater, and after the audience voted, broke in.   They overran the stage and the boxes and committed sufficient damage to prevent the next day's scheduled performance from taking place.[20]

The press reacted to the rioting as did the parties most involved: theater owners, theatergoers, and the authorities.   Neither the theater manager nor the actor made any active attempt to incite a riot, and, in the second Anderson incident, most theatergoers supported the actor, yet the judge and the press both failed to suggest that it might be more proper either to restrain the mob or to protect the actor.   Ultimately, none insisted on suppressing the rioting.   From the first, the *Gazette and General Advertiser* stated it would not comment on the extent to which the audience was justified in its disruptive behavior.[21]   The *Commercial Advertiser* reacted similarly; failing to criticize the rioters, the paper simply acknowledged that the actor could not expect to perform in New York City again. After the first riot, the *Commercial Advertiser* concluded, "we trust that he will have too much good sense to attempt it under any circumstances;"[22] after the second riot, it testily decided itself "tired of seeing this gentleman's name and of having to record the disturbances to which his obtrusion on the public has. . .occasioned."[23]

Other newspapers, which criticized the audience's behavior, noted that a dispute between an actor and a citizen was a private matter, so long as the actor behaved properly on stage;[24] that those who opposed Anderson should simply have stayed away from the theater;[25] and that the audience should have allowed Anderson to make his apology.[26] After the 1832 riot, however, even the newspapers critical of the rioters changed their stance.

The decision of the mob that Anderson not appear went unchallenged although the audience disagreed with the mob. Several newspapers simply did not report the incident.[27] The *Evening Post*, on the other hand, admitted the obvious: "this probably decides the question of Mr. Anderson, . . .we can but hope that he will not again attempt to come before an audience; for it is not probable he can collect one of which a portion shall not be willing to forget dignity and propriety for the sake of a row."[28]

There were *direct* links between both the anti-Sabbatarian agitation and the anti-English theater riots and violent anti-abolitionism. The link was most apparent when rioters stormed the Bowery Theater, July 9, 1834. On that night, a portion of the mob that had invaded the Chatham Street Chapel earlier in the evening, proceeded to the theater where a crowd had already gathered to protest against William Farren, the English-born stage manager who had described Americans as "a damned set of jackasses." A combined mob of about 500 persons separated themselves from the larger crowd and invaded the building to shout down the performers. Anglophobia and anti-abolitionism merged and fed on each other as an American singer, to quiet the rioters, sang the popular minstrel song, "Zip Coon," a disparaging account of a Negro dandy.

Leonard Richards credits the theater riot to the rioters linking the English to abolitionism.[29] This occurred, but most of the crowd about the theater—5,000 strong—did not come from the Chatham Street Chapel,[30] and attempts to end the rioting appealed more to the rioters' nationalism than to their racism. At one point, Thomas S. Hamblin, the Bowery's manager, came on stage waving an American flag in each hand.[31]

The *Sun*, which leaned to the abolitionists, encouraged the mob. Arousing its Anglophobia, the newspaper reported stage manager Farren's remarks and suggested violence: "if the story. . .is true. . .Mr. Farren may possibly be enabled to discover that if he has gulled the damned Yankees as he calls them, with their consent, he will not be allowed to beat and knock them down with impunity."[32]   The *Sun* was sympathetic to the abolitionists; yet the paper would not condemn mob violence in the midst of anti-abolitionist rioting.

The paper's editorial course called for an imperturbable stance. On July 2, the *Sun*, in a prescient article apparently directed against the *Courier and Enquirer* (although the article named no newspaper), warned against raising up mobs.   It argued that mobs could be gotten together easily and that if the laws are "trampled under foot, there is no safety for any citizen."   On July 10, the *Sun* claimed "it has been our undivided purpose, as the unbending advocates of order and law .to endeavor to discourage every act of tumult and violence."

The *Sun* exempted the Bowery affair as "a genuine expression of public opinion," unlike, it said, the July 4 disruption.   On July 11, the paper argued that if riots "be justifiable with the American people," it was when foreigners, depending upon the Americans for their livelihood, assailed the character of the country.   The *Sun* concluded with the inflammatory remark that "this will teach English play actors a lesson they will long remember.   There are one or two worthies we intend to expose before long."

The anti-abolitionist link to anti-Sabbatarianism is more tenuous, but it is there. The disruption of the anti-slavery meeting of July 4, 1834 was not the first of its kind.   An earlier disruption (which served as a precedent) makes it very clear that the abolitionists did not suffer a unique fate.

In October 1833, an attempt was made to disrupt the anti-slavery society's organizational meeting.   General Robert Bogardus chaired a meeting opposing the abolitionists, *as, in 1821, he had chaired the anti-Sabbatarian meeting*; but the meetings differed in that the plans of the militant abolitionists went awry.   A crowd gathered at Clinton Hall where the abolitionists had scheduled their meeting, but the site was secretly changed to the Chatham Street Chapel to avoid interference.   The anti-abolitionist crowd was thwarted, but not dispersing, it adjourned to Tammany Hall where Bogardus held his meeting.

A resolution was passed that no actions should be taken without the support of the South.   The whereabouts of the abolitionists, however, were learned, and this led some of the anti-abolitionists to leave Tammany Hall for the chapel.   As a mob, they invaded the building, only to find that the abolitionists, who had been there, had eluded them again. So, with apparent good humor, the anti-abolitionists appointed a black man the mock chairman and passed emancipation and amalgamation resolutions.[33]

Leonard Richards argues that the colonizationists expected a disturbance of the kind that occurred.[34] He dismisses the assertion of colonizationist John Neal that "I am for mild, firm and effectual measures,"[35] as out of keeping with the mood of the New York anti-abolitionists. (Neal's comment was contained in a letter to R. R. Gurley, the secretary of the American Colonization Society.) A contrary interpretation, however, would look to John Lang's militant editorializing in language similar to that used by the anti-Sabbatarians in 1821: he trusted "that the friends of order and good government, who know the motives, and feel the consequences likely to result from the agitation of this subject (abolition) will go to the meeting and by a firm but discreet interference, put a stop to the injudicious and ill-advised course of these deluded individuals."[36] General Bogardus was acting in this vein when he chaired the Tammany Hall meeting. In opposing the suggestion that they adjourn to the Chatham Street Chapel, he warned his listeners that they would be labeled disorganizers.[37]

II

Yet, if there was toleration of some types of rioting and rioting in particular situations, we still may wonder why certain newspapers—with all their influence—actively abetted the rioters while others passively looked on. The answer lies in the general willingness of certain editors to use the mob to influence public policy and opinion. The same newspapers which in April had anticipated and published the most inflammatory accounts of the rioting, in July encouraged the mob to disrupt abolitionist meetings.

In this role of riot abettor, James Watson Webb of the *Courier and Enquirer* stood preeminent. In April, Webb had urged the Whigs to take countermeasures against the anticipated Jacksonian use of bullies, and in the midst of the election, he personally led a force of citizen volunteers into the Irish dominated sixth ward.[38] In June, he raised the issue of amalgamation with respect to Cox's sermon and spread false rumors, goading the mob to violence.

The *Commercial Advertiser*, edited by Stone, actively encouraged rioting in neither April nor July, but used language that could only have encouraged that result. The *Evening Star*, edited by Mordecai M. Noah, inflamed the mob nearly as much as the *Courier and Enquirer*, although this paper was not willing to see the mob out. Noah, perpetually fearful of the mob getting out of hand, early turned against the mob in the July rioting and, in the midst of the April rioting, subdued his inflammatory war imagery. Redwood Fisher, one of the *Mercantile Advertiser's* three editors, was identified by Commissary-General Henry Arcularius as one of twenty-three men who in April took a leading part in the seizure of the arsenal.[39] In July, his paper encouraged the mob. Representing the Democrats, the *Standard* in April and the *Times* (which continued the policies and personnel of the *Standard*) in July took far more belligerent stands than the *Post*, the other leading Democratic paper.

The fixed attitudes towards rioting which made the press reaction to the election and anti-abolitionist disturbances predictable, did not likely originate in 1834. In the cases of Stone and Noah, there is conclusive evidence of their earlier support for mob violence.

In 1825, Stone encouraged the mob that prevented the English actor, Edmund Kean, from appearing on the New York stage. In 1821 in Boston, Kean had refused to go ahead with a scheduled performance because he thought there were too few people in the audience. This offense to the American public ended his tour of the United States, but when he returned in 1825, the Americans did not forget the insult. Americans were also aware of Kean's much publicized affair with the wife of a London alderman. The audience shouted Kean down when he premiered in New York and refused to hear his apology. About one-fourth pelted the actors with oranges and rotten apples. When the curtain fell at the end of the play, the offending actor was called for. Informed that he had already left the theater, the audience broke benches and fixtures and did other damage. Outside, a large crowd tried to break in, but about twenty or thirty watchmen arrived in time to prevent them.[40]

The *Commercial Advertiser* edited by William Leete Stone, played a major role in the affair and took up the cudgels against Kean more than six weeks before his scheduled appearance. The paper made a suggestion: "let the males, if they will go, hiss him off with indignation."[41] The paper continued its opposition throughout the the following weeks, but did a turnabout in its stand as the performance neared. Kean's opponents were now urged to stay away from the theater to avoid violence.[42] The *Commercial Advertiser* reversed itself again after the riot. It was surprised that one-quarter of Kean's audience objected to him. The actor's supporters were accused of attempting for weeks to pack the theater. It reported rumors that applauders were hired. Stone called Kean's appearance "a bold experiment" and he defended the right of the audience to hiss, provided no actual riot occurred.[43]

Stone's changing position in 1825 paralleled his stance in 1834 in opposing the abolitionists.   In both instances, strong and persistent editorializing against violators of his morality significantly contributed to a riotous climate; but once the explosive situation came into being, Stone did not continue to encourage violence.   After the rioting ended, the right to shout down a public speaker was stoutly defended.[44]

Noah was an influential figure in Tammany Hall until his desertion in the early 1830s.   He supported the regular nominations chosen by nominating committees against insurgent candidates.   On three occasions during the 1820s, strong-arm tactics, acceptable to Noah, were used to elect the chairman—the man who would control the meeting:

> We trust that no tumult will prevail—that the question will be taken upon each name—that speakers may be heard and answered with decorum—that none but men recognized and considered as members of the democratic party will be permitted to vote or mingle in the deliberations of the party.

When individuals who were not "recognized and considered as members of the democratic party" attempted to influence or control party proceedings, there were appropriate measures to be taken:

> Of late not more than thirty members of Tammany Society have attended the regular meetings; and a few malcontents, taking advantage of this slender number, have ventured to intrigue a little in the name and under the influence of the Society.   We have permitted them to amuse themselves without opposition because it was quite harmless.   If any thing serious to the party grew out of these petty speculations, this presidential game of push pin for Mr. Calhoun, we were ready to sound the alarm, and call out old Tammany, to the tune of 1,000 members, when these speculators would cut and run with more avidity than Gardner did behind the barn at the battle of Chippewa.[45]

In 1823, the People's party tried to take over Tammany Hall:

> A sudden rush was made upon our right, our sides were near being stove in, and we discerned the passing fragments of the Secretary's chair, which had been torn from under him, and was borne triumphantly off by the cohort who had made this successful dash among the enemy.   We immediately perceived the chairman in motion, and judged from his movements, that he was about to leave the chair; and such was indeed the fact, for in spite of piercing shouts "no! no! don't give up the ship! support the chair!" he gave up his dangerous eminence, and sunk undistinguished amidst the tumultuous waves that surrounded it. . .we beheld, rising above the sea of heads, the tall and erect form of the people's chairman. . ."leave the chair! pull him out! pull him down!" To say the

> truth—the General seemed not altogether at ease. . .He looked around and seemed to expect an attack. . .a band, which had suddenly rallied, made its way past as, with vehement gestures, and in a few minutes, chair and chairman were bro't down together, and for a season chaos reigned.[46]

Party meetings resembled the disruptions that Noah supported in July 1834. In each case, the objection of the tumult was limited—control of the meeting. While most editors did not object strenuously to such affairs, Noah actively encouraged them.

One editor who literally took to the streets was Webb. Personal disputes, already noted, led him to physically assault his antagonists.[47] In 1836, in an ironic reversal of roles, he declined a duel. Webb had encouraged a mob to drive an English actor off the stage because the actor had offended an American actress whose part Webb took. The chagrined actor challenged the editor to a duel.[48] In the April 1834 election riot, Webb organized and led a force of volunteers to protect the Whigs' right to vote in the sixth ward. In a more passive advocacy, Webb, in October 1833, issued a call for a mob to put down the anti-slavery society's organizational meeting.[49]

III

Press accounts plus analyses after the fact provide us the information necessary for measuring the extensiveness and seriousness of the anti-abolitionist disturbances.[50] Summarized chronologically in Table 1 are the various incidents comprising the riot, beginning July 4 and ending July 11.

On the number of rioters, newspaper estimates ran as high as several thousand—for the night of July 11.[51] Only several hundred rioted on July 10,[52] and, on July 9, about the same number broke into the Chatham Street Chapel;[53] a somewhat larger number, about 500, stormed the Bowery Theater.[54] Spectators, intrinsic to the scenes and encouraging to the more active rioters, massed together in crowds: on July 9, the Bowery Theater was surrounded by 5,000 persons and the Chatham Street Chapel by 2,000 - 3,000. These crowds, however, were not larger than other crowds of the period. Several thousand persons collected together on a number of other occasions for sundry reasons.[55] Theater riots repeatedly involved crowds of 5,000.[56]

TABLE 1

MAJOR ANTI-ABOLITIONIST INCIDENTS JULY 4-11, 1834

Date	Incident	See Text Pp.
July 4	Disruption of the anti-slavery meeting in Chatham Street Chapel	38-39
July 7	Disruption of the Negro meeting in Chatham Street Chapel (Sacred Music Society incident)	39-40
July 8	Disruption of Moral Lyceum meeting in Clinton Hall	40
July 9	Assault on Lewis Tappan's house	33
	Forceable entry into Chatham Street Chapel	41
	Forceable entry into the Bowery theater and disruption of the performance	41,65-66
July 10	Assault on Rev. Samuel H. Cox's church	34
	Assault on Rev. Samuel H. Cox's house	34-35
July 11	Assault on the store of Arthur Tappan & Co.	34
	Assault on Rev. Samuel H. Cox's church	35
	Assault on Rev. Henry G. Ludlow's church	35
	Rampage against Five Points Negroes	75-78

Property destruction, of course, must also be considered. Historians, most recently Leonard Richards, have been impressed by the rioters' attack on a great number of abolitionist homes, businesses, and churches. The rioters are also charged with indiscriminately attacking Negro homes in the neighborhood of the infamous Five Points. This view exaggerates the violence. The intensity of violence, it is true, increased greatly on July 10 and 11 when the mob attempted to destroy the abolitionists' property; but if we consider the number of targets, rioting did not increase anywhere near the "hundredfold" that Richards suggests.[57] On the two days taken together, the major targets, excepting the Negroes, numbered only four. On July 10, the mob concertedly attacked only the Reverend Cox's house and church. On the following day, rioters turned to Tappan's store and churches of the Reverends Henry G. Ludlow and Samuel H. Cox. Many windows were broken, but extensive damage was done only to Ludlow's church.

As for black homes in the (racially mixed) Five Points, wholesale destruction also did not occur. The mob randomly attacked the homes of many Negroes, but there was no razing and ransacking of the area. The mob attacked the Centre Street church of Peter Williams, a black minister and an officer of the anti-slavery society. When it met no opposition and gutted the church, it assaulted the building next door and several across the street. Windows were smashed, doors broken in, and some or all of the buldings entered. A Negro barkeeper, sustaining the most damage, had his bar equipment and house furnishings destroyed. This amounted to about $800 worth of damage, a sizable sum.

In the hours between 11:00 p.m. and 2:00 a.m., July 11-12, rioters damaged several houses in several streets. The *Sun* listed four houses attacked in Centre Street, and also an additional one in Leonard, six in Orange, two in Cross, and two in Mulberry—fifteen in all.[58] The *Transcript* reported a total of about twenty-five buildings attacked, including fifteen in Orange Street, three in Leonard, three in Centre, and three or four in Anthony.[59] The mob went on a spree in Orange Street, breaking windows in a number of houses which the *Transcript* counted, but the *Sun* did not. This is the major difference between the two accounts. The *Daily Advertiser*, without providing an explicit breakdown, reported that twenty Negro famlies lost all their possessions in the rioting and that city-wide rioters attacked twenty houses and seven churches.[60]

The mob did create great havoc—perhaps 500 blacks, fearing further rioting, left their homes on Saturday, July 12—but in all, relatively few Negroes suffered directly.[61] The New York riot conformed to the pattern of pre-industrial violence. Many kinds of disturbances, including election riots, theater riots, and disruptions of public meetings entailed minimal property damage, and when mobs did assault property, their targets were related specifically to their discontent.[62] In the case of the anti-abolitionists, the mob attacked the homes and churches of the three abolitionists who most offended them. Selectivity broke down in the case of Five Points blacks only; but anti-black mobs generally were an exception to the rule. Such mobs, once aroused, victimized all Negroes, regardless of their roles in the precipitating incidents. In Providence in 1831, rampaging mobs, in four nights of rioting, attacked more than thirty buildings which Negroes owned or inhabited;[63] in Philadelphia in August 1834, mobs, in three nights of rioting, attacked between thirty and thirty-five such buildings.[64] The New York riot, involving damage to approximately twenty or twenty-five Negro owned or inhabited buildings committed in the course of one night's rioting, did not match the destructiveness of these other major anti-Negro mobs.

Despite the duration of the rioting, the numbers involved, and the resistance of the authorities, very few serious injuries resulted. In the fighting about Reverend Ludlow's church, "a good many persons," reportedly, "were more or less hurt."[65] In the anti-black rioting in the Five Points area, a black woman fell and broke her leg while fleeing out the back way of her house.[66] A white rioter was shot by a black barber defending his home from assault (he allegedly was the only black to resist the mob).[67]

Neither the rioters nor the militia used firearms, and no one was killed. Altogether in the 1820s and early 1830s, only two deaths resulted from rioting in New York. During the 1834 charter election, a watchman was killed,[68] and, in 1825, eight members of a youthful gang murdered a wealthy citizen.[69] Nationally, however, fatalities were more frequent because riots occurred where authorities shot into crowds. In Providence in 1831, the militia killed five;[70] and in Baltimore in 1835, a citizens' guard killed five during an anti-bank riot.[71] According to David Grimsted, between 1828 and 1835 seventy-three incidents of riot in the nation resulted in sixty-one fatalities.[72]

Ultimately, however, our frame of reference determines whether or not we consider the New York anti-abolitionist riot "serious." Were we to adopt the view prevalent in the 1830s, any riot involving property damage would be a major one; but on any objective scale of magnitude, the New York riot was not the most serious of the era.

However, whatever the true "seriousness" of the riot, many New Yorkers reacted with undue hysteria—and this reaction is probably more important than any objective measure of the scale of the riot. The press (misleading future historians), expressed their fear of impending anarchy, and several papers called on the authorities to put down the mob at all costs—to shed blood if necessary. The *Post*, the most alarmist, wanted those rioters who made "the first movement towards sedition [to] be shot down like dogs."[73] The *Daily Advertiser* opined, "it cannot be disguised. . .the City Government was overawed, and for the time at an end;"[74] and the *Star* asked:

> Who is safe? Whose property may not be assailed? Whose store may not be destroyed? You cannot reason with a mob; decision and energy are necessary to sustain the majesty of the laws to restore order.[75]

The mayor, agreeing with the press, decided after the rioting of July 11 that only the strongest actions would end the violence. He issued a second proclamation—with a less urgently worded one proving ineffective—calling upon the citizenry and the ."whole body of the military" to patrol the streets.[76] A command post was established at City Hall to which military commanders stationed about the city forwarded their reports. Thirty volunteer aides assisted the mayor. Most remained with him at the command post, but some were stationed at danger points in the city. The mayor, responding to the incoming reports, sent small detachments of troops to possible targets.[77] The rioters, believing that the militia could not fire without orders from the governor, the commander-in-chief of the militia, were warned by the mayor that if the disturbances continued, there would inevitably be deaths. The mayor's actions may have forestalled further rioting, but they did not end it in any literal way; on July 12, there was no mob to suppress and no large crowds to disperse.

A post-mortem to the riot was provided by Recorder Richard Riker, the city's criminal judge. He used the sentencing of the few persons convicted of rioting as an occasion to describe the violence as "of a very atrocious character." Its "infamous proceedings amounted almost to insurrection." Riker lectured the rioters in a tone characteristic of the press at the height of the violence. He reminded the rioters that magistrates could have ordered them shot, and he offered his own view on the wisdom of a hard line:

> Many good men had thought it best to fire blank cartridges at first; and no doubt this would be best if effectual, but experience had shown that such a measure only exasperated and emboldened a mob the more, and the result was the loss of more lives, than would have followed from administering the fatal remedy at first.—The majority of those who had promulgated opinions on the subject, were in favor of using balls at first; and though he might be wrong, he confessed he inclined to this opinion himself. He was averse to calling upon the military at all, unless they were to act with vigor; for it was unjust to expose them to be stoned by a mob unless they had the power of repelling such attacks.[78]

Riker also made a comment which mirrored the *Post's* after-word on the election riot:

> All who reflected on the character of a mob, knew that it was a mere brute force which any bold and bad man might direct as an engine to gratify private revenge, and for the worst of purposes. It was devoid of descrimination and reflection; so that no matter how innocent or excellent a man might be, he is liable to become its

victim. It was impossible to describe its evils. Hurried on by a blind fury, every thing became subject to its force, and the rights of property and personal security were lost and swept away, as it were, in an ocean of madness.[79]

The hysteria accompanying the charter election subsided quickly once the polls closed. Preoccupation with the anti-abolition disturbances, in contrast, lingered on. The press assumed an accusatory posture and apportioned blame.[80]   In the middle of August, when a race riot occurred in Philadelphia and an anti-Catholic riot in Charlestown, Massachusetts, the papers linked the two events to their own riots as manifestations of the increase in disorder nationally.[81]

August 1834 is a benchmark in the history of the 1830s. Throughout the next several years, nationwide occurrences biased New Yorkers in their reactions to local disturbances; and the two major New York riots of 1834 served as a backdrop. The specter of the unleashed mob overshadowed public discussion and policy making alike; but it was a specter that seemed to come and go.

NOTES

[1]On the press attitude to early labor strife, see below, Chap. 5. When eight ruffians murdered a respectable and wealthy citizen in 1825, the press and the authorities reacted harshly and without hesitation. See the *New-York Commercial Advertiser*, June 3, 4, 7, 21-24, July 2, 1825.

[2]A. J. G. Perkins and Theresa Wolfson, *Frances Wright Free Enquirer, The Study of a Temperament* (New York, 1939), *Commercial Advertiser*, January 8, 1829. When Frances Wright lectured in Philadelphia during this same tour, a caricature was published which called on the public to hiss her down. See LITHOGRAPH, "A Downright Gabbler, or a goose that deserves to be hissed—" (Philadelphia, ca. 1830), Print Division, New-York Historical Society.

[3][Lewis Tappan], *The Life of Arthur Tappan* (New York, 1871), pp. 112-17; Phyllis Mary Bannan, "Arthur and Lewis Tappan: A Study in New York Religious and Reform Movements" (Ph.D. dissertation, Columbia University, 1950), pp. 62-63; *Commercial Advertiser*, August 15, 16, 1831.

[4]*Commercial Advertiser*, July 20, 24, 1821.

[5]*New-York Evening Journal, And Patron of Industry*, July 25, 1821.

[6]*New-York American*, July 24, 1821.

[7]*Evening Post* (New York), July 24, 1821.

[8]*Mercantile Advertiser and New-York Advocate*, July 25, 1821.

[9]*American*, July 26, 1821; *Evening Journal*, July 26, 1821; *National Advocate* (New York), July 26, 1821.

[10]Gardiner Spring, *Personal Reminiscences of the Life and Times of Gardiner Spring*, 2 Vols. (New York, 1866), 2:142-43.

[11]*National Advocate*, July 28, 1821.

[12]Ibid.

[13]Ibid.; *American*, July 27, 1821; *Evening Post*, July 25, 26, 1821.

[14]*Commercial Advertiser*, August 1, 1821.

[15]Gardiner Spring, *Personal Reminiscences*, 2:144; *American*, July 28, 1821; *National Advocate*, July 28, 30, 1821; *Evening Post*, July 25, 26, 1821.

[16]David Grimsted, *Melodrama Unveiled: American Theater and Culture 1800-1850* (Chicago, 1968), pp. 65-75.

[17]The riots against English actors are discussed below, but for the other theater riots, see the *Commercial Advertiser*, January 9, August 17, 1822, December 2, 1825, July 21, 1827, February 23, 1830, March 15, 1833.

[18]For anti-English riots, in addition to those described in this chapter, see Richard Moody, *The Astor Place Riot* (Bloomington, Ind., 1958); Grimsted, *Melodrama Unveiled*, pp. 65-75.

[19]*American*, October 14, 17, 18, 1831; *New-York American Advocate*, October 14, 17, 18, 1831; *New-York Gazette and General Advertiser*, October 14, 17, 1831; Philip Hone, *The Diary of Philip Hone, 1828-1851*, ed. Allan Nevin, new and enl. ed. (New York, 1936), p. 50 (October 17, 1831).

[20]*Commercial Advertiser*, March 19, 20, 1832; *Gazette and General Advertiser*, March 20, 1832; *New York Standard*, reprinted in the *Evening Post*, March 20, 1832.

[21]*Gazette and General Advertiser*, October 14, 1831, March 20, 1832.

[22]*Commercial Advertiser*, October 17, 1831.

[23]Ibid., March 20, 1832.

[24]*American*, October 14, 1831; *American Advocate*, October 17, 1831.

[25]*Evening Post*, October 14, 1831.

[26]*Standard*, October 15, 17, 1831.

[27]*American*; *American Advocate*.

[28]*Evening Post*, March 20, 1832.

[29]Richards, *"Gentlemen of Property and Standing,"* p. 69.

[30]On a crowd gathering at the Bowery Theater while an anti-abolitionist mob was still at the Chatham Street Chapel, see the *Morning Courier and New-York Enquirer*, July 10, 1834; *Evening Star* (New York), July 10, 1834.

[31]*Sun* (New York), July 11 1834; *Evening Star*, July 10, 1834.

[32]*Sun*, July 8, 1834.

[33]Richards, *"Gentlemen of Property and Standing,"* pp. 26-30. In Edward Pessen, "The Wealthiest New Yorkers of the Jacksonian Era: A New List," *New-York Historical Society Quarterly* 54 (April 1970): 156, Bogardus is listed, in 1828, with assessed wealth at between $50,000 and $100,000—among New York's top 202 fortunes. Bogardus was a Federalist and Whig lawyer (see Donald M. Roper, "The Elite of the New York Bar as Seen from the Bench: James Kent's Necrologies," *New-York Historical Society Quarterly* 56 (July 1972): 233-34). His title of general was acquired during his service in the militia during the War of 1812.

[34]Ibid., p. 27.

[35]Ibid.

[36]*Gazette and General Advertiser*, October 2, 1833.

[37]Ibid., October 3, 1833.

[38]Above, pp. 7, 12-13.

[39]New York (State), Assembly, *Report of the Commissary-General to the Committee on the Militia and the Public Defence, in Relation to the Arsenal in the City of New-York,* Doc. 389, 57th sess., 1834, p. 8.

[40]*American,* November 15, 1825; *Commercial Advertiser,* November 15, 1825; *Gazette and General Advertiser,* November 15, 1825; *National Advocate and New-York National Advocate,* re-printed in the *Evening Post,* November 15, 1825. On anti-Kean rioting in Scotland—the result of his affair—see *Dictionary of National Biography;* Grimstead, *Melodrama Unveiled,* p. 66.

[41]*Commercial Advertiser,* September 29, 1825.

[42]Ibid., October 15, 28, 29, 31, November 2, 11, 1825.

[43]Ibid., November 15, 17, 1825.

[44]Ibid., July 12, 1834.

[45]The quotation is from Noah's paper, the *National Advocate,* September 24, 1823. The meetings are reported in Jerome Mushkat, *Tammany: The Evolution of a Political Machine 1789-1865* (Syracuse, N. Y., 1971), pp. 84, 113; *Commercial Advertiser,* October 31, 1822, October 28, 1823, November 1, 1828; *American,* October 28, 1823, October 28, November 1, 1828; *National Advocate,* October 28, 1823; *Evening Post,* October 31, 1822, October 28, 1828; *New-York Enquirer,* October 28, 31, 1828.

[46]*Commercial Advertiser,* October 28, 1823.

[47]Above, p. 6.

[48]T[homas] Allston Brown, *A History of the New York Stage: From the First Performance in 1732 to 1901,* 3 Vols. (New York, 1903), 1:44; *Courier and Enquirer,* May 25-28, 1836.

[49]*Courier and Enquirer,* October 2, 1833.

[50]For a list of sources and secondary works, see above, Chap. 2, n. 1.

[51]*New-York Daily Advertiser,* July 12, 1834, estimated the Five Points mob at "some thousands;" the *New York Times,* July 12, 1834, estimated it at 2,000-3,000. The *New York Transcript,* July 12, 1834, describing two separate mobs, estimated one at 1,000 and the other at 300.

[52]The *Evening Post,* July 11, 1834, always prone to exaggerate the extent of rioting, described several mobs at 500-2,000 persons each, but both the *Daily Advertiser* and the *New York Journal of Commerce,* July 11, 1834, estimated the mob at several hundred. The local press probably reprinted the local news accounts of the *Journal of Commerce* more often than they did those of any other paper—the accounts of this paper were generally both the most reliable and the most detailed.

[53]*Courier and Enquirer,* July 10, 1834; but the *Journal of Commerce,* July 10, 1834, claimed the number of rioters to be 2,000-3,000. Other estimates: "there could not have been less than five thousand people" surrounding the Theater (*Mercantile Advertiser and New-York Advocate,* July 10, 1834); "more than 1,000 persons" stormed the Theater (*American,* July 10, 1834).

[54]*Sun,* July 11, 1834; *Daily Advertiser,* July 10, 1834; *Mercantile Advertiser,* July 10, 1834; *Times,* July 10, 1834.

[55]As spectators frequently encouraged active rioters, estimates of the size of mobs legitimately can vary widely. During the anti-abolitionist rioting, apparently, most members of the mob did not actually engage in property destruction. Most rioters merely went along. Counting only active rioters reduces the mob considerably. The *Courier and Enquirer,* July 15, 1834, discounting the importance of the rioting for which it was responsible, makes this argument. The paper alleges that only 100 men and boys rioted, but that "some thousands" followed them. The *Mercantile Advertiser,* July 14, 1834, and the *Daily Advertiser,* July 12, 1834, also refer to the large number of spectators as do the mayor's two proclamations. New York (City), Board of Assistants, *Communication from His Honor, the Mayor, Relative to the Late Riots, Etc., Accompanied with Two Prclamations, Issued by the Mayor, on the 11th and 12th of July, 1834,* Doc. No. 11, Vol. I (1834).

In 1827, a mob of 2,000 attacked stores staying open after twilight (see the *Commercial Advertiser,* November 2, 3, 9, 1827). The *Commercial Advertiser,* September 29, 1834, reported a brawl among non-Americans which involved 100 active rioters and 1,000 onlookers, and the paper observed that "there appeared to be more persons engaged than in any of our July riots." The week before the anti-abolitionist rioting, a mob attacked a shoe store after a woman was arrested for stealing a pair of shoes. While 200 rioters smashed the window and destroyed the carpet and awning, 2,000 spectators watched (see the *Commercial Advertiser,* July 1, 1834; *Courier and Enquirer,* July 1, 2, 1834). In the early morning hours of New Year's Day, 1828, a mob numbering about 4,000 fought the watch as they committed various acts of depredation. *Evening Post,* January 2, 1828.

[56]*Evening Post,* March 20, 1832 (second Anderson riot); *Courier and Enquirer,* October 17, 1831 (first Anderson riot). In 1849, in the most famous American theater riot, a New York mob of as many as 15,000 persons collected outside the Astor Place Theater to oppose the British actor William MacCready. Richard Hofstadter and Michael Wallace, eds., *American Violence: A Documentary* (New York, 1970), p. 454.

[57]Richards, *"Gentlemen of Property and Standing,"* p. 118.

[58]*Sun,* July 14, 1834.

[59]*Transcript,* July 14, 1834.

[60]*Daily Advertiser,* July 14, 1834.

[61]*Man,* July 14, 1834; *Transcript,* July 14, 1834.

[62]David Grimsted, "Rioting in Its Jacksonian Setting," *American Historical Review* 77 (April 1972): 379-80; Richards, *"Gentlemen of Property and Standing,"* passim.

[63]*Providence Journal*, reprinted in *Commercial Advertiser*, September 23, 24, 1831; *Providence Journal*, reprinted in *Gazette and General Advertiser*, September 26, 28, 1831; *Providence American*, reprinted in *Commercial Advertiser*, September 24, 1831; *Commercial Advertiser*, September 26, 1831.

[64]*Pennsylvania Inquirer*, reprinted in *Hazard's Register of Pennsylvania* 14 (August 23, 1834): 128; "Report of the Committee Appointed at a Town Meeting of the Citizens of the City and County of Philadelphia," *Hazard's Register* 14 (September 27, 1834): 202; *New-York Observor*, August 23, 1834.

[65]*Journal of Commerce*, July 12, 1834.

[66]*Transcript*, July 14, 1834.

[67]*Courier and Enquirer*, July 12, 1834.

[68]Above, p. 16.

[69]*Commercial Advertiser*, June 3, 1825.

[70]*Providence Journal*, reprinted in *Gazette and General Advertiser*, September 28, 1831.

[71]Grimsted, "Rioting in Its Jacksonian Setting," p. 377.

[72]Ibid., pp. 362, 364.

[73]*Evening Post*, July 12, 1834

[74]*Daily Advertiser*, July 12, 1834.

[75]*Evening Star*, July 12, 1834.

[76]New York (City), Board of Assistants, *The Late Riots*.

[77]Cornelius Lawrence File on the Anti-Abolitionist Riots, New York City Miscellaneous Manuscripts, 1834, Manuscript Division, New-York Historical Society.

[78]*Commercial Advertiser*, July 23 1834. Reporters at this time did not quote their sources word for word. Thus, the press' report of Riker's speech is only a close approximation of his exact words.

[79]Ibid. Grimstead, "Rioting in Its Jacksonian Setting," pp. 364-74 and passim; Richards, *"Gentlemen of Property and Standing,"* chap. 4, passim.

[80]*Commercial Advertiser*, July 15, 17, 23, 24, 1834; *Courier and Enquirer*, July 14, 15, 18, 21, August 9, 1834; *Journal of Commerce*, July 16, 19, 1834; *Man* (New York), July 16, 17, 19, 21, 26, 1834; *Evening Post*, July 15-18, 21, 22, 24, 25, 1834.

[81]*Daily Advertiser*, August 16, 1834; *American*, August 14, 15, 1834; *Commercial Advertiser*, August 26, 1834; *Man*, August 16, 1834; *Evening Post*, August 15, 19, 1834; *Star*, August 15, 1834; *Sun*, August 14, 15, 1834.

CHAPTER FOUR

THE DEMAGOGIC VIEW OF RIOTING

I

Rioting tore through the nation in 1835; more than twice the number of incidents of violence made the news than in 1834.[1] Abolitionism, nativism, and labor discord remained the central causes; and a partial listing of the violence would include the race riots in Philadelphia, and the anti-abolitionist or anti-black riots in Boston; Washington, D. C.; Hartford, Connecticut; and Utica, New York. Also, there were anti-Irish and anti-Catholic riots in Detroit, Buffalo, and Newburgh, New York, and labor violence along the canals of Indiana and New York State and on the railroads in the District of Columbia.[2]

In New York City, fifteen disturbances were locally reported in the eighteen months between the anti-abolitionist riot and the next call up of the militia—the period August 1834-January 1836.[3] Fights between Irishmen and nativists erupted in September and October 1834 and in January and June 1835. In March 1835, Irish Catholics disrupted a meeting of the New York Protestant Association, and five months later, in August, Irishmen attacked a watchman taking one of their countrymen to the watchhouse. Seamen, pianoforte workers, and stonecutters all staged violent strikes. In August 1835, a mob attacked a Negro-owned barber shop.[4]

In the biggest New York riot, in June 1835, mobs of as many as 500 nativists and Irish fought each other and the watch for three days in what has since become known as the "Five Points Riot." A bystander, a doctor on his way to a patient, was hit by a brick, knocked to the ground and beaten. Several days later, he died from his injuries. Rioters also gutted a tavern, and a police justice and several watchmen were slightly wounded. Sharply departing from mob behavior generally, rioters fired several shots.[5]

Given the extent of local mob violence and the nationwide alarm over the issue, the action of the civil authorities more often than not was lethargic. The mayor's response, in the case of New York's "Five Points Riot," was to urge the citizens to observe the Sabbath. (The riot had begun on a Sunday.) A warning was issued to liquor sellers that they could be fined, imprisoned, and deprived of their licenses—a warning indeed irrelevant.[6]

Any effective measures to limit or prevent violence in this case or others would have required the police system to be reorganized on more military lines, as had already occurred in London with the appointment of "bobbies." The majority of Americans were not yet prepared to take this step. They often expressed a fear of a permanent "military" force—a standing army. They did not want to chance damaging their republican institutions. By militarily suppressing riots and establishing a permanent military-style police force, Americans believed they might bring this unfortunate result about.[7]

II

The lower classes turned on their betters only when goaded by demagogues, according to the traditional view, and rioting of this sort happened rarely.[8] The many riots of 1835, from this vantage point, were a temporary aberration which had started with the "fanaticism" of the abolitionists and the rabble rousing of their opponents: the leaders caused the rioting.

The press generally accepted this analysis—although paradoxically the press itself was the greatest rabble-rouser. When contemporaries condemned demagogues, they meant newspaper editors and others whose advocacies found their way into print. In a society without other means of mass communication, the printed word had great import and influence. When the press, on occasion, credited itself with the ability to arouse mobs, it was only expressing pride or stating a fact about what others criticized: the press's shaping of public opinion and its ability to trigger mob violence.[9]

The 1834 anti-abolitionist violence was analyzed in this vein most fully by the *Journal of Commerce.* The mob wanted plunder, but this factor ranked sixth among seven. Well ahead of it were the immoderate zeal of the abolitionists and the incitements of some of the press, particularly the *Courier and Enquirer,* the *Times,* and the *Commercial Advertiser.* (The *Journal of Commerce* also charged that conspirators had planned the riots and that "respectable" men anticipated if they did not actually instigate them. Other factors the paper listed as encouragements to the mob were the impunity of the rioters during the Charter election, the spirit of "agrarianism" and "infidelity," and the attempts that had been made to connect the rioting to other popular issues.)[10]

The *Man* agreed with the *Journal of Commerce,* though on other political or religious issues the two newspapers could be poles apart. In this case, the *Man* concurred that some newspapers had sought to arouse the mob and actors behind the scenes also were involved. Both papers assumed that the mob did not have a mind of its own. George Evans' editorship of the *Man*—Evans also edited the *Workingman's Advocate*—made no difference. The fear of racial amalgamation, emphasized by Richards, the most recent historian of the anti-abolitionist riot, was seen by contermporaries as dormant until demagoguery awakened it.[11]

The "Five Points Riot" made the demagogic role of the New York City press again an issue. The press itself blamed several newspapers, the *Herald* detailing the charges most fully. The paper reported that the groups of well-dressed persons who had gathered in front of the police office blamed the riot on the newspapers that "influenced the minds of the Irish against the Americans." In support of that charge, the *Herald* said that the *Star*, the *Courier and Enquirer*, and the *Journal of Commerce* had held the Irish up to scorn.

The *Star*, in particular, had appealed to "the mobbish feelings . . .almost every other day, for the last three months"; and the *Courier and Enquirer* "on several occasions . . .almost called the people to riot by express language."[12] The *Herald* did not exonerate the Irish, but placed their share of the responsibility on the Catholic clergy who had failed to elevate the Irishmen's "ignorant, riotous, outbreaking" character.[13]

The *Gazette* and the *Commercial Advertiser* did not disagree on the role of the press and refused as a matter of policy to elaborate on the disturbances. The papers feared exciting further violence. "We are too heartily sick and disgusted with these miserable evidences of our unsound and unsafe condition, with such elements of discord and violence rankling among us, and but too many who ought to know and to do better, ready to excite them into fearful activity, to go into the details."[14] As for the *Post*: the "opposition papers . . .[were to] beware what they are doing." The paper had refrained at first "from saying one word about the riot . . .and we should still refrain, were not the comments of the opposition wholly unjustifiable in their character, and so obviously calculated to work the direst mischief."[15] The press, generally, made a concerted effort to make it seem that the authorities controlled the situation; personal injuries and property damage were minimized. The *Journal of Commerce*, which prided itself on accuracy, and the penny papers, just beginning publication, were exceptions to the consensus.[16]

The press, in previous years, occasionally had been self-conscious about its ability to arouse a mob and its responsibility to exercise restraint (following the anti-Sabbatarian incidents, for example); but in 1835, it seemed especially desirous of maintaining calm.[17] The newspapers disassociated themselves universally from the "Five Points Riot," although the riot can be traced directly to the tensions arising from the anti-immigrant politics in which a number of editors were taking part.[18] Violence was not so great as to cause the press to report rumors as facts, and this careful reporting stands in sharp contrast to the handling of the anti-abolitionist rioting of July 1834. (In August 1835, the press, in alarmist tones, reported a major riot in Baltimore after having minimized it: a threshhold of magnitude was reached which turned reporters into "fearmongers."[19] This is what happened in New York in the case of the abolitionists.)

III

Charges of demagogy issued from both the Jacksonian and Whig press, and while the sentiment was greatest among Whigs,[20] it was not totally absent among Democrats. The *Evening Post*, the newspaper of the Democratic radicals, consistently expressed more fear of an aroused rabble than any other paper in the city: "no rational man," it claimed characteristically, "would go to work deliberately to light a fire among" the "combustible" Irish; "nothing but blood will cool" "infuriated mobs."[21]

The concern with demagogy emerged from a well defined philosophy of the relationship between politics and the well ordered society: neither political parties nor electioneering—in the abstract—were approved. This philosophy, based ultimately on eighteenth century English political concepts, was manifest in United States history as early as the first party system of the 1790s.[22]

The Federalists of the period regularly objected to the Republicans' method of acquiring political power. The Republicans concurred with the Federalists in their organic view of society. The Republicans, however, acclaimed the masses a virtuous and patriotic people who prevented aristocrats from subverting republican institutions;[23] and thus they created a rationale for themselves for organizing politically while simultaneously rejecting political parties. The Federalists called this demagogy.

In 1794, Republican merchants and lawyers in New York founded a Democratic Society open to all classes, and there was Federalist criticism at permitting "the lowest order of mechanics, laborers, and draymen" to attend its meetings.[24] The next year, another Federalist spoke of "our demagogues always fixing their meetings in order to take in all mechanics and laborers—over whom they alone have influence."[25] The Republicans, by 1800, had successfully won over the less well-off mechanics and the poor immigrants, many of whom were destined for the almshouse. On several occasions, the Federalists did not compete at all.[26] They also threatened the mechanics with the loss of their jobs and challenged the eligibility of naturalized citizens to vote. Republicans, in answering Federalist criticism of the mechanics' participation in politics, signed their newspaper articles "one of the swinish multitude" and "only a mechanic and one of the rabble."[27] The federalists both scorned and feared the "mob."

The Clintonians were a Republican faction. Named after De Witt Clinton, mayor of New York from 1803 to 1815 and subsequently governor of the state, they feared an urban rabble as distinguished from "the people" who did not threaten society's well-being.[28] Clinton reported to the grand jury, in 1811, that although New York had only one tenth of the state's population, it had almost half its criminal convictions; and he attributed this poor record, in part, to a foot-loose underclass, "the constant migration of bad men from one great and opulent city to another."[29] After 1812, the Clintonians, no longer allied with the Tammany Republicans and seeking Federalist support, increasingly labeled the Republican opposition as the "Jacobin party"—as men who sought power through the use of mobs.[30] The Clintonian paper, the *New York Columbian*, warned explicitly that demagogues posed a special danger to society:

> How great a fire a little spark may kindle! In All well regulated cities, it is forbidden to place fire in stoves dangerously situated, and in some it is not permitted to smoke segars in the streets—but in none is it allowed to keep powder in the midst of population and danger from accident. Although he is not excusable who supplies the match, are they unblamable who inflame the atmosphere and prepare the combustible materials? Those who wilfully excite and provoke disorder and violence cannot be wholly guiltless of their effects. And where there is no regard to decency, duty and honour, there should at least be some thought of common prudence.[31]

According to Craig Hanyan, Clinton increasingly defined himself as an "omnicompetent patrician" appealing to those "who felt increasingly confronted by an urban Jacobinism that seemed to augur anarchy and oppression." The Clintonians denied the legitimacy of partisan politics, and sought to restore a balance in government—and society—"by giving a renewed spirit and sense of leadership" focused about learned and benevolent societies.[32]

The Clintonian faction collapsed with the death of its leader in 1828. In the 1830s, anti-partyism was to be found in the Whig party. Unlike 1834, in 1835 a local issue, water supply, dominated the charter election; and the Whig party did not vigorously oppose Tammany's control of city government. The Whigs did not contest Democrat Lawrence's reelection to the mayoralty, and in three of the fifteen wards, they actually endorsed the Democratic candidates for alderman—two incumbents and one Democrat elected as an assistant alderman in 1834. (The Democrats, on the other hand, did not endorse any of the Whig candidates for alderman or assistant alderman, although they failed to field tickets in two strongly held Whig wards.)[33]

Thus, the Whigs, when confronting a well-run political organization, as in the charter election of 1834, still relied upon anti-partyism and the anti-demagogue caveats that had been used for forty years. Although politicians such as Webb and Noah, ex-Jacksonians who did not subscribe to this ethic, may have manipulated this sentiment for their own political purposes,[34] the Whigs as a party saw the 1834 election rioting in terms of a loss of control to the Tammany Hall "demagogues" resulting in indiscriminate destruction by their following, the mob. Neither the Whig preventive assault on the arsenal in 1834 nor the Whig attempt to bypass the mayor and obtain the intervention of federal troops makes sense from any other perspective.

Tammany Hall, the Republican, then the Democrat party, was a political organization in continuous existence since the 1790s. For the anti-party Whigs, this very continuity and the perennial—not just sporadic—baiting of the people with anti-aristocratic, anti-rich rhetoric threatened the republic especially gravely. Political riots were of great concern. Hence, the disruption of a nonpartisan political meeting upset the Whigs more than any other incident between July 1834 and February 1836.

Leading Democrats and Whigs organized a meeting, in March 1835, to protest a bill then before the state legislature that would have transferred the power to license ferries between New York and Long Island from the Common Council to a state commission. A coalition of Long Islanders, Democratic radicals, and uptown real estate interests had been instrumental in having the bill proposed. The issue cut across party lines. At the meeting, radical Democrats—aided perhaps by some Brooklynites—disrupted the proceedings in which the regular Democrats had expected to play the leading role. The radicals compelled the regulars to accept ex-mayor Gideon Lee as chairman in place of their original choice, Preserved Fish, a wealthy Democratic merchant. Then when the regulars sought to present their anti-commission resolutions, they found themselves drowned out by their opponents. Following this, radical Democrats Joel Seaver and Alexander Ming, Jr. harangued the crowd with anti-monopolist invective as a prelude to the radical resolutions in support of a state commission which the meeting ultimately approved. Finally, having obviously no hope of regaining control, the regular Democrats and their Whig supporters abandoned the hall to the radicals and published an official report, including the resolutions they had intended presenting, in the city's newspapers.[35]

Several traditional Whig papers were incensed. "Respectable" citizens, including some of the city's wealthiest merchants,[36] had been prevented by the Democratic popular following from speaking for the community in one voice on an issue allegedly of vital concern to all New Yorkers. The *Commercial Advertiser* charged that "the disorder was the result of the growing spirit of agrarianism, anarchy and confusion," and added that "public meetings in New-York, except those of a mere partisan character, are a farce. . . .The tendency—the end of these things,—it is fearful to contemplate."[37]

Philip Hone was similarly indignant. The former mayor noted in his diary that "it might be supposed," that the meeting "would meet the approbation of all New Yorkers." Instead, an "organized opposition":

> Opposed their political leaders; they would not have their own great man Preserved Fish, the ornament of the Democracy for President of the meeting. . .and they had their own orators, the embryo Robespierre's. and Marat's who found their accustomed avenues to the hearts of their auditor's by abusing the men of property as Monopolists and aristocrats, designating one of the Vice Presidents, Jacob Lorillard, as a man with an Hundred thousand Dollars.

Hone continued,

> Now then is the 'poisoned chalice, condemned to the lips' of such men as Preserved Fish, Gideon Lee, Walter Bowne and Jacob Lorillard, and now is the prophecy about to be realized, which I made. . .after the fall Election. The opposition to Virtue, talents and wealth no longer skulks in bye places, but comes openly forward in the wigwam of the faithful, and using the power which their leaders have given them, throws off the restraint heretofore imposed upon the rank and file of our city Democracy, by the small remains of Honesty among the officers.[38]

Hone, an ardent anti-party Whig, on occasion blamed mobs of all kinds on the Tammany Hall demagogues. In April 1835, during a journeyman carpenters' strike, he wrote that "the Devil is in the people." "Encouraged by those who want their support at Elections [they] seem determined to rule the roust." And in December 1835, after New York's great fire destroyed much of its business district, Hone expressed alarm at the poor prowling about the fire's ruins and making a run on the Bank of Savings, founded and managed by the rich. He wrote that their anti-aristocratic

> cant is the very text from which their leaders teach their deluded followers. It forms part of the warfare of the poor against the rich, a warfare which is destined I fear, to break the Hearts of some of the politicians of Tammany Hall, who have used these men to

answer a temporary purpose and find now that the dogs they have
taught to bark, will bite them as soon as their political opponents.

Singling out the Irish, Hone added that their importance in elections

is derived, from the use which is made of them by political
demagogues who despise the tools they work with. Let them look to
it, the time may not be very distant, when the same brogue which
they have instructed to shout "Hurrah for Jackson"! shall be used to
impart additional horror to the cry of "down with the natives."[39]

For Hone then, and for the other anti-party Whigs holding the
Democrats responsible for the mobbish spirit abroad in the nation, the
riots of the mid 1830s were almost inevitable, given the rise of a political
system based on mass appeal.

IV

The anti-party Whigs—expecting periods of major
rioting—believed that while an anarchic society was imminent, it had not
yet arrived; and, perhaps paradoxically, Whigs and Democrats viewed
many riots in the same light. Many riots, because of the refusal to take
seriously the lower class mob acting independently, were played down or
ignored. The "Five Points Riot," since demagogues played no immediate
role in arousing the mob, was seen essentially as a large scale brawl, of
no great importance. The press seemed concerned as much with the
"disgrace" that such riots brought on the city's reputation as with their
effect on the stability of society. Prior to the riot period, the phrase
"disgraceful riot" was used almost routinely, and it continued in use into
the mid 1830s The *Commercial Advertiser,* for example, described the
"half-jesting mood," in which it reported the "Five Points Riot" as "the
mirth of sorrow, humiliation and despair."[40] The *Courier and Enquirer*
commented in a similar vein that the Irish were "amusing themselves
with these manly sports," and that it was "high time that these
disgraceful scenes should be put a stop to."[41]

Historians have noted three New York disturbances of lesser
magnitude than the "Five Points Riot" as also particularly contributory
to the social conflicts of the period July 1834-February 1836. The press,
in character, gave them little consideration. Two incidents involved the
Irish.

In one, Irish laborers attacked on-duty firemen. The firemen,
fighting a blaze on an unusually cold night in January, sought to warm
themselves over a fire they had built on the property of a nearby gas
company, and this incursion aroused the wrath of the company's Irish

laborers. When the Chief Engineer, James Gulick, intervened to settle
the dispute, a laborer assaulted him with a hot poker and inflicted a
minor wound. In the melee that followed, both laborers and firemen
suffered serious injuries; and eventually ten to twenty laborers were
arrested. All the newspapers reported the incident, but they concentrated
on the fire; the *Post* referred briefly to a "fight"; the *Times* to "some
difficulty." Many papers probably noted the disturbance only because of
Gulick's injury, and of all the papers examined, only the *Commercial
Advertiser* reported that the laborers were Irish.[42]

The press also minimized the riotous disruption of a New York
Protestant Association meeting in March 1835—the Irish responsible were
not blamed. The association met to debate the question, "Popery is
compatible with civil liberty." After the doors were closed, 100 to 200
Catholics forced their way into the filled hall and began an
indiscriminate attack on the audience. Many women screamed and some
fainted; when the audience tried to get out of the rioters' way, several
women were injured. The sexton was also slightly injured, but the
clergymen responsible for the meeting escaped through a private exit. As
the audience fled, the invaders tore up benches and smashed windows
and lamps.

Only seven of the twelve newspapers examined carried accounts
of the disturbance, [43] and four of these delayed their reports, indicating
that they probably did not regard it as very serious. The meeting took
place on Friday evening, March 13 , and only three papers, the *Man*, the
Sun, and the *Courier and Enquirer* reported it on Monday. The *Gazette*
reprinted the *Courier and Enquirer's* account on Tuesday; and on
Wednesday and Thursday, the *Commercial Advertiser* and the *Journal of
Commerce* printed the official version, released by the New York
Protestant Association's directors.[44] The directors were moderate in tone,
but on the defensive. Their public questioning of Catholic civil liberties
was questioned. The *Star* wanted the rioters punished, but saw no point
in discussing "Popery's" compatibility with civil liberty, since the
Catholics undeniably had civil rights.[45] On Friday, March 20, the
evangelistic *Journal of Commerce*, unable to brook even-handed
sentiments, denounced both the *Star* and the *Courier and Enquirer*.
After this anti-Irish outburst, the press let the issue drop.

Stonecutters figured in the third riot the historians have
mentioned. Several hundred of these workers marched up Broadway, the
city's main street, in late October 1834, and attacked the buildings which
a Mr. Bloomer had recently erected with prison-made marble.[46]
Windows were smashed and the doors and marble pillars battered. The
arrival of a "strong posse" of watchmen prevented the mob from
breaking in. The following evening, the watch, on orders from the

mayor, again guarded the buildings. In general, the press did not devote much attention to the disturbances, and only four newspapers of the ten examined reported it.[47]   Thus, again we see that the press did not emphasize a riot which has since been frequently mentioned.[48]

The reporting of two of the incidents may have been affected, to a degree, by the political situation existing in 1834-1835.   Both the Protestant Association meeting and the stonecutters' assault occurred several weeks prior to elections.   The *Star,* which expressed concern for Catholic civil liberties, could still in March, at the time of the meeting, have hoped for Catholic support, even if after the April election it played an important role in the emerging nativist movement;[49] and the case of the stonecutters was another locally explosive issue.   Both Whigs and Democrats deferred to the stonecutters and opposed the use of prison labor in stonecutting.

Yet, popular violence was consistently under-reported in the 1820s and early 1830s and the more heated political atmosphere of the mid-1830s made little overall difference.   For example, a riot occurred on the anniversary of the Battle of the Boyne in July 1824.   The disturbance, between Irish Catholics and Protestants, let to thirty-three arrests and a grand jury call for an end to celebrations of the battle (riotous celebrations were not uncommon).[50]   Yet only three of seven newspapers examined reported it.[51]   In May 1831, a journeyman cabinetmkers' strike turned into a disturbance.   Striking workers surrounded the shop of a cabinetmaker who was paying nonstriking workers wages lower than what the strikers were asking.   The strikers harassed the working journeymen, and when the cabinetworker asked the police to disperse the strikers, the latter beat up the man sent to the police with the request.   A dozen strikers were arrested, but typically, only four of eight newspapers reported the incident.[52]

Diarist Philip Hone was in accord with the press.   He too ignored many riots originating with the lower classes.   He condemned the Democratic party and the effects of its demagogic appeals, but ordinarily wrote little when rioting was politically unrelated.   He hid neither his disdain for the Irish nor his hostility to trade unionism, but the disruption of the New York Protestant Association meeting, the stonecutters' riot, and even the three-day long "Five Points Riot" received no mention from him.   Hone, when he wrote of the fight between the firemen and the "amiable Irishmen," probably noted it only because of the injury to his "good Friend," Chief Engineer Gulick.[53]

V

From the editors' and officials' point of view, there was another reason for reacting complacently to the disturbances of the mid 1830s. The number of riotous incidents occurring in New York City was not greater in 1835 than in the previous two years, and most riots had traditionally been viewed with complacency. Statistics show a steady increase in rioting from the early 1820s through the mid 1830s, with a peak in 1834—so rioting in 1835 actually declined from the previous year. (See Table 2. The statistics are based on the reports of the *Commercial Advertiser*.)

TABLE 2

INCIDENTS OF RIOT IN NEW YORK CITY 1821-1837

Year	Number of Incidents
1821	2
1822	5
1823	3
1824	3
1825	5
1826	6
1827	8
1828	10
1829	5
1830	6
1831	5
1832	6
1833	10
1834	13
1835	10
1836	9
1837	10

SOURCE: Calculated from the *Commercial Advertiser*, 1821-37. Riots of more than one day's duration are counted as single incidents.

Between 1833 and 1835, a number of incidents occurred which have not been remembered, but which were equal in scale to all except the biggest historians have previously written about. In March 1833, twenty to forty ruffians entered at least four ins along the suburban road popular among sleighing parties in what was described as a frolic. They beat the proprietors and inflicted injuries on at least six persons.[54] In late June 1834, after the authorities arrested a woman for stealing a pair of shoes, about 200 rioters, shouting "State Prison monopoly!" attacked the shoe store, destroyed the awning, smashed the windows and, after the watch intervened, rescued some of the arrested rioters from the clutches of the law. Two thousand persons allegedly watched this scene.[55] In mid September 1834, a rumor spread that a "respectable" girl had been seduced and then, when she came down with cholera, turned out to die. In response, a mob of 200 to 300 marched upon the alleged brothel, and about a dozen persons, encouraged by their compatriots, entered and destroyed the premises.[56] In late September 1834, a brawl occurred involving upwards of 1,000 persons. At least to an extent, the fight was between Irish Protestants and Irish Catholics: "Swarms of half naked and more than half drunken vagabonds poured out of the neighboring rookeries."[57] In April 1835, a seaman was murdered, and about 100 seamen attacked and destroyed the furnishings of the boardinghouse where the murder occurred.[58]

Undue importance has been given to the eight riots of the 1833-35 period that historians have noted. They have been wrenched out of their context: considerable small-scale violence (thirty-three known riots). Moreover, the riots that have been noted (with the exception of the "Five Points Riot") are those where a mob assaulted an organization or the authorities: in 1833—the anti-abolitionist riot in October;[59] in 1834—the charter election riot in April, the anti-abolitionist rioting in July, and the stonecutter's riot in October;[60] in 1835—the assault on the firemen in January,[61] the disruption of the New York Protestant Association meeting in March,[62] and, in October, the meeting at Tammany Hall where radical Democrats lit locofoco matches after party regulars blew out the gas lights.[63] Contemporaries were not so much concerned with the goal of a mob as with its structure and source of motivation—were demagogues responsible?—and their listing of important riots differed substantially from the above, garnered from secondary sources.

In 1835, New Yorkers were further encouraged in their complacency by local rioting occurring a full year before the peak in rioting nationally. No major violence, against the abolitionists or otherwise, disrupted the city's peace in the summer and fall of 1835 when rioting was most in the news.[64] For the nation, excluding New York City, the *Commercial Advertiser* reported seven riots in the first half of 1834 and thirteen in the second half; for 1835, it reported ten in the first half and thirty-nine in the second half, thirty-three between July and October alone.

The year's interval between the city's and the nation's major riots allowed both the authorities and the press the time to regain their usual perspective. Thus, New York's leaders greeted the election and anti-abolitionist disturbances when they occurred with what amounted to hysteria, but soon they realized that they had become alarmed unjustifiably—that their alarm had originated in the fear that demagogues had unleashed the uncontrollable fury of the rabble. In May 1834, the committee the Whigs appointed to write an account of the election riot readily, perhaps defensively, reported that fears fed by the rumors circulating the city led them to attack the arsenal.[65] On July 14, 1834, Mayor Lawrence reported to the Common Council that the anti-abolitionist disturbances had resulted in no deaths, no serious personal injuries, and that "the amount of property destroyed is much less than has been generally apprehended."[66]

By mid 1835, Philip Hone had come around to criticizing the prevalence of lynch law in the South and West. There, the "inflammable spirit" had found "more combustible matter" than in the East where it had caused "excitement and tumult in a less dangerous degree."[67]

In August 1835, New Yorkers met to denounce the abolitionists, but opposed "fanatics" and demagogues of all kinds. The *Evening Post's* editor, having been shown the resolutions in advance, happily stated that "calm and dignified," the resolutions' "sentiments and tone are such as ought to proceed from this great community."[68] The meeting, called to assuage the South, passed resolutions which did anything but that. The city's leaders returned to their tolerant position of 1833, defending the rights of the abolitionists to a far greater extent than they had the previous July; at the same time, they condemned southern violence against the mails.[69] The meeting was carefully orchestrated, with the mayor presiding. The lieutenant governor and the judges of the Court of Errors were introduced as they took their seats on the podium. Hone, who came back to the city from his summer retreat nearby, despite his daughter's ill health, still believed that he and his kind could effectively deal with any threat to the community's good order if they made a determined effort to exert their moral influence:

> I am desirous that persons of character should be present in the greatest possible number, with the two fold object of convincing the people of the South that incendiaries constitute an inconsiderable proportion of our citizens, and to prevent any violence which might possibly be attempted by turbulent persons ever on the look out for a row, for it is certain that in the present state of feeling, the least

spark would create a flame in which the lives and property of Arthur Tappan and his associates would be endangered.[70]

VI

The prevalent belief that serious rioting was inevitably triggered by demagogic incitements kept New Yorkers from considering the need for an effective police force. The belief, although weakened by the anti-abolitionist rioting, prevailed. Only after labor agitation in early 1836 did the city's political leadership feel compelled to reappraise their ability to manage a mob.

NOTES

[1] Leonard L. Richards, *"Gentlemen of Property and Standing": Anti-Abolition Mobs in Jacksonian America* (New York, 1970), pp. 10-12, 16-18; David Grimsted, "Rioting in Its Jacksonian Setting" *American Historical Review* 77 (April 1972): 362. According to Richards, 4 riots occurred in 1838, 20 in 1834 and 53 in 1835. Grimsted reports "some 20" riots from 1828 to 1833; in 1834, 16; and in 1835, 37. My own compilation, derived from an examination of the *New-York Commercial Advertiser*, yields the same conclusions: excluding New York City mobs, the newspaper reported 9 mobs in 1833, 20 in 1834 (13 of these in the last half of the year), and 50 in 1835.

Unlike Richards and Grimsted, who attempt to come to some approximation of the total violence committed during this period. I offer my own compilation only to measure in an objective way how the New York public perceived rioting. Richards and Grimsted both do not give enough consideration to the increased newsworthiness of riots in the mid 1830s and the bearing this had on exaggerating the upswing in violence. Richards' data is derived solely from *Niles' Weekly Register*; Grimsted's, from the *Register* in addition to local histories, the *National Ingelligencer*, and "scattered reading in other newspapers, journals, and manuscripts." *Niles' Weekly Register*, a Baltimore newspaper which Richards credits with a reputation for national coverage, was perhaps more concerned with Southern vigilantism not directed against the blacks or abolitionists than was the *Commercial Advertiser*. Poor communication, as well as geographical orientation, probably led to the very few reports of riots in the Northwest.

[2] *Commercial Advertiser*, July 16-18, December 29 (Philadelphia); October 24 (Boston); August 14, 15, 18 (Washington); June 11-13 (Hartford); October 24 (Utica); July 17 (Detroit); August 15 (Buffalo); August 10 (Newburgh);August 31 (Indiana); August 15 (New York State); March 11, 1835 (District of Columbia).

[3] *Commercial Advertiser.*

[4] Ibid. For nativist-Irish mobs, see September 29, October 4, 1834, January 5, March 18, June 22-24, August 20, 1835; for labor disturbances, July 23, October 27, 1834, November 11, 1835; for the anti-Negro mob, August 26, 1835.

[5] Ibid., June 22-24, 1835; *New-York American*, June 22-24, 1835; *Morning Courier and New-York Enquirer*, June 22-24, 1835; *Morning Herald* (New York), June 23-24, 1835; *Sun* (New York), June 22-25, 1835; *New York Transcript*, June 23-25, 1835.

[6] *Commercial Advertiser*, June 26, 1835.

[7] James F. Richardson, *The New York Police: Colonial Times to 1901*, The Urban Life in America Series (New York, 1970), pp 21-22; Grimsted, "Rioting in Its Jacksonian Setting." pp. 395-97.

[8] Allegedly the party of the "people," Republicans (Democrats) eschewed the use of the word "deamgogues," but not the assumptions which lay behind it. They merely substituted "aristocrats" for the traditional word. They proclaimed that the people in their wisdom would not be misled, but when rioting erupted, explained it as the result of effective demagoguery. See Thaddeus Stevens, *An Address Delivered on the Fourth*

of July, 1835, at an Anti-Masonic Celebration of the Anniversary of American Independence, Composed of About 2000 Substantial Citizens of Pennsylvania, in Pursuance of Invitations Given by Citizens of Pittsburgh, &c [Pittsburgh, 1835], p. 2, A. F. Cunningham, *An Oration Delivered before the Trades Union of the District of Columbia, in the City of Washington, in the Baptist Church, on the Fourth Day of July, 1835* (Washington, 1835), p. 8; Myer Moses, *Oration, Delivered at Tammany Hall, on the Twelfth May, 1831, Being the Forty-Second Anniversary, of the Tammany Hall, or, Columbian Order* (New York, 1831), passim.

On the historical roots of the fear of demagoguery, see Bernard Bailyn, *The Origins of American Politics,* The Charles K. Colver Lectures, Brown University, 1965 (New York, 1968), pp. 72, 152-58, and passim: Michael Wallace, "Idealogues of Party in the Ante-Bellum Republic" (Ph.D. dissertation, Columbia University, 1973), passim. On the eighteenth and early nineteenth century belief in the ideal of political unanimity, see Richard Hofstadter, *The Idea of a Party System: The Rise of Legitimate Opposition in the United States, 1780-1840,* Jefferson Memorial Lectures (Berkeley, Cal. 1970), passim.

[9]For comments in the 1830s that the press had a particularly pernicious influence, see Moses, *Oration,* pp. 19-21; George W. Bethune, *Our Liberties: Their Danger, and the Means of Preserving Them. A Discourse* (Philadelphia, 1835), p. 14; Levi Hubbell, *Oration Delivered before the Young Men's Association of the City of Albany, at the First Presbyterian Church,* July 4, 1835 (Albany, N. Y., 1835), p. 13; Jacob Broom, *Oration Delivered on the 4th July, 1835, before the Union Literary and Debating Society* (Washington, D. C., 1835), p. 11. Echoing these beliefs about the efficacy of the press, Theophilus Parsons urged the educated men of the country to use the press for their own ends, to cultivate "just views and principles" in the "mass of the people" (*An Address Delivered before the Phi Beta Kappa Society of Harvard University, 27 August 1835. On the Duties of Educated Men in a Republic* [Boston, 1835], p. 12).

Richards explains the widespread and generally irrational fear of the abolitionists during 1835 as the result of the abolitionists utilizing the printing revolution, which had dramatically reduced the costs of printing, to create a "propaganda machine" ("*Gentlemen of Property and Standing,*" pp. 51-62, 71-75, 167-69). In the early years of the nineteenth century, a scurrilous popular press emerged as an electioneering tool. (See David Hackett Fischer, *The Revolution of American Conservatism: The Federalist Party in the Era of Jeffersonian Democracy* [New York, 1969], pp. 129-49.)

[10]*New York Journal of Commerce,* July 16, 1834.

[11]*Man* (New York), July 17, 1834.

[12]*Herald,* June 24, 1835. James Gordon Bennett, editor of the *Herald,* joined the staff of James Watson Webb's Tammany Hall organ, the *Courier,* in the late 1820s and rose to the position of associate editor of its successor paper, the influential *Courier and Enquirer,* edited by Webb and Mordecai M. Noah. Bennett resigned from the paper and founded the *Herald* when Webb abandoned his support for Jackson in 1832. *Dictionary of American Biography.* Noah also went his own way, and, in 1835, edited the *Star.*

[13]*Herald,* June 25, 1835.

[14]*Commercial Advertiser*, June 23, 1835, the source of the quotation, and the *New-York Gazette and General Advertiser*, June 25, 1835.

[15]*Evening Post* (New York), June 23 , 1835.

[16]See especially the *American*, June 24, 1835; *Commercial Advertiser*, June 24, 1835; *Courier and Enquirer*, June 24, 1835; *Evening Post*, June 24, 1835; *Journal of Commerce*, reprinted in the *Man*, June 25, 1835. Two cheap papers taking notable exception to the consensus view: *Herald*, June 24, 25, 1835; *Sun*, June 22, 23, 24, 25, 1835.

[17]See the discussion of the anti-Sabbatarian meeting in 1821, above, pp. 57-60.

[18]Leo Hershkowitz, "The Native American Democratic Association in New York City, 1835-36" *New-York Historical Society Quarterly* 46 (January 1962): 45-49.

[19]*American*, August 11, 12, 1835; *Commercial Advertiser*, August 10, 11, 12, 1835; *Gazette and General Advertiser*, August 11, 12, 1835; *Evening Post*, August 10, 11, 1835; *New York Times*, August 10-12,1835; *Transcript*, August 11, 12, 1835.

[20]Whig anti-partyism in New York is discussed below. On anti-partyism being crucial to the formation of the Whig party nationally, see Lynn L. Marshall, "The Strange Stillbirth of the Whig Party" *American Historical Review* 72 (January 1967): 445-68. On politicians of both major political parties using anti-party rhetoric in the mid 1830s, see David J. Russo, "The Major Political Issues of the Jacksonian Period and the Development of Party Loyalty in Congress, 1830-1840" *Transactions of the American Philosophical Society Held at Philadelphia for Promoting Useful Knowledge* New series, 72, part 5 (1972): 5-6.

[21]*Evening Post*, April 12, 1834.

[22]Hofstadter, *Idea of a Party System*, pp. 74-211.

[23]See for example, Moses, *Oration*, passim.

[24]William Woolsey to Oliver Wolcott, Jr., March 6, 1794, cited by Alfred Young, "The Mechanics and the Jeffersonians, 1789-1801" *Labor History* 5 (Fall 1964): 256.

[25]Benjamin Walker to Joseph Webb, July 24, 1795, cited by Young, "Mechanics and Jeffersonians," p. 259.

[26]The New York City Federalists in 1797, 1801, and 1805 failed to run candidates for the state assembly, although in every assembly election but one between the mid 1790s and 1815, they received at least 44 percent of the vote (the exception was 1801 when the Republicans received a winning percentage of 61.6). The Republicans, on the other hand, fielded a candidate in every election, even in, and following, years of decided Federalist victories: 1799 and 1811 when they garnered 59.4 percent and 57.5 percent respectively. (Edmund P. Willis, "Social Origins of Political Leadership in New York City from the Revolution to 1815" [Ph.D. dissertation, University of California, Berkeley, 1967], pp. 72,75,77 [Tables II-11, II-15, II-17].)

On the frequently ineffective attempts of the Federalists to emulate Republican electioneering techniques, see Fischer, *Revolution of American Conservatism*, pp. 91-109. Howard B. Rock, "The Independent Mechanic: The Tradesmen of New York City in Labor and Politics during the Jeffersonian Era" (Ph.D. dissertation, New York University, 1974) confirms that Federalists' attempts at electioneering in New York City were as amateurish as in the nation generally.

Subsequently, the continuing failure of the anti-Republicans to form a lasting coalition, despite their potential electoral majority, was a major theme of New York (State) politics between 1820 and 1837 (see Richard P. McCormick, *The Second American Party System: Party Formation in the Jacksonian Era* [Chapel Hill, N.C., 1966], pp. 112-24).

[27] *Argus*, April 8, 1799, cited by Young, "Mechanics and Jeffersonians," p. 207.

[28] Craig R. Hanyan, "De Witt Clinton and Partisanship: The Development of Clintonianism from 1811 to 1820" *New-York Historical Society Quarterly* 56 (April 1972): 123; Hofstadter, *Idea of a Party System*, p. 223.

[29] Cited by Hanyan, "De Witt Clinton and Partisanship," p. 114.

[30] Ibid., pp. 116-17.

[31] Ibid., p. 117.

[32] Ibid., p. 130.

[33] *American*, April 10, 12, 1834, April 18, 1835; *Evening Post*, April 18, 1835.

[34] Both Noah and Webb sought to revive the fortunes of the Whig party by allying it in 1835 with political nativism (Hershkowitz, "Native American Democratic Association," pp. 46-54, 59). As a Tammanyite, Noah in particular had long called for party regularity. On his functioning as a party wheel horse, see Isaac Goldberg, *Major Noah: American Jewish Pioneer* (New York, 1937), pp. 132, 137-38, 152-54,157-60, 224-25, 234-35. On changing attitudes respecting the desirability of political parties, see Michael Wallace, "Changing Concepts of Party in the United States: New York, 1815-28" *American Historical Review* 73 (December 1968): 453-91

[35] *Commercial Advertiser*, April 1, 1835; Philip Hone, MS Diary, April 1, 1835, Manuscript Division, New-York Historical Society; Leo Hershkowitz, "The Loco-Foco Party of New York: Its Origins and Career, 1835-1837" *New-York Historical Society Quarterly* 46 (July 1962):: 314-16.

[36] The 21 signers of the call for a meeting included 8 merchants—2 Whigs and 6 Democrats. Six of the merchants, including both Whigs, had wealth assessed at $25,000 or more in 1828. One other signer, Hugh Maxwell, a lawyer and one-time district attorney, was also among New York's wealthiest citizens. (A Jacksonian in 1829, a Whig in 1838, it could not be determined when he changed his party affiliation.) I am indebted to Brian J. Danforth for information on the merchants.

See also Edward Pessen, "The Wealthiest New Yorkers of the Jacksonian Era: A New List" *New-York Historical Society Quarterly* 54 (April 1970): 155-61.

[37] *Commercial Advertiser,* April 1, 1835; *Gazette and General Advertiser,* April 2, 1835. Strictly speaking, "agrarianism" was the socialism advocated by such reformers as Frances Wright and Robert Owen. Radical Democrats were supporters of laissez-faire.

[38] Hone, MS Diary, April 1, 1835.

[39] Ibid., April 29, December 17, 1835. The *Commercial Advertiser,* April 7, 1835, also warned wealthy Democrats, such as merchants Gideon Lee and Cornelius Lawrence, that they too would suffer when their anti-rich rhetoric finally aroused the mob to violence.

[40] Ibid., June 22, 1835.

[41] *Courier and Enquirer,* June 22, 1835.

[42] The newspapers examined included the *Mercantile Advertiser and New-York Advocate,* January 5, 1835; *Commercial Advertiser,* January 5, 1835; *Courier and Enquirer,* reprinted in the *American,* January 5, 1835; *Gazette and General Advertiser,* January 5, 1835; *Man,* January 6, 1835; *Evening Post,* January 5, 1835; *Sun,* January 5, 1835; *Times,* January 5, 1835. See also Hone, MS Diary, January 4, 1835.

[43] The five papers not reporting the incident were the *American,* the *Mercantile Advertiser,* the *Evening Post,* the *Times,* and the *Transcript.* The religious weekly, the *New York Evangelist,* also did not report it.

[44] *Commercial Advertiser,* March 18, 1835; *Journal of Commerce,* March 19, 1835.

[45] *Evening Star,* March 19, 1835.

[46] The incident has frequently been cited as occurring in August 1834, but no stonecutters' riot occurred at that time. (For the August reference, see, for example, Richards, *"Gentlemen of Property and Standing,"* p. 113; Benson J. Lossing, *History of New York City, Embracing an Outline Sketch of Events from 1609 to 1830, and a Full Account of its Development from 1830 to 1884,* 2 vols. [New York, 1884] 1: 341; Charles H. Haswell, *Reminiscences of an Octogenarian of the City of New York (1816 to 1860)* [New York, 1897], p. 290. The August misdating probably originates with William L. Stone, *History of New York City from the Discovery to the Present Day* [New York, 1872], p. 466.

[47] The newspapers reporting the incident include the *Commercial Advertiser,* October 27, 1834; *Courier and Enquirer,* October 27, 1834; *Sun,* October 28, 1834; *Transcript,* October 28, 1834. The following papers did not report the incident: *American, Gazette and General Advertiser, Man, Mercantile Advertiser, Evening Post,* and *Evening Star.*

[48] The U. S. Violence Commission historical survey refers to the religious and ethnic violence of the Five Points area in general and specifically mentions the stonecutters' riot (Richard Maxwell Brown, "Historical Patterns of Violence in America," in *Violence in America: Historical and Comparative Perspectives,* A Report Submitted to the National Commission on the Causes and Prevention of Violence, ed. Hugh Davis

Graham and Ted Robert Gurr [New York, 1969], pp. 53-54; 79, n. 47). Richards, *"Gentlemen of Property and Standing,"* p. 113, also mentions the stonecutters; riot.

Older secondary works which have been turned to by historians and other writers and which describe the stonecutters' riot in some detail include Herbert Asbury's *The Gangs of New York: An Informal History of the Underworld* (New York 1928) and a number of others from the late nineteenth century: Joel T. Headley, *The Great Riots of New York, 1712 to 1873* (New York, 1873); William L. Stone, *History of New York City* (New York, 1872); Charles H. Haswell, *Reminiscences;* Benson J. Lossing, *History of New York City.* Most of the other major histories of New York City written in the last third of the nineteenth century, a period of great labor strife and large scale immigration, also describe the stonecutters' riot.

The riot between the firemen and the Irish gasworkers is given attention in fire department histories: George W. Sheldon, *The Story of the Volunteer Fire Department of the City of New York* (New York, 1882), pp. 329-30; Augustine E. Costello, *Our Firemen. A History of the New York Fire Departments. Volunteer and Paid* (New York, 1887), pp. 175-76; and Lowell M. Limpus, *History of the New York Fire Department* (New York, 1940), pp. 46-47. While firemen frequently fought amongst each other long before 1835, Limpus describes the gashouse riot as the first of a series between the firemen and gangsters.

On the disruption of the New York Protestant Association meeting, see Ray Allen Billington, *The Protestant Crusade, 1800-1860: A Study of the Origins of American Nativism* (New York, 1952) pp. 59-60; and Louis Dow Scisco, *Political Nativism in New York State,* Studies in History, Economics and Public Law, vol. 13, no. 2 (New York, 1901), pp. 22-23.

[49]Above, n. 34.

[50]*Commercial Advertiser,* August 20, 1824.

[51]The newspapers reporting the incident include the *Commercial Advertiser,* July 15, 1824 and the *Gazette and General Advertiser,* July 16, 1824, both reprinting the account of the *National Advocate* (New York), July 15, 1824. The following papers did not report the riot: *Daily Advertiser, American, Evening Post, New-York Statesman.*

[52]The newspapers reporting the incident include the *American,* May 5, 1831, and the *Commercial Advertiser,* May 5, 1831, both reprinting the account of the *Journal of Commerce,* May 5, 1831; and the *Courier and Enquirer,* May 5, 1831. In addition, the *Daily Advertiser* mentioned the incident in its regular police column. The following newspapers did not report the incident: *Gazette and General Advertiser, Evening Post, New York Standard.*

[53]Hone, MS Diary, January 4, 1835.

[54]*Commercial Advertiser,* March 9, 1833.

[55]Ibid., July 1, 1834.

[56]Ibid., September 13, 1834.

[57]Ibid., September 29, 1834; *Man,* September 29, 1834.

[58]*Commercial Advertiser,* April 27, 1835; *Gazette and General Advertiser,* April 27, 1835.

[59]See above, pp. 11-13.

[60]See above, pp. 7-20, 33-45, 74-77, 105, 118-19.

[61]See above, p. 103.

[62]See above, pp. 103-105.

[63]See Hershkowitz, "The Loco-Foco Party of New York," pp. 306-310.

[64]Richards contends that violence erupted when an abolition society was first organized; and New York City, with one of the first such societies, missed the peak of organizational activity (*"Gentlemen of Property and Standing,"* pp. 75-81).

[65]*Mercantile Advertiser,* May 2, 16, 1834.

[66]New York (City), Board of Aldermen, *Communication from the Mayor, Relative to the Late Riots;* and *[A] Proclamation* and *[B] Proclamation,* Doc. No. 17, vol. I (1834).

[67]Hone, MS Diary, August 2, 1835.

[68]*Evening Post, August 27, 1835.*

[69]Ibid., August 28, 1835. For the attitude of the New York press at the time of the anti-abolitionist riot of 1833, see above, pp. 66-68.

[70]Hone, MS Diary, August 26, 1835.

CHAPTER FIVE

LABOR STRIFE: NEW AND OLD

I

Inflation overshadowed the American economy through much of the 1830s. Between April 1834 and February 1837, wholesale commodity prices jumped 50 percent,[1] the biggest increases coming in the cost of necessities—food, housing, and fuel.[2] In New York, flour selling for $4.81 a barrel in April 1834 sold for $7.00 a barrel in February 1836 and $11.31 a barrel in 1837. During the same period, beef rose from $9.50 to $10.06 to $14.06 a barrel; and coal from $6.00 to $8.00 to $10.50 a ton.[3] Rents also increased alarmingly. In December 1835, a fire destroyed a large part of the business district, exasperating a housing shortage. New construction was diverted in 1836 from residential sections to rebuild the "burnt district,"[4] and New Yorkers scrambled for living quarters as early as February 1837, two to three months ahead of the May 1 moving day. Outraged editorialists urged tenants to refuse to pay the increases demanded by the landlords.[5]

The city's workers responded to skyrocketing costs in two distinct ways. They held mass protests to demand that commodity prices be lowered. (In early 1837, the Locofocos organized three such protests which drew crowds of more than 5,000 persons.)[6] Secondly and more effectively, they formed unions and went on strike, either for higher wages or against a reduction in wages. Thirty-three of the thirty-four strikes known to have occurred in New York between 1834 and 1837 centered on the issue of wages.[7]

On two occasions, the opposition to rising prices led to violence which provoked the authorities to call out the militia. These events turned the community against mob violence, but the growing determination to suppress rioting did not bring about a consistent policy.

The first series of incidents leading to violence were the strikes of February 1836. On Monday afternoon, February 22, stevedores and riggers struck to raise their daily wage 25 cents from its current level of $1.25-$1.50 per day. To publicize their strike, the ship workers paraded the streets; to broaden its base, they went from ship to ship until they had pulled some 300 men off their jobs. Apparently some employers consented to meet the workers' demands, but no agreement was reached because the employers refused to guarantee the higher pay for a year in advance. No violence occurred on this first day of the strike.

On the strike's second day, police intervention precipitated a disturbance. Two police officers confroned some 200 striking workers, urging them to disperse and warning them against pressuring nonstrikers to join the protest. The workers ignored the warning. One officer was "insulted." When an attempt was made to arrest the offender, the strikers came to his aid. One of the officers picked up a stick, and the strikers, armed with pipe staves, rushed the two police. They knocked one unconscious, and, victorious, went on their way. The authorities, in response, made seven arrests by day's end.

A second unrelated strike also occupied the authorities that day. Laborers clearing the rubbish from the area of New York's catastrophic December fire struck to raise their daily wage from $1.00 to $1.25. The turnout spread quickly as laborers went from site to site within the compact twenty block area. In short order, the majority of construction laborers in the area, some 500 to 800 men, were off the job.

Although they roughly handled a police officer when he attempted to prevent the strike from spreading, the affair did not present any real problem to the authorities. High Constable Hays, heading a small force of police, persuaded the strikers to end their walkout. He told them that they had the right to strike, but not to interfere with the rights of other workers. The laborers cheered Hays for his support of the strike principle, and they disbanded.

The ship workers' strike also collapsed quickly, despite the episodes of violence. By Tuesday evening, the crowds had dispersed and some laborers were already at work. The regular watch, reenforced by twenty additional men, had no trouble maintaining order. The entire affair did not amount to much—a walkout of unskilled laborers who dispersed at the first appearance of the police, a strike of ship workers which the police suppressed simply by arresting ringleaders. On Wednesday, after the call-up, the strikers gathered in small groups along the wharves but made no effort to prevent nonstrikers from working. By Thursday, the men were back at work, their demands apparently unmet.[8]

II

The authorities, however, did not take the affair lightly. Although few people today would classify the strikes as riots, they were seen in that light at the time. When it was heard that stevedores were threating to prevent a packet ship from sailing, the mayor ordered out the militia; and between Tuesday night and Wednesday morning, two regiments (eighteen companies) were called up and given ammunition. While the troops did no more than appear on parade in City Hall Park, the call-up was historic. It marks the first known use of the militia to quell a strike.[9] Although many of the disturbances of the preceding two years had been far more destructive, the New York authorities viewed these relatively peaceful strikes as a turning point. The city's leaders now felt that they could no longer take the "mob" lightly. For the third time in two years, they felt sufficiently threatened to call up the militia, and this time they did not let the issue of public order drop.

In the immediate aftermath of the strikes, steps were taken to regularize the militia's use.   The twenty-seventh regiment received standing orders to be prepared to suppress rioting.[10] Then, early in March, the regiment's Board of Officers, taking advantage of the city's gratitude, memorialized the state legislature to exempt members of the regiment from jury duty for life; and the regiment's commander was authorized to lobby on behalf of the memorial in Albany.[11]

The proposal sailed through the legislature, less than a week elapsing between its introduction as a bill and its passage into law. An exemption bill was referred to committee by the state senate on March 17 and the following day it was reported out—unamended—passed, and forwarded to the assembly. The assembly passed the bill 105 to 2, eight of the eleven member New York City delegation voting yea and the other three not voting. A law was enacted on March 22. It exempted militiamen living in New York City from jury duty after one year's service and so long as they actively served. It also specifically authorized the mayor to order the militia to "quell riots, suppress insurrection, to protect the property, or preserve the tranquillity of the city."[12]

The lightning passage of the jury exemption and its liberal provisions testify to a suddenly heightened fear of serious rioting. Similar jury exemption proposals had been advanced for years, but little had come of them: the limited jury exemption law finally passed the previous April required seven years service for a permanent exemption, did not allow a temporary exemption for active militiamen, and applied only to the horse artillery.[13] The section in the 1836 act in which the mayor was specifically delegated the authority to call out the militia clarified an issue that had arisen and then been dropped at the time of the anti-abolition riots of July 1834. The rioters believed at the time that only the governor could call out the militia, but the recorder, in support of the mayor and backed by the press, warned the rioters and potential rioters that theirs was a mistaken impression. The raising of the matter again in the spring of 1836 indicated that the authorities were not as certain on the law as they had pretended, but that only the laborers' and ship workers' strike of February 1836 jarred them into clarifying the mayor's authority to deal with mob violence.

Strengthening the militia system and clarifying the mayor's right to use the militia could not be a permanent solution to the problem of disorder. Regular use of the military, even a citizen's militia, had no place in a republican government. Mayor Lawrence warned of this in his annual address to the Common Council in July 1836. Repeated use of the militia had called into question the "propriety," although not the legality, of the existing means for maintaining order.

Lawrence, however, considered the system basically sound. Rather than proposing major reform, he suggested that the number of police be increased considerably, that the watchman's pay be raised, and that the watch begin one-half hour earlier at night. These actions would mean higher taxes, but Lawrence predicted the public would accept this necessity "with the most cheerful unanimity."[14]

The mayor received the bipartisan support of the Common Council: the Board of Aldermen approved a resolution allowing the councilmen to appoint as many as six Sunday officers in each of their wards. The vote was 11 to 2. Three members did not vote. The Whigs voted 8 in favor and 1 opposed; the Democrats, 3 for and 1 against. Although the Democrats divided over the issue (the 3 nonvoting councilmen were all Democrats), partisanship was not dominant.[15] The Board of Aldermen also approved—this time unanimously—a resolution to station two police officers in the Five Points neighborhood during the hours when the night watchmen were not on duty.[16] The Board of Assistant Aldermen concurred in these proposals and passed several additional resolutions. Modifying one of the mayor's proposals, the Democratic assistant alderman of the sixth ward proposed setting the watch one hour earlier than it was set currently and having it continue on duty one hour later in the morning.[17]

Up to this point, police reform was no more than a patchwork; but the authorities quickly lost their timidity and began considering a drastic overhaul of the system. In early August, a Democratic assistant alderman, Abraham V. Williams of the twelfth ward, proposed that the police committees of both boards investigate the necessity of reorganizing the police department. The board approved the resolution and Mayor Lawrence requested Oliver M. Lownds, a police justice, to make recommendations. In mid September, the mayor transmitted Justice Lownds' plan to the Common Council, which established a joint special bipartisan committee of both boards to consider it.[18] Lownds recommended replacing the existing constables and night watch with a twenty-four hour professional police. He based his plan on the London police, organized by Robert Peel in 1829. The justice argued that such a force could suppress "a tumult or riot" without the assistance of the military "except in extreme cases." Lownds recommended equipping the station houses with bells for signaling a riot and informing the special constables, the (day) patrol, and the watch that they had to report to their station houses. This would reduce as much as possible the time needed to collect a force large enough to suppress mob violence. (The day-to-day function of the bells, however, would be to make it known that a fire had broken out.) Lownds also specified the riot duties of the city's officials, in a reorganized department; the mayor would command and direct the police force, and he could, if the situation required it, request the aid of the military. The aldermen and assistant aldermen were to assist the mayor.[19] The mayor forwarded Lownds's plan to the council with his approval, although it went far beyond his own previous recommedations. He again expressed his confidence that the community would willingly pay for a more effective police in the interests of civic order.[20]

The press agreed with the mayor. At the end of August, anticipating the Lownds report, the newspapers charged that law and order had broken down, that "almost daily," New York was "disgraced with rows, riots, or disturbances of one kind or another."[21] Democracy in America had become "licentious;" it disregarded the "social compact;" only a more effective police system could prevent disaster.[22] To effect this reform, the press diligently sought to educate the city on the benefits and operation of the London police.[23]

The London "bobbies," according to the press, did not infringe upon the people's liberty. They went unarmed and uniformed—in no way a military force or a secret police. Rather they were polite, restrained peacekeepers who would settle a potentially disruptive dispute by calmly interrupting: "let me be the judge, gentlemen, or sir."[24] One erstwhile "European" recalled a Trades' Unionist demonstration when 40,000 persons marched peaceably through the streets to petition the king. Because of the police, not "a single soldier was in attendance, nor did the slightest breach of the peace occur."[25]

Opposition to radical police reform finally surfaced when the Common Council referred the Lownds report to its joint police committee in late September; and a London-style police force was not effected.[26] When the report emerged from committee in January 1837, it did not resemble the original. Some police reform, however, was deemed necessary. The committee, while not urging a total reorganization, suggested that the existing system of daytime constables and nighttime watchmen be expanded. New Yorkers no longer could hope that their city would remain untouched by the serious rioting which had been occurring nationwide. The community's leaders could no longer consider the election and anti-abolition riots as aberrations: they now accepted serious rioting as an occasional but continuing threat, and their solution was a compromise between their past do-nothingism and Justice Lownds's activism.

The Common Council's joint special committee on the police adopted the view that the Lownds proposal for police reform was an extravagance which did not reflect the limited danger that serious rioting actually posed. It agreed with Justice Lownds that a police force should emphasize the prevention of crime rather than its detection and punishment, but it dissented from his proposal for a sweeping reorganization. The committee specifically rejected a London-style police force with its around-the-clock patrols on the grounds that riots, occurring only occasionally, merely required the mayor to have the power to organize a strong posse in particular situations. For the prevention of ordinary crime, the city did not need an expensive day police with regular patrols.

The police committee, in its substitute proposal, asked that the state legislature be petitioned to grant the mayor the authority to appoint as many special constables as he deemed necessary. It recommended giving these special constables the same power to make arrests as the marshals and the elected constables already possessed. It was claimed that with these special constables, the regularly constituted police could prevent most riots, breaches of the peace, and other crimes of which they had advance knowledge, without the aid of their military. The added manpower would enable the authorities to organize special patrols and to station men where they expected trouble to develop. The police committee also recommended that 192 additional watchmen be appointed, with the title of the existing roundsmen, but with greater responsibilities. Besides deterring crime by making the "rounds" within their districts, the new roundsmen would observe the regular watchmen and report back to their captains if they saw anyone neglecting to do his duty. Other committee recommendations included extending the watch limits north of the current Twenty-Sixth Street line into the less populated part of the city and replacing overage watchmen and others unable to fulfill their duties with more competent men.[27]

On February 1, 1837, the Board of Aldermen passed a bill incorporating the committee's major recommendations. Before the Board of Assistant Aldermen could act on it, a flour riot occurred, overshadowing the impact of the February 1836 strikes. The mayor once again called out the militia, and, the very next day the pressured assistant aldermen passed the watch act that they had been sitting on for almost two weeks.[28]

III

The authorities and the press were alarmed by these strikes because they did not expect orderly and purposeful behavior from unskilled workers. Such workers did not strike: they "rioted." They only could gather in "rum-drinking assemblages."[29] To the leaders of the community, it was clear that trade union "demagogues" over whom the leaders had no influence had joined up with the mob to threaten serious rioting.

These two elements—demagogues and mobs—had combined before, most notably in the election and anti-abolition riots of 1834, but the situation this time was potentially more dangerous. The demagogic leaders of these earlier riots had been "respectable" citizens. As conservative politicians or newspaper editors—often wealthy ones—such rabble-rousers would naturally refrain from inflaming a mob further when it threatened to get out of hand. The same restraint could not be expected from the trade union leaders accused of fomenting the ship workers' and laborers' strikes.[30] They were more dangerous than the Tammany Hall demagogues. As Philip Hone saw it, the militia had "restored order for the present," but "the elements of disorder" were still at work. "Bands of Irish and other foreigners, instigated by the mischievous councils of the trades-union and other combinations of discontented men, are acquiring strength and importance which will ere long be difficult to quell."[31]

Yet, even though Hone and other leading citizens frowned upon trade unions, they did not as a rule act to suppress them. Trade union leaders without a mobbish following posed no urgent threat to society; and skilled artisans, in their role as workers, did not belong to the mob. For this reason, the organization of workers into unions proceeded apace without the interference of the authorities. Conversely, unskilled workers could strike (or riot) without causing great alarm—so long as they remained unorganized.

Moreover, journeymen long had a sense of worth to which the political leadership of the city catered. As early as the 1790s, they had formed their own organizations.[32] During the trade union resurgence of the mid 1830s, both Democrats and Whigs appealed to them as members of particular crafts (although the Democrats more frequently appealed to the laboring classes in general).[33] When unionized artisans struck, the authorities usually did not interfere. Between 1833 and the end of 1835, New York's artisans organized at least forty-three unions and called at least eighteen strikes.[34] The employers formed their own associations to crush the unions and to resist the demands of their journeymen for higher wages,[35] but they were not unanimously backed by the elite. Much of the press acknowledged the workers' right to organize and even to strike. In the aftermath of the ship workers' strike, the newspapers supported the journeymen's demands for a "just increase in their wages."[36] When the cost of life's necessities increased faster than wages, workers had the right to combine and demand that their wages be raised.[37]   Those who would deny these demands were "pseudo christians" and "would-be patriots" who only sympathized with the rich merchant and the master craftsman.[38] The *Commercial Advertiser*, which urged employers not to raise wages even if the situation justified a wage hike, was criticized for its willingness to stand aside while "the hapless child" cried to "its starving and agonized mother," while "wretched parents with. . .aching hearts" watched "their offspring gradually expire of want and hunger."[39]

Even where nonstrikers were coerced into joining strikes and unions were unacceptable, the authorities responded with discretion, not calling upon the militia.[40] The 1836 laborers and ship workers' strike was the one exception. The journeymen tailors showed, in February 1836, that workers could muster support outside of their craft.[41] The journeymen struck and the master tailors took them to court and won. An unsympathetic Judge Ogden Edwards found twenty-five of the striking tailors guilty of riot and conspiracy and levied fines totaling $1,400. On the day of sentencing, a crowd, variously estimated at from 1,500 to 30,000, collected in City Hall Park to protest the tailors' conviction.[42] It listened to speeches and hung Judge Edwards and another judge in effigy. At no time during the affair, however, despite the threatened disregard of the court's decision, did the authorities use force, either to circumvent the courts or to prevent protest from turning into violence. Despite incendiary handbills posted in advance, the authorities made no attempt to prevent the June protest meeting. When the meeting adjourned, the police appeared—but only to disperse the lingerers.[43] It is apparent that the militia was not used to break strikes; rather, the authorities went to the courts to test union strength.

The greatest parallel to the ship workers' strike of 1836 were strikes in 1825 and 1828 that the authorities put down easily and calmly. In these earlier strikes, stevedores, riggers, and ship laborers walked out over wages—in the first instance to demand a raise, in the second to prevent a reduction. In each strike, several hundred workers went from wharf to wharf to spread the walkout, calling upon nonstrikers to join them and allegedly using force when peaceful persuasion failed. In 1825, the strikers "soon amounted to a mob, and committed some excesses."[44] In 1828, they threw stones at a ship which they had unsuccessfully attempted to board. They wounded one of its officers and later threatened to attack it. Both strikes of the 1820s, like the strike of 1836, ended soon after the police made an appearance and arrested the ringleaders. However, in contrast to the 1836 strike, the authorities in the 1820s felt no need to call out the militia. The issue of demagogy did not arise. In 1825, the press complacently noted that laborers from outside the city would happily take the strikers' places, and one paper therefore called the strike "obviously impolitic."[45] In 1828, the reaction was somewhat sharper, the recorder (a judicial official) warning the rioters that the civil magistrates could call out the militia if they wished. The authorities, however, took no action in this direction, and the threat was an empty one.[46]

It would seem, then, that the strikes of February 1836 were unique: they touched a raw nerve. The city's leaders were not aroused by the violence per se. They were alarmed because the strikes were led, as they saw it, by demagogues who were outside the mainstream of society and would not hesitate to use the very lowest orders in society to create havoc in order to achieve their ends. Trade union leaders manipulating the mob were even more dangerous than Tammany Hall politicians doing the same thing.

IV

When the flour riot came in 1837, it did not result in an increased fear of the mob, nor did it quicken the move for judicial reform. On the contrary, it eased fears the 1836 strikes had aroused because it was a "traditional" riot; those involved only wanted their due and did not dream of disrupting the established order.

In February 1837, the Locofocos (a group of antimonopoly free trade politicians who had temporarily parted ways with the Democratic party) sought to turn the continuing inflation to their own political advantage. To this end, they planned a meeting in City Hall Park and placarded the city with inflammatory handbills:

BREAD, MEAT, RENT, FUEL!
THE PRICES MUST COME DOWN!

The Voice of the People shall be Heard, and Will Prevail!

The People will meet in the PARK, *Rain or Shine*, at 4 o'clock, on MONDAY AFTERNOON

To inquire into the Cause of the present unexampled Distress, and to devise a suitable Remedy. All Friends of Humanity, determined to resist Monopolists and Extortioners, are invited to attend.[47]

The day of the meeting, February 13, was perhaps the most bitter of the entire winter, with winds allegedly of hurricane strength making the cold almost unbearable.[48] Nevertheless, a large crowd estimated at between 2,000 and 6,000 persons gathered in City Hall Park to hear the Locofoco haranguers.[49]

All the speakers blamed the banks and the monopolists for the high rents and high prices, but their anti-speculator rhetoric notwithstanding, the Locofocos did not speak to the crowd's concerns—they never really had the meeting in hand. Throughout the crowd, small knots of people stopped listening to the politicians on the platform and turned their attention to soapboxers within the crowd instead.[50] Then after the meeting had gone on for some time, a man whose identity has never been ascertained,[51] delivered a speech from the rostrum which turned a portion of the crowd into a mob. The speaker told his listeners to go to the store of flour merchant Eli Hart, who was said to have hiked prices by keeping 50,000 barrels of the commodity off the market, and to offer him $8.00 a barrel for his flour. As the speaker seemed about to urge the crowd to take the flour if they could not buy it at this price,[52] someone on the platform touched him on the shoulder and the speaker, after a pause, told his listeners to leave Hart's store peaceably even if Hart refused their offer.

After the Locofoco meeting adjourned, a crowd ranging from 100 to 1,000 persons proceeded immediately to the Hart store and began attacking it.[53] The authorities tried several times unsuccessfully to restore order. The mob threatened to attack Police Justice John M. Bloodgood and some half dozen police officers. Mayor Lawrence personally tried to reason with the rioters, but they shouted him down and barraged him with barrel staves, heading sticks, stones, and balls of flour. The mob ransacked the store unhindered for several hours. The rioters threw some 200 barrels of flour and 1,000 bushels of wheat into the street and broke open the containers. They also entered the counting room, smashing the desks and scattering the company's papers. At the height of the disturbance, one rioter, as he threw a number of barrels out of an upper story window, shouted "here goes flour at eight dollars a barrel!"[54] In the meantime, women in the street carried the precious flour away—in boxes, baskets, and in their aprons.

At about dusk, the rioters headed as a body towards the flour stores in the first ward, a distance of about a mile. They stopped first at E. & J. Herrick's on South Street, but they did not attack the store because the Herrick representative persuaded them that the company had sold its stock at low prices. The rioters moved on, stopping next in Coenties Slip at the store of S. H. Herrick & Son. They broke into the building and began throwing barrels of flour into the street. They had taken hold of some twenty barrels when an agent from the owner appeared and promised the rioters that the company would give every barrel in the store to the poor. The ploy worked and the rioters left peaceably. As they were deciding on their next target, a force of 100 marshals and watchmen finally met up with them and easily suppressed the disturbance. In fact, by this time, the crowd had almost disintegrated of its own accord: when the police arrived, 100 spectators were watching a mere 15 to 30 rioters.

The mayor called up the militia soon after the riot began, but the troops took several hours to assemble. When the authorities sent them to Hart's store, the mob had already moved on; so the troops returned to City Hall. The militia remained on active duty the next day. In the aftermath of the riot, large crowds gathered outside Hart's store and in City Hall Park (outside the police office where the authorities were charging the arrested rioters). The mayor stationed the troops at these points as well as at several others to prevent further rioting; but calm soon returned to the city, and the troops avoided a violent confrontation with the crowds.[55]

Although the authorities had obviously tried to suppress the rioting, much of the press charged that they had done too little, too late. A force of twenty-five or fifty men, "energetically applied on the first violators of the peace, would have quelled all disturbance;" and calling out the militia after rioting had already begun was like "shutting the stable. . .door after the horse had been stolen."[56] The authorities should have expected trouble, given the rumors floating about the city and the Locofoco call for a protest meeting. They simply had refused to heed the danger signals: "if the dead should rise from the grave to warn them, it is doubtful whether the supernatural visitation would rouse our magistrates into timely activity."[57]

The *Journal of Commerce* even charged that the authorities had concrete advance knowledge of the riot. On the morning after the disturbance, the newspaper reported that the mayor had come into possession of several letters threatening Hart and Company, which he had shown to Hart, but which neither he nor the flour dealer considered seriously. According to the *Journal of Commerce* report, one letter in particular should have forewarned the authorities. This unsigned letter addressed to a W. Lennox,[58] described how a "large party" intended to plunder the Hart building. The rioters would attack at night and they would sound false fire alarms to draw the police and the watch away from the targeted store.[59] The Lennox letter was wrong in almost all its details and gave no clues that would have enabled the authorities to anticipate the rioters' movements. False fire alarms were not reported, the riot occurred in the late afternoon and not at night, and the letter did not specify on what day the attack would occur.

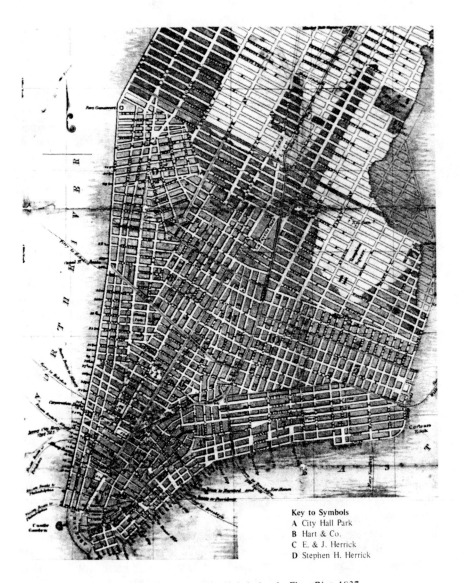

Key to Symbols
A City Hall Park
B Hart & Co.
C E. & J. Herrick
D Stephen H. Herrick

Fig. 1. Targets of the Mob during the Flour Riot, 1837.

V

Yet the Lennox letter had its effect when subsequently the authorities sought to prevent crowds from getting out of hand. In early March, when the Locofocos held a second meeting to protest high prices, the mayor called out the militia in advance of the meeting so that troops would be on hand should trouble develop. (They guarded the flour stores, but carefully stayed away from the area of the meeting so as not to incite the protesters to violence by their presence.)[60] The following May, when the banks suspended payment in specie, the mayor called out the militia before the run on the banks could develop into a riot.[61] In neither instance did the crowd show any inclination to violence, but the principle of riot prevention had been established. In the future, when the authorities considered mob violence to be a possibility, they ordered out the watchmen in advance. In November 1837, after anti-abolitionists martyred Elijah P. Lovejoy, the Illinois anti-slavery editor, New York's anti-slavery society held a memorial meeting with a force of watchmen on hand from the beginning.[62] And in the fall of 1838, violence threatened to erupt several time. In the first instance, the police protected Frances Wright from mobs threatening to disrupt her series of Sunday night lectures. For the last four of her six lectures, people thronged the street in front of the building, but the presence of police force discouraged violence.[63] In the second case, during the November election, watchmen protected the homes of several election inspectors who were threatened because they had ballot boxes in their possession.[64]

This policy of actively using the police and the militia to prevent violence represented a distinct departure from past practice. Previously, the authorities either ignored the possibility of rioting or took only minimal precautions to guard against it. Each of the situations involving a preventive police in 1837-1838 had an earlier counterpart in which the authorities had acted far less vigorously. The March 1837 Locofoco meeting, of course, was the counterpart of the Locofoco meeting of the month before. The suspension of specie payments in May 1837 resembled the bank failures of 1819, when the authorities detained the watch after their night's duty until two o'clock in the afternoon, but did not call upon the militia.[65] In 1837, the authorities protected an inflammatory meeting of the anti-slavery society, whereas in 1833 and 1834 they denied that disrupting a meeting was riotous behavior and refused to provide police protection even after the abolitionists requested it.[66] In 1838, the authorities protected Frances Wright, but in 1829, a noisy crowd frequently disrupted her talks and the police were noticeably absent.[67]   Finally, the authorities, in 1838, guarded the ballot boxes, while in 1834 they did so only after rioting had begun.

This new policy emphasizing prevention rather than suppression stemmed from increased concern over rioting; but, paradoxically, it also reflected the authorities' confidence in their ability to control crowd behavior. The fears that had given rise to the alarmist rhetoric and the harsh suppressive reactions of the 1834-1836 period were not evident in 1837-1838.   Community leaders now advocated using the existing constable and watch system more efficiently instead of instituting wholesale police reform. The press's assertion in the aftermath of the flour riot that the authorities could have easily suppressed or prevented that disturbance set the tone for the rest of the decade.

The conversion of riot control and prevention into a political issue indicated the community's more relaxed attitude.   During 1836, police reform appeared urgent and therefore had bipartisan support. But in 1837, rioting no longer posed so serious a threat to the social fabric; thus disagreement on what steps to take led to inaction, with the tacit sanction of community leaders. The flour riot disguised this long range trend for a time. On the day following the flour riot, the Board of Assistant Aldermen approved the police act which the aldermen had passed earlier in February, as an aftermath of the February 1836 strikes, and the mayor assented three days later. In April, the Common Council and the mayor voted to open discussions with the governor for the removal of the arsenal from its downtown site to a more remote part of the city.[68]   The flour riot, however, did not have a continuing impact. The arsenal vote was the last law and order vote taken without partisan debate. Police reform did not receive bipartisan support again until the early 1840s when crime and disorderly behavior became too prevalent to ignore.

The April 1837 mayoralty campaign first revealed the change in attitude. The parties fought the election mostly on national issues, but the Whigs also appealed to the electorate as the party of law and order. They depicted the Democratic candidate, John I. Morgan, as too feeble to lead the police in quelling riots. The Democrats responded by charging that the Whig candidate, Aaron Clark, lacked the "respect" of the community because he had formerly sold lottery tickets.[69]   The new importance of partisanship was confirmed in July 1837, when the question of continuing the sixth ward's two day policemen came before the Board of Aldermen. In July 1836, the Board had unanimously approved the introduction of the day police into this heavily Democratic ward, but the vote, the following year, correlated with party affiliation.

Fig. 2. "The Would-Be Mayor Preparing to Quell a Riot" (Lithograph)

Table 3 shows the results of a first vote, when the outcome was still in doubt and table 4 the results of a succeeding vote after it became apparent that the aldermen would vote to continue the day police.[70] The vote also shows disunity among the Whigs.

These indications of partisanship and disunity portended trouble for major police reform. The reorganization of the police was rejected by the state legislature; and Mayor Aaron Clark, by urging the Common Council to readopt the rejected measure or pass a similar one, was acting on a campaign promise which his own party did not fully support.

TABLE 3

VOTE TO ABOLISH SIXTH WARD DAY POLICE

	Whigs	Democrats
Ayes	3	4
Nays	8	0
Not Voting	1	1

TABLE 4

VOTE TO CONTINUE SIXTH WARD DAY POLICE

	Whigs	Democrats
Ayes	10	0
Nays	1	3
Not Voting	1	2

Clark made recommendations for making police reform even more effective than originally suggested: survivors' benefits for the families of watchmen dying in the line of duty and additional pay for extra service (such as would be required to suppress a daytime riot). Material relating to the London police was forwarded as supporting documentation. Clark warned that "at any and every hazard, the peace of this great commercial metropolis of the country will be maintained."[71]

Clark's appeal was made in May 1837, but the Whig-controlled Common Council, disagreeing with the mayor's sense of urgency, did not resubmit the police reorganization proposal to committee until the following January. When the joint police committee acted speedily and issued a favorable report in February, the whole council did not at once accept it. The Board of Aldermen tabled a motion that would have forwarded the reorganization proposal to the state legislature, and, instead, debated each section in turn. Three more months elapsed before a new watch law was passed. The board agreed with the committee that the preservation of the public peace and private property required a "thorough system of subordination and close and active inspection" of the watch, and it approved the appointment of 132 sergeants, a new category of watchman, intended to oversee closely the ordinary members of the department.[72]   But the board rejected, after debate, for unascertainable reasons, a provision granting the Common Council the power to appoint an unlimited number of special police justices. The number of minor offenses the courts could handle remained limited. The Whigs, by splitting on the issue doomed the measure to defeat.[73]

Mayor Clark expressed much greater satisfaction with the state of the city in his second annual address, delivered in May 1838, than he had in his first. He approved of the recent modest reorganization of the police department and observed, with satisfaction, that the militia had not suppressed a riot "for more than a year past." He gave credit for this comparative peace to various governmental bodies—the courts, the police, the watch, and the Sunday officers; but he also commended "the exertions of all good citizens."[74]

TABLE 5

UNLIMITED APPOINTMENT OF SPECIAL POLICE JUSTICES

	Whigs	Democrats
Ayes	4	0
Nays	5	3
Not Voting	3	2

Issac L. Varian, a Democrat elected mayor in April 1839, picked up on this latter theme: law and order depended upon "good citizens" "discharging their duties." This was as important as magistrates forceably suppressing rioters. The citizens had to provide the necessary "aid, support and assistance" to magistrates enforcing the law. The authorities could not act contrary to community wishes, for when the community supported "vicious" rioters—"even silently"—and the "public press does not frown upon, but rather encourages attempts to excite popular feeling, the arm of the law becomes at once, in a measure, powerless."[75] In other words, if the community supported the authorities and the press behaved responsibly, no radical police reform would be needed.

VI

The police reform movement made no substantial progress because the social climate offered no cause for alarm. The national fury had dissipated itself: seventeen riots in 1836 and twenty in 1837 compared to the far more ominous fifty in 1835.[76] The local situation was also changed.

The flour riot encouraged the authorities to believe that future disturbances could be handled: the violence took a traditional form and upheld traditional values. Historically, rioting occurred—as it did in February 1837—when prices were not "fair" or "just;" municipal government was expected to regulate commodity prices, especially the price of bread.[77] Although New York abolished the latter regulation, called the assize, in 1801,[78] the idea of price control lingered on. Price control was only one direction which commodity regulation took. Municipal government in the 1830s still regulated weights, measures, quality, and conditions of sale.[79]

Many "respectable" citizens of the Jackson era, aware of government's past responsibility, saw inflation as offering a choice—between morality and laissez faire economics. They condemned the riot while sympathizing with the rioters. The riot? It was the worst "in violence and infamy" since the 1834 anti-abolitionist riot. The rioters? They were "inoffensive, hard working men."[80]

Philip Hone was the foreman of the grand jury which investigated the riot. He thought the riot "alarming," and claimed credit for the indictment of John Windt, a Locofoco politician allegedly involved; but he also sympathized with the "poor devils" who made up the mob. Hone's diary for February 18 reads, in part, as follows: "What is to become of the labouring classes. . .It is very cold now, if it continues so for a month, then will be great and real suffering in all classes. . .the present unnatural state of things cannot continue."[81]

Before the flour riot, several of New York's conservative newspapers even applauded a protest meeting in Portland, Maine that the February 13 meeting in New York later resembled. The leading citizens of Portland, led by their mayor, gathered to protest high prices for which they held speculators responsible, and flour, the Portland citizens resolved, should be sold at a "fair" price. If the merchants would not accede, there would be no sales, for flour would not be purchased at the market price. In New York, the Whig *Gazette* called these resolutions "in the right spirit to show a determination not to submit to unjust exactions from any quarter."[82]   The *Express*, also a Whig paper, described the Portland citizens as "benevolent and enterprising;" and the paper claimed that if only "their spirit of kindness and determination" were spread throughout the country, "much may be done to alleviate the suffering of the Poor."[83]

This endorsement of the meeting by several Whig newspapers probably reflected their belief that a united community could effect a "fair" price without violence. They sought to establish the same time-honored consensus that community leaders had used so successfully against the Sabbatarians in 1821 and with unintended riotous consequences against the abolitionists in 1833 and 1834. When rioting broke out again in 1837 because the concept of a "fair " price was not universally acceptable, the conservatives who supported lower prices before the flour riot turned silent or reversed their position afterwards.[84] They would not risk uncontrollable violence by making inflammatory demands.

The new cheap press, on the other hand, printed angry editorials on inflation before the riot, and continued printing them afterwards, despite the possible consequences of their agitation. The *Herald*, before the riot, detected "an atrocious and wicked conspiracy by rich speculators. . .to grind to the earth the great mass of society."[85]   It urged tenants who were unable to afford the soaring rents to stay in their apartments after their leases expired on May 1.[86]   After the riot, the paper did not back down: it warned the city that it could escape further disturbances only if rents and prices fell. Otherwise, "the whole body of the people" would be driven "out of all sense and all moderation."[87] The *New Era*, another cheap paper, also castigated "monopolists," describing them as "veritable vermin who preys upon the community;"[88] and the paper urged a series of schemes, all intended to bring down the high prices and high rents. On one day, the paper appealed to "the feelings of justice and humanity" on the part of the landlords; on the day following, it suggested that "benevolent and public spirited landlords" erect small one family dwellings to alleviate the housing shortage, even urging the city to intervene if private efforts proved inadequate. Next, the *New Era* exhorted tenants to resist rent increases individually.[89]   In another instance, the paper called for the formation of an anti-monopoly association—without middlemen—which would do its

own purchasing and its own banking, and which would sell flour and
fuel cheaply.[90]   After the flour riot, the paper continued its attack,
eventually trying to start a boycott by publishing the names of five
"monopolistc" flour dealers.[93]

VII

A paternalistic attitude was inherent in the press attacks on
inflation. The flour riot was a just protest. And paternalism explains
also why the New York elite continued to assume that the elite
controlled riots just as it controlled other, more ordinary aspects of
community life.

NOTES

[1] See the *New York Times* and *New-York American* for ads announcing the selling and letting of homes, rooms, stores and offices (February-April, 1837). Peter Temin, *The Jacksonian Economy*, The Norton Essays in American History (New York, 1969), pp. 68-69, and passim; for New York City in particular, including a chart of wholesale commodity prices, see George Rogers Taylor, *The Transportation Revolution, 1815-1860*, The Economic History of the United States, vol. 4 (New York, 1951), pp. 330-31.

[2] Taylor, *Transporation Revolution*, pp. 332-33.

[3] Arthur Harrison Cole, *Wholesale Commodity Prices in the United States 1700-1861; Statistical Supplement: Actual Wholesle Prices of Various Commodities* (Cambridge, Mass., 1938), pp. 249, 252, 257-58, 261-62, 265. Coal, at this time, was replacing firewood as a home fuel (see the *New-York Commercial Advertiser*, March 8, 1833).

[4] Unfortunately, no index of rents exists; but construction records help somewhat to fill in the gap. The number of new buildings erected in New York City increased from 1,259 in 1835 to 1,826 in 1836, but the latter figure includes buildings replacing structures destroyed by the fire of December 1835. Some 670 buildings burned in that fire, and between January 1st and September 12th, 1836, 506 buildings were erected in the first ward, the ward where the fire occurred. In contrast, only 106 buildings were erected in this ward for all of 1835. New York (City), Board of Assistant Aldermen, *Report of the City Inspector, Relative to the Number of Buildings Erected and Erecting in the City of New York, from 1st Day of January, 1836, to the 12th Day of September, 1836*, Doc. No. 114, Vol. VIII (1836): 325-27; in addition, city wide residential construction appears to have declined slightly. Therefore, unless the rate of population growth also declined between 1835 and 1836—and no population data bearing on this point exists—the fire of December 1835 contributed to a housing shortage. New York (City), Board of Assistant Aldermen, *The Report of the City Inspector to the Common Council, of the Number and Class of New Buildings, Erected in the City of New York, from the First Day of January, 1836 to the First Day of January, 1837*, Doc. No. 59, Vol. X (1837), 193-98; New York (City), Board of Alderman, *Annual Report of the City Inspector of the New Buildings Erected in the City and County of New York*, Doc. No. 63, Vol. VI (1840) 621-28; *New-York As It Is, in 1837* (New-York, 1837), p. 22; *Herald* (New York), December 21, 1835.

[5] *Herald*, February 4, 1837; *New Era* (New York), February 1, 2, 6, 10, 1837; *Sun* (New York), February 2, 4, 10, 1837.

[6] F. Byrdsall, *The History of the Loco-foco, or Equal Rights Party, Its Movements, Conventions and Proceedings* (New York, 1842), pp. 99-101, 109, 113.

[7] Edward B. Mittelman, "Trade Unionism (1833-1839)," Part III of *History of Labor in the United States*, by John R. Commons et al., 4 vols. (New York, 1921-35), 1:appendix II, 478-84.

[8] The press is the best source of information on the strikes: *New-York American*, February 24-25, 1836; *New York Commercial Advertiser*, February 23-24, 1836; *Morning Courier ad New-York Enquirer*, February 23-26, 1836; *New-York Gazette and General Advertiser*, February 23-25, 1836; *Herald*, February 24-25, 1836; *New York*

Journal of Commerce, February 24-25, 1836; *Mercantile Advertiser and New York Advocate,* February 25, 1836; *Evening Post* (New York), February 24, 1836; *Evening Star* (New York, February 23-24, 1836; *Sun,* February 24-25, 1836; *New York Times,* February 24-25, 1836; *New York Transcript,* February 23-25, 1836. For a map of the "burnt area," see the *Herald,* December 21, 1835.

Other useful sources include the following: Emmons Clark, *History of the Seventh Regiment of New York 1806-1889,* 2 vols. (New York, 1890), 1:243; Philip Hone, MS Diary, February 24-25, 1836, Manuscript Division, New-York Historical Society; New York (State), 27th Regiment Artillery, Fourth Company, MS Orderly Book 1828-39, February 1836, Seventh Regiment Collection, New-York Historical Society.

[9]There is no positive evidence, just none to the contrary.

[10]Clark, *Seventh Regiment,* 1:243-44.

[11]Ibid.

[12]New York (State), Senate, 59th sess., *Journal,* March 17-18, 1836, pp. 238, 243; New York (State), Assembly, 59th sess., *Journal,* March 18, 21, 1836, pp. 581, 589, 592; New York (State), *Laws* (1836), c. 66.

[13]New York (State), *Laws* (1835), c. 49.

[14]New York (City), Board of Aldermen, *Proceedings,* XI (1836), 52-55.

[15]Ibid., p. 75.

[16]Ibid.

[17]New York (City), Board of Assistant Aldermen, *Proceedings,* VIII (1836), 65-66, 79.

[18]Ibid., pp. 88, 124; *Times,* Sepember 19, 1836.

[19]New York (City), Board of Aldermen, *Communication from His Honor the Mayor, Transmitting from Mr. Justice Lownds, a Plan for a Reorganization of the Police Department,* Doc. No. 25 Vol. III (1836-37), 139-51.   Under the existing watch law, the mayor and the councilmen had the right to give orders to the watchmen "for the purpose of preserving the peace and good government of this city," but they were not specifically charged with the responsibility of suppressing mobs.   New York (City), *Laws and Ordinances* (1834), c. 33, title II, sec. 7.

[20]New York (City), Board of Aldermen, *Reorganization,* p. 140.

[21]The citation is from the *Herald,* August 30, 1836.

[22]*Commercial Advertiser,* August 26, 1836.

[23]See especially the *Evening Post,* August 30-31, 1836; *Commercial Advertiser,* August 26, 30-September 3, 14-15, 1836; *Times,* August 25, 30-September 3, 6, 1836.

[24]*Times,* August 25, 1836.

[25]Ibid., August 30, 1836.

[26]*Courier and Enquirer*, September 24, 1836; *Sun*, September 20, 1836; James F. Richardson, *The New York Police: Colonial Times to 1901*, The Urban Life in America Series (New York, 1970), p. 37; *Herald*, September 20-21, 1836.

Public opinion on the issue appears to have been mercurial. The press, which had so vociferously favored a London style police in late August and the first half of September fell suddenly and permanently silent during the second half of the month. The *Herald*, the one newspaper which continued to speak out on the issue, indicates a quick and drastic change in the public's thinking. On September 20, the paper praised the Lownds report, particularly pleased at the idea of policemen walking regular beats. It observed approvingly that the police "are to be ready at all times to aid in quelling any disturbance or riot, and are to be always on the alert and ready for action." But the *Herald* retracted its support the following day, reporting that the justice's plan had met with widespread dissatisfaction and that the *Herald*, after examining it critically, agreed with public opinion. The paper now claimed that the courts, by their leniency, brought on the disorder plaguing the city.

[27]New York (City), Board of Aldermen, *The Joint Select Commitee, to Whom Was Referred the Subject of the Reorganization of the Police Department, Together with the Annexed Communications Relative Thereto, Presented the Following Report Thereon, and the Annexed Law*, Doc No. 88, Vol. III (1836-37), 561-95; on the duties of the roundsmen prior to 1837, see A[ugustine] E. Costello, *Our Police Protectors. History of the New York Police from the Earliest Period to the Present Time.* Published for the Benefit of the Police Pension Fund ([New York], 1885), p. 69.

[28]New York (City), Boards of Aldermen and Assistant Aldermen, *Proceedings Approved by the Mayor*, IV (1837), 183-84.

[29]*Herald*, February 24, 1837.

[30]*Evening Star*, February 24, 1836; *Journal of Commerce*, February 27, 1836; *Herald*, February 26, 29, 1836.

[31]Philip Hone, *The Diary of Philip Hone, 1828-1851*, ed. Allan Nevins, new and enl. ed. (New York, 1936), p. 200 (February 24, 1836).

[32]Howard B. Rock, "The Independent Mechanic: The Tradesman of New York City in Labor and Politics During the Jeffersonian Era" (Ph.D. dissertation, New York University, 1974), pp. 53-59, passim.

[33]Leo Hershkowitz, "New York City, 1834 to 1840, A Study in Local Politics" (Ph.D. dissertation, New York University, 1960), pp. 28-37, 42-3.

[34]Mittelman, "Trade Unionism (1833-1839)," 1:Appendixes I and II, 472-84.

[35]Walter Hugins, *Jacksonian Democracy and the Working Class: A Study of the New York Workingmen's Movement, 1829-1837*, Stanford Studies in History, Economics, and Political Science, 19 (Stanford, Cal., 1960), p. 62.

[36]*Herald*, February 19, 1836.

[37] *Sun,* February 25, 1836.

[38] *Transcript,* February 24, 1836.

[39] Ibid. For opposition to the workers' right to organize, see the *American,* February 26, 1836; *Commercial Advertiser,* February 24, 1836.

[40] For support of unionization which did not extend to the use of "coercion," see the following: *Courier and Enquirer,* February 24, 1836; *Times,* February 25, 1836; New York (City), Board of Aldermen, *Proceedings,* X (1836), 274; Hugins, *Jacksonian Democracy and the Working Class,* p. 61; Hershkowitz, "New York City," p. 155; Joseph G. Rayback, *A History of American Labor,* expanded and updated ed. (New York, 1966), p. 59.

[41] Hugins, *Jacksonian Democracy and the Working Class,* p. 62; Rayback, *A History of American Labor* pp. 81-82.

[42] The *Commercial Advertiser,* June 14, 1836, gives is own estimate of the size of the crowd and the estimates of several other newspapers.

[43] *Commercial Advertiser,* June 14, 1836.

[44] *American,* March 22, 1825.

[45] *New-York National Advocate,* March 23, 1825.

[46] On the 1825 strike, see the *New-York Daily Advertiser,* March 22, 1825; *American,* March 22, 1825; *Commercial Advertiser,* March 22, 1825; *Evening Post,* March 22, 1825; *New-York Statesman,* March 22, 1825. On the 1828 strike, see the *American,* July 14-16, 21, 1828; *Commercial Advertiser,* July 15, 21, 1828; *Gazette and General Advertiser,* July 15-16, 1828; *Evening Post,* July 14, 1828.

[47] *The Sun,* February 13, 1837.

[48] Hone, *Diary,* p. 241 (February 13, 1837).

[49] For crowd estimates, see the *Courier and Enquirer,* February 14, 1837; *Sun,* February 14, 1837; *New-York Daily Express,* February 14, 1837; *Commercial Advertiser,* February 14, 1837.

[50] *Journal of Commerce,* February 14, 1837; *Commercial Advertiser,* February 14, 1837.

[51] The grand jury indicted John Windt, a leading Locofoco, for inflammatory language which excited the populace to commit acts of violence, but the district attorney quashed the indictment. Hone, MS Diary, February 13, 16, 20, 1837; *Herald,* February 18, 1837; *Sun,* March 15, 1837.

[52] Contemporary accounts did not refer to a "fair" price, but Byrdsall, describing the event in 1842, did attribute this traditional term to a speaker on the platform (Byrdsall, *Equal Rights Party,* p. 103).

[53]For crowd estimates, see the *Evening Post*, February 14, 1837; *Commercial Advertiser*, February 14, 1837; *Gazette and General Advertiser*, February 14, 1837; *Express*, February 14, 1837; Byrdsall, *Equal Rights Party*, p. 103.

[54]*Commercial Advertiser*, February 14, 1837; *Courier and Enquirer*, February 14, 1837.

[55]The sources for crowd estimates and for particular aspects of the riot are cited in nn. 48-54. The complete list of sources used for the events of February 13th and their aftermath follows: *Commercial Advertiser*, February 14-15, March 23, 1837; *Courier and Enquirer*, February 13-15, 1837; *Express*, February 14, March 15, 18, 1837; *Gazette and General Advertiser*, February 14, 1837; *Herald*, February 13, 15, 18, March 14-15, 1837; *Journal of Commerce*, February 14-15, 1837; *New Era*, February 13-15, 1837; *Evening Post*, February 14, 1837; *Sun*, February 14-15, 18, March 15, 24, 1837; *Times*, February 14-15, 1837; Byrdsall, *Equal Rights Party*, pp. 99-105; Hone, MS Diary, February 13-16, 20, 1837; New York (State), 27th Regiment Artillery, Fourth Company, MS Orderly Book 1828-39, February 14, 1837; New York (City), Board of Aldermen, *Communication from His Honor the Mayor in Relation to the Precautionary Measures Adopted by Him to Secure the Public Peace at the Recent Election in This City, with Documents, and a Report from the Comptroller Relative to the Expenses Incurred during Said Election*, Doc. No. 29, Vol. V (1838-1839), 303-304, 335-36.

[56]*Gazette and General Advertiser*, February 15, 1837.

[57]*Plaindealer* (New York), February 18, 1837. For similar sentiments, less graphically stated, see the *Courier and Enquirer*, February 14, 1837; *American*, February 14, 1837; *Herald*, February 15, 1837; *Evening Post*, February 14, 1837; *Times*, February 16, 1837.

[58]In *Longworth's American Almanac, New-York Register, and City Directory*, 1836-37, a William Lenox (73 Mott Street) is listed as a baker.

[59]*Journal of Commerce*, February 14, 1837.

[60]*Herald*, March 6, 1837; *New Era*, March 4, 6-7, 1837; Brydsall, *Equal Rights Party*, pp. 109, 113.

[61]New York (City), Board of Aldermen, *Precautionary Measures*, pp. 304-306; Hone, *Diary*, pp. 257-59 (May 10, 1837).

[62]New York (City), Board of Aldermen, *Precautionary Measures*, p. 306.

[63]Ibid., p. 307.

[64]Ibid., pp. 307-10.

[65]*Evening Post*, July 2, 1819.

[66]Above, pp. 11-13, 38-39; *Commercial Advertiser*, July 5, 1834; *Journal of Commerce*, July 7, 1834.

[67]A. J. G. Perkins and Theresa Wolfson, *Frances Wright, Free Enquirer. The Study of a Temperament* (New York, 1939), pp. 231-32.

[68]New York (City), Boards of Aldermen and Assistant Aldermen, *Proceedings Approved by the Mayor*, IV (1837), 184, 236.

[69]Lithograph, "The Would-Be Mayor Preparing to Quell a Riot" (New York, 1837), Print Room, New-York Historical Society; *Courier and Enquirer*, March 18, 1837; *Express*, March 20, 28, 1837; *Gazette and General Advertiser*, April 11-12, 1837; *New Era*, March 20, April 5, 1837; *Plaindealer*, March 18, 25, 1837; *Evening Post*, March 15-16, 18, 20, 28, 30, April 11, 1837; *Times*, April 13, 1837.

[70]New York (City), Board of Aldermen, *Proceedings*, XIII (1837), 227, 274-75.

[71]Ibid., pp. 25, 28, 31-32, 35.

[72]New York (City), Board of Aldermen, *Proceedings*, XIV (1838), 190, 197; New York (City), Board of Assistant Aldermen, *Proceedings*, XI (1837), p. 286; New York (City), Board of Aldermen, *The Committee on Police &c. of Both Boards, to Whom was Referred the Resolution Relative to the Re-organization of the Police Department, Presented the Following Report*, Doc. No. 62, Vol. IV (1837-1838), 489-502; New York (City), Boards of Aldermen and Assistant Aldermen, *Proceedings Approved by the Mayor*, V (1838), 219-26. Title I, secs. 5, 12, deal with the number and duties of sergeants.

[73]New York (City), Board of Aldermen, *Proceedings*, XIV (1838), 431. The number of complaints lodged at the police offices increased from 14,548 for the 1834 calendar year to 18,956 between September 1, 1836 and September 1, 1837. In the latter year, of 5,491 complaints forwarded to the courts of general and special sessions (the criminal courts), 3,346 remained unacted upon. See New York (City), Board of Aldermen, *Report from the Special Justices of the City of New York, in Pursuance of a Resolution of the Board Passed September 25, 1837*, Doc. No. 42, Vol. IV (1837-38), 293-96.

[74]New York (City), Board of Aldermen, *Proceedings*, XV (1838), 24-25.

[75]Ibid., XVII (1839), 23.

[76]Compiled from the *Commercial Advertiser*. See above, chap. 4, n. 1.

[77]Carl Bridenbaugh mentions the Boston bread riot of 1713 and pressure for price regulation (see *Cities in the Wilderness: The First Century of Urban Life in America, 1625-1742* [New York, 1938], pp. 196-97).

[78]On the abolition of the assize and the increasing unpopularity of price regulation, see Sidney I. Pomerantz, *New York: An American City, 1783-1803, A Study of Urban Life*, Studies in History, Economics and Public Law, no. 442 (New York, 1938), pp. 170-78. For references in 1837 to the history of bread rioting, see the *Commercial Advertiser*, February 14, 1837; *New Era*, February 14, 1837.

[79]Bridenbaugh, *Cities in the Wilderness*, pp. 50-52, 201-203, 356; Pomerantz, *New York*, pp. 170-78; Carl Bridenbaugh, *Cities in Revolt: Urban Life in America, 1743-1776* (New York, 1955), pp. 83-84; Bayrd Still, "Patterns of Mid-Nineteenth Century Urbanization in the Middle West," *Mississippi Valley Historical Review* 28 (September 1941): 187-206.

See also New York (City), *By-Laws and Ordinances of the Mayor, Aldermen and Commonalty of the City of New York, Revised A.D. 1838-1839* (1839)—c. 12, on the public markets, including the regulation of weighmasters and butchers; c. 45, on the inspection of weighing and measuring instruments; c. 46, on weighmasters, measurers, and gaugers; c. 48, on the sale and manufacture of bread; c. 49, on the sale of coal; c. 50, on the sale and inspection of firewood; c. 51, on the sale of hay and straw; c. 52, on the sale of lime.

[80]*Times,* February 15, 1837.

[81]Hone, MS Diary, February 14-16, 18, 1837.

[82]*Gazette and General Advertiser,* February 8, 1837.

[83]*Express,* February 2, 1837. The official proceedings of the Portland meeting can be found in the *Express* of this date. Indicative of the widespread existence of "fair" price ideas, the Portland meeting requested that the New York City newspapers reprint the account appearing in the local papers, presumably because the New York press circulated nationally and the Portland citizens sought to set an example for the rest of the country.

[84]*Gazette and General Advertiser,* February 16, 18, 1837.

[85]*Herald,* February 9, 1837.

[86]Ibid., February 4, 1837.

[87]Ibid., February 15, 1837.

[88]*New Era,* February 2, 1837.

[89]Ibid., February 1-2, 6, 1837.

[90]Ibid., February 7, 1837.

[91]Ibid., February 17, 20, 1837.

CHAPTER SIX

SOCIAL CONTROL

I

The unruly scene at President Jackson's inauguration in 1829 has become a familiar anecdote: the "people" ruled. A mob "*literally* nearly pressed [the President] to death and almost suffocated" and tore him "to pieces" at the reception after the ceremonies in their eagerness to shake his hand; and Jackson was forced to flee the White House. The crowd, in its eagerness to get to the spiked punch, smashed cut glass and china worth several thousand dollars. Tubs of punch, wine, and ice cream were brought to the garden to avoid further destruction. The studied simplicity of early inaugurations had become a thing of the past.[1]

II

This famous incident had its parallel in New York. On New Year's Day of 1837, Mayor Lawrence kept open house as had the city's mayor "from time immemorable." An unwritten code of behavior had always determined the visitors' conduct: "Gentlemen visited the mayor, saluted him by an honest shake of the hand, paid him the compliments of the day, and took their leave; one out of twenty perhaps taking a single glass of wine or cherry bounce and a morsel of pound cake or New Year's cookies." The "rabble" of 1837 refused to observe this etiquette. They rushed the house at ten in the morning, took the refreshment tables "by storm," and emptied the bottles "in a moment." The "confusion, noise, and quarreling" that followed were so great that the mayor had finally to call upon the police to clear the house; and until he had removed "every eatable and drinkable," he kept his doors locked.[2]

The combination of rowdyism, treating, and politics was nothing new, nor was disrespect on the part of the lower classes; but this rowdyism against political leaders by their own followers seemed more than an expression of egalitarianism. It suggested a deliberate flaunting of disrespect for authority. The man who would wear his hat in the mayor's presence, "smoke and spit on his carpet, . . . and wipe his greasy fingers upon the curtains," would not heed the mayor's advice,[3] and certainly not that of lesser authorities, and in the New York of the 1830s, it was crucially important that the common man respect the words of public officials. The maintenance of law and order depended on it.

When large crowds gathered, the mayor would frequently lead the police (with aldermanic assistance) in suppressing disturbances. For example, the mayor took a personal hand in putting down the ship workers' strike of 1828, the Anderson theater riot of 1831, the election riot of 1834, and the flour riot of 1837. When the banks suspended payment in specie in May 1837, the mayor may have prevented an angry crowd from turning into a riotous mob.[4] Few, if any, persons in positions of influence had questioned the wisdom or propriety of the mayor's peacekeeping role; it was one of the customary functions of his office. The riots of the mid thirties, however, caused the issue of direct mayoral involvement to be aired.

In March and April 1837, the Whigs charged that John I. Morgan, the Democratic candidate for mayor, was too feeble to command the respect of the city's rowdies. In their allegations, the Whigs made frequent use of a political cartoon: "The Would-Be Mayor Preparing to Quell a Riot" (see figure 2). In the background, watchmen with nightsticks were portrayed battling a mob; in the foreground, Morgan—tall, thin, and sickly—approached assisted by three liveried servants. One servant held open an umbrella, a second carried a chair, and the third, a young Negro, carried two horse pistols. The rowdies in the background mocked their pampered would-be mayor:

> Well, poor Tammany is done over when such a skeleton is to represent the great democracy!
>
> Do'nt! whistle in the face of the new Mayor, he may catch the grippe!
>
> Vel, vot ov it, who care for Mr. Morgan: a good puff will blow him away.—Go it my corris!!
>
> Here comes Mr. Morgan the new Mayor. Pat, knock the nagur [nigger? or mayor?] down!—[5]

"They tell us," the *Daily Express* typically jeered, "that Mr. Morgan has a great horror of rain, out door, muddy boots, riots, rows, and so on, which will, without doubt secure him strong support in some quarters." Also scoffing was the *Courier and Enquirer.* Morgan was "a harmless, inefficient and inoffensive man," and better qualified to be a bishop's private secretary than the mayor of New York.[6]

The Democrats' rejection of the Whig criticism was frequently in kind. Sometimes they claimed that Morgan's health was irrelevant, but at other times that Aaron Clark, Morgan's Whig opponent, could not himself command the rowdies' respect. If Morgan's health was questionable, so was Clark's prior occupation. Clark had once sold lottery tickets, an activity illegal since 1834, so what right did the Whigs have for being righteous?

> The man who enjoys the respect and confidence of the community will sooner quell a popular disturbance than he who is regarded with contempt. What will such a mountebank as Clark do to quell a riot? Will he issue proclamations in his old style of 'Huzzah for Clark:' 'Clark's ponies distance every thing,' and sign them 'Fortune's Favorite?' The populace would pelt him with rotten eggs.

And the *Times* echoed:

> And this man is to be the conservator of public morals! He is to suppress riots! What security is there that he will attempt to do so? Can a man accustomed to resort to base acts for gain have elevated views?. . .If he should try to do his duty, how can he be efficient? How can a volunteer mountebank and charlatan command public respect?[7]

Finally, the Democratic press questioned Clark's credibility. Where had he been when the mob attacked Eli Hart's flour store (located in his ward)? He should have led the police in quelling the riot, but he stayed away, preferring friendly shelter to a hostile mob.[8]

III

Using "respect" to govern was an issue again when public executions were prohibited. In New York State this occurred in May 1835.[9] The practice had once been invested with much pomp and circumstance, but in the 1830s the people no longer stood sufficiently in awe of their leaders for the ceremonious hanging of criminals to any longer serve a useful purpose. Instead, executions, ostensibly serious occasions, had become sportive events and posed the danger of becoming riotous affairs.[10]

A prototype of an execution was that of a twenty-two year old seaman, James Reynolds. He was publicly hanged in 1825 for murdering his ship's captain; he committed the deed with a single blow of an axe to the head. (Other New York executions of the period, in 1824, 1829, and 1834, were degenerations—near riotous affairs.)

On the day of Reynolds' hanging, crowds began collecting in the vicinity of the prison behind City Hall at about 9:00 a.m.[11] The authorities—the High Constable, the sheriff and his deputies, marshals, a batallion of infantry, a company of dragoons, and representatives of the ministry—made their appearance about one hour later; and at 10:30 a.m.

the prisoner was led from his cell to a seat on a small stage in the prison yard. Dressed in white trousers, a white frock, and a white cap trimmed with black (but wearing a cloak of nondescript color to protect him from the cold), Reynolds made a dramatic appearance.

With the scene thus set, the Reverend John Stanford, the minister to the city's humane and criminal institutions,[12] delivered a "very solemn and affecting" sermon, addressed to both the spectators and the condemned man: it "caused the tear to flow from many an eye." As Stanford prayed for Reynolds' soul, Reynolds "listened attentively." Although he wept "little," he tried to suppress the emotions which convulsed his body. He father stood by him. The elder Reynolds did not cry, but he obviously was weighed down with grief. When the service ended at 11:05 a.m. the condemned man shook hands with a number of persons whom he had met in prison.

The procession to the site of the execution was led by the sheriff and one or two of his deputies on horseback; outside the prison yard gates, the military joined them. Next came Reynolds' coffin carried in a wagon followed by Reynolds himself in an open carriage with two ministers and a doctor. The marshals brought up the rear and the crowd fell in. The procession moved slowly, taking more than an hour to travel the distance of two miles.

At the scaffold, the sheriff read the warrant for the execution. Reynolds then requested and received permission to address the "multitude." In the company of two officers and two clergymen, the condemned man climbed the steps to the scaffold so that the crowd below him could better see and hear him. He paused for a moment after reaching the top, but once he began, he spoke "in the most cool, clear and collected manner." Reynolds repeated himself and his language revealed that he was not an educated man, but he told a classic tale of moral degradation. According to the published accounts, Reynolds claimed "that he had led a comparatively moral life" until he began frequenting the brothels at Corlaer's Hook, a section of New York known for its crime and depravity. Then he began to drink and mingle with evil company and "was thus led on in the paths of guilt, step by step," in the same way as he had ascended the scaffold on which he then stood. Reynolds ended "by an exhortation to youth, and a fervent prayer," admonishing his listeners "to take warning by the awful spectacle, and shun the paths of vice."

The ceremony slowly began to draw to a close. The Reverend Somers sang two verses of a psalm (while Reynolds sang along) and delivered "an appropriate and impressive address." He was followed by another minister, Reverend William Roy, who concluded the religious exercises with a prayer. Reynolds now with only a few minutes to live, asked to speak to his father. The elder Reynolds ascended the scaffold, and, after a moment's conversation, shook his son's hand and descended. Next, each minister spoke to the prisoner and also shook his hand. The sheriff and under sheriff were the last to ascend: telling Reynolds that the end was near, they removed his cloak. Interjecting an unplanned element, Reynolds requested and received permission to speak to the crowd again. He repeated what he had said before, ending "by a sort of ejaculatory prayer." The ceremony at the scaffold finally ended at 12:45 p.m., about one half hour after it had begun, and more than two hours after Reynolds had entered the prison yard. The cap was drawn over the prisoner's eyes and he was hanged while "earnestly praying to God for pardon."[13]

Until the 1820s, it was alleged that public hangings could be put to "a wise and good Use." The claim was that "awful" scenes, such as in the Reynolds case, would strike "terror" into the hearts of spectators—that those who saw men die on the scaffold, would be deterred against committing capital crimes. When, ironically, crowds gathered at executions only out of "vain Curiousity,"—for "Sport and Merriment"—to sympathize with or torment the condemned criminals, the spectators rather than the ceremonies themselves were faulted.[14]

Increasingly, after 1820, there was dissent from this traditional view. The object lesson in public executions was now seen by many as ineffectual. Viewing shocking scenes only made the witnesses morally insensitive; it accustomed them to the taking of life.

Partly, the rise of humantarianism explains this new attitude, but other factors were also involved. Curiosity and a carnival atmosphere attracted huge crowds with which local governments could not deal. A Cooperstown, New York newspaper editor lamented: "these public executions always bring with them more or less disasters."[15] In Canton, Ohio, a city with a population of about 1,500, the gathering of 30,000 to 40,000 spectators led to a major disaster. On the evening prior to an 1833 execution:

> Multitudes flocked into town to such an extent that not one fourth obtain lodgings, and the residue were compelled to remain in the streets, and under the naked canopy of heaven, during the night. A watch was ordered to patrol the town to prevent disorder and disturbances. By break of day the prison was so thronged that it became necessary to guard the doors, and the military were compelled to remove the crowd at the point of the bayonet.[16]

The New York authorities had to deal with crowds of even larger size. In 1824, a crowd estimated at about 50,000 people thronged the execution procession route several hours in advance of the starting time. Traffic was blocked for distance of half a mile. It took the authorities an hour to clear a path for the marchers, and even then the procession "could not proceed more than a few yards at a time" without the military having to "clear away the rabble."[17]

As New York's population continued to grow, the authorities sought to limit the crowds, and they hit upon an ingenious solution. In 1829 and again in 1834, the city executed criminals on small islands (Blackwell's [now Roosevelt (Welfare)] and Gibbet [now Ellis]), several miles from the heart of the city. The authorities put themselves in the ludicrous position of fleeing overeager spectators. In 1829, they had hoped to leave the prison "with such rapidity as to prevent the rabble from keeping pace with the cavalcade"; but by the time the procession started, at least several thousand persons—"all animated by the strange, savage, and fierce desire to see the disgusting spectacle,"—had collected. Five years later, the authorities were more successful. They outwitted the crowd by taking the condemned man to the site of his execution four hours earlier than scheduled. Neither execution, however, was in fact really private. In 1829, four or five steamboats cruised back and forth and 200 to 300 small boats lined the shore. In the course of the afternoon, at least three boats overturned, dumping their passengers into the river. In 1834, "a vast multitude" found their way to the island, while others watched from "on board boats of every description," of which "there was a greater number than. . . was, perhaps, never [sic] seen in our harbor at one time."[18]

From the mid 1830s, humanitarianism combined with the new concern over mob violence to end these execution spectacles in many parts of the country. Pennsylvania was the first state to abolish public hanging (in April 1834); and New Jersey, New York, and Massachusetts followed suit in March, May, and November 1835 respectively. New Hampshire came next in January 1837, and still other states voted to end public executions in the course of the next decade.[19]

Previously, most Americans had opposed private executions as tyrannous abuses of power. For this reason, opponents of capital punishment dominated the movement to abolish public hanging. Most political leaders saw a choice between two extremes: public executions, with all their attendant evils, or no capital punishment at all, even for the heinous offenses of murder and rape. Presented with these two choices, they invariably chose the first. In the 1830s, however, private executions became acceptable. The riots of the 1830s presented Americans with a choice between disorderly execution crowds that could turn into mobs and the possible abuse of private execution power by tyrants who wished to eliminate political enemies. Many politicians viewed the second potential evil as the more remote. Thus the movement against public hanging triumphed because of a coalition between the opponents of capital punishment and those supporters of the death penalty who opposed the execution spectacle but not the punishment itself.

Several notorious incidents helped bring about this change in policy. In January 1835, a public hanging in Augusta, the capital of Maine, led to riot. The Maine legislature investigated the incident; a year later, the Massachusetts legislature's committee on capital punishment remembered the incident:

> Those whom it would be desirable to affect solemnly, and from whom we have the most reason to fear crime, make the day of public execution a day of drunkenness and profanity. These, with their attendant vices, quarrelling and fighting, were carried to such an extent in Augusta, (at Sager's execution) that it became necessary for the police to interfere, and the jail, which had just been emptied of a murderer, threw open its doors to receive those who came to profit by the solemn scene of a public execution.[20]

The same Massachusetts committee also cited a Hopkinton, New Hampshire hanging which may have influenced the latter state to vote to end its own public executions. In that case, "the riot of a mob thirsting" for the condemned man's "blood" and desirous of taking "revenge with their own hands, rather than lose the spectacle of that wretch's last agonies, resulted in the death of a tender wife, daughter, and mother."[21]

IV

Public executions and riot control by the mayor both illustrate the use of respect as a governing tool. There were differences between them, however, that underline the fate of deferential politics in the 1830s.

Execution spectacles were imposing ceremonies that no longer inspired fear. They intertwined church and state, ministers and politicians, while the separation of the two and freedom of religious choice had become the conventional wisdom.[22] In 1833, Massachusetts became the last state to discontinue its official support of the religious establishment; and clergymen, with less influence over their congregations, were espousing eternal damnation less and free will and salvation more.[23]

Public execution ceremonies placed government officials physically as well as symbolically above and apart from the people. When an execution crowd grew boisterous, it could not easily turn on the criminal or his executioners.

Riot control, in contrast, used respect, but not in such a structured way. The officials had to physically confront the rioters. When the officials' presence and the reading of the riot act could not restore order, the crowds might bombard them with rocks and other objects and sometimes assault them. In riot control, the expectation of respect was softened by personal involvement—the same kind of involvement that, later, ward politicians revealed.[24]

• In truth, although political machines did not develop until after 1850, earlier elite politicians often performed many of the functions assumed by lower class ward heelers. Even the most prominent citizens, even though they demanded respect, did not stand apart from the rest of society. Their control of city affair brought them into continuous contact with all classes. Two case histories—one drawn from the 1820s, the other from the 1840s—illustrate just how extensive this contact was.

Stephen Allen, who served as mayor from March 1821 to January 1824, stands at the crossroads in the history of the New York City mayoralty. His predecessors used the office to reach out to all segments of the community. They presided over the Court of General Sessions, the city's major criminal court. They personally licensed a wide array of occupations serving the public, specifically the owners and drivers of hackney and stage coaches, cartmen, public porters, pawnbrokers, second hand dealers, junk shop keepers, and chimney sweepers; and they shared with the aldermen the responsibility for licensing intelligence (employment) offices and taverns. They directed firemen at fires and led the police at disturbances.[25] In addition, these early mayors, men of great wealth and prestige, customarily played a leading and formative role in the city's cultural and philanthropic life. DeWitt Clinton, mayor for most of the years between 1803 and 1815, took an active part in the Free School Society, the American Academy of Fine Arts, and the New-York Historical Society.[26] Cadwallader Colden, Allen's immediate predecessor, was active in the Society for the Reformation of Juvenile Delinquents, the Society for the Prevention of Pauperism, and the Bloomingdale Asylum for the Insane.[27]

Starting with Allen, New York's mayors abdicated some of their responsibilities. They no longer presided over the Court of General Sessions, they did not appear at fires and riots as regularly, and they did not particularly devote themselves to the city's private institutions.[28] Yet the mayors did not by any means isolate themselves from city life. We have noted their presence at large scale disturbances. In addition, they controlled significant patronage positions which they still meted out personally. It is in this respect that Mayor Allen's papers are particularly instructive.

The ordinances specifying the mayor's power to grant licenses followed a common form. That for hackney coachmen is typical:

> The mayor of the City for the time being shall from time to time
> issue licenses under his hand and seal, to so many and such persons

as he shall think proper to keep Hackney Coaches and Carriages for
hire in the said City, and to revoke all or any of the said licenses.

The Mayor of the said City may administer to any person applying
for a license, an oath or affirmation, and shall examine such orally,
touching said application and qualifications to receive said license.[29]

There were hundreds of applications each year, consuming a great deal
of the mayor's time and distracting him from his other business. For
example, on one occasion, Allen felt himself obliged to apologize for
being so involved with a particular license case that he ignored a
communication that the mayor of Philadelphia had sent him by special
messenger:

> I was in the performance of the most perplexing and irritating
> business of my offfice, to wit, the issue of the License for retailing
> spiritous Liquers [sic] in this City. I had at that moment several
> persons—waiting for an answer to their application, and had just
> refused one who had irritated me by his solicitude while a complaint
> was before—me for his irregular conduct.[30]

Later mayors, beginning with Fernando Wood in the 1850s,
flagrantly abused their control of patronage in order to build up personal
followings, but Allen, aside from any political considerations which may
have motivated him, clearly had the public good in mind. At one point,
he urged the state legislature to restrict the number of grog shops, public
gardens, shows, plays, and hackney coachmen by raising the license fee.
When the city's delegation refused to push the issue, Allen responded
testily,

> I have had some experience in these matters, . . .and I have
> therefore come to the conclusion, that in a City with a population so
> numerous, and of such mixed character, . . .evils will exist to a
> greater or Less extent according to circumstances, but at the same
> time, that they may be lessened by compelling the persons who
> follow the business which is the cause of producing them, to take
> out a License, the amount to be paid for which, to be regulated
> according to the circumstances of the case.

Allen drew upon the city's past experience:

> In proof of the good effects of this system I beg leave to refer you
> to some instances of recent date—It is but a few years—ago that we
> had in this City a great nuisance resulting from the Lottery
> offices/amounting to some scores/that was working the ruin of
> families, and affecting the morils of Society, but since the act
> compelling them to take out a License annually, the evil has ceased,

and at this time there is but six or seven offices in the City, and no complaints are heard of any irregular or improper conduct in any of them.

If there existed no authority to License pawn brokers, of the price of a License was $10 instead of $50, the result would be that the City would be filled with them, and inducements would not be wanted for pilfering and numerous other evils, but there are at present only six of them under License, and they are generally respectable. The results are the same from the authority granted to License—intelligence offices [employment agencies specializing in domestic help], and would be equelling benificeal, were we permitted to fix a proper amount on the License to the grog shops, public gardens, Shows, Plays, and Hackney Coachmen.[31]

In most cases, the mayor could revoke as well as grant licenses, and the hearings he conducted in his office offer us an insight into the kind of behavior that most violated community norms—for the revocation of a license meant denying a man his livelihood. A plurality of cases reaching the mayor involved cartmen: the charges included driving recklessly, too fast, and without a license; while other cartmen allegedly engaged in immoral conduct, falsely claimed a residence in the city, or failed to live up to carting agreements. The mayor, however, also adjudicated a number of cases involving complainants who refused to tolerate a cartman's abusive language; and taken together, these last cases show the premium the community placed upon respectful behavior. They also show that the cartmen did not hesitate to assert their independence. (See the Appendix for a summary of all cases heard by the mayor.)

In the case of cartman John Latour and complainant John Morey, Latour asked Morey whether he wanted wood. Morey did not answer, and "Latour called him a damn impudent puppy or rascally puppy." Morey took down the number on Latour's cart and left, but returned, upset by the cartman's arrogance, to ask the cartman why he used such language. Latour denied having abused Morey earlier, "but said if he had done it he would do it again." Mayor Allen did not revoke Latour's license but warned him that he would indeed do so if Latour had another complaint lodged against him.[32]

A similar case involved Peter Bridsall and cartman Peter Nodine. Bridsall complained to Nodine that the latter had backed his cart against the curb stone in front of the Bridsall house. Nodine's reply was insolent. He "used much abusive language . . . and said that he would back and load there when he pleased and would do it to day [sic] again if he pleased, and called him [Bridsall] abusive names." In this instance, again, Mayor Allen reprimanded the offending cartman.[33]

One cartman whose license was revoked had the misfortune of unknowingly insulting an alderman. Alderman Henry Mead ordered cartman Chris Teel to slow down; when Teel refused, the alderman went after Teel to make a note of the license number on the cart. At this point, Teel grew abusive, and when Mead asked Teel whether he knew to whom he was speaking, Teel answered "yes I know you are a damnd raskel and he used other abusive and unbecoming expressions."[34]

Aside from the cartmen, the cases heard by the mayor most often involved chimney sweeps and their servants. Only in this occupation did the mayor have the right to interfere between masters and servants. (Perhaps because the plight of chimney sweeps was a major humanitarian concern in Great Britain,[35] humanitarians in the United States may, for this reason, have taken up the cause of the sweeps more than historians now generally recognize.)[36] In New York, servants of chimney sweeps had to be at least eleven years old and their masters had to "comfortably clad" them and provide them with sufficient "good and wholesome food." In addition, the servants could work only between the hours of 6:00 a.m. and 4:00 p.m. in winter and 5:00 a.m. and 6:00 p.m. during the rest of the year. If a master sweep violated the law, the mayor could revoke his license.[37]

In several extreme instances, Mayor Allen did indeed protect the servants involved. In one such case, one sweepmaster accused another sweepmaster of employing a boy under eleven years of age. According to the complainant, the offending master forced his servant to go up the chimney, but the boy "cried and refused going up, but Smith [his master] forced him, and when the Lady of the house desired him to desist he replied that he like to see Ladys frightened." The boy was brought forward for the mayor to see and Allen noted for the record that the sweepboy was apparently two to three years under age. As a result of the flagrant violation of the law, the mayor revoked the sweepmaster's license.[38]

In an even more appalling case, the complainant testified that a sweepmaster, Henry Williams, beat his boy "so that the blood ran from him, he is badly cloathed, has only a torn trowses [sic] through the winter c." Williams denied brutalizing the boy, but he justified inflicting corporal punishment (a leather strap had already been produced in evidence): "the boy was sick on his hands," he had run away frequently, "and is a bad boy." Although the boy (perhaps out of fear) came to his master's defense, testifying "that he is well and has no complaint to make against his master—," the mayor agreed with the complainant. Allen warned Williams "to use the boy better"; he told "the boy to behave himself," but he also advised him that "if he was cruelly used to apply to me for redress." The mayor obviously intended that Williams take his warning seriously, for four months later, when another complainant charged this sweepmaster with beating his boy and confining him without food or drink, the mayor revoked the sweepmaster's license and ordered the boy to appear before the Alms House commissioners.[39]

Allen could support the master as well as the servant. So it was in a case where the sweepboy himself lodged the complaint. Charles Orr charged that he "was ill used, . . . and kept improperly in cloathing etc.," by his master and brother, John Orr. Allen, however, concluded that the boy had "done many improper acts, and in several instances deserved correction." He told the boy "to behave better" and the master "to correct him with judgment or to bring him before me when [he] committed another fault."[40]

Although to a steadily lessening extent, the mayors of New York practiced personal government into the 1840's. In 1845, for example,[41] the city established a police force and created 800 new positions; and Mayor William F. Havemeyer personally examined hundreds of applicants. The mayor, a Democrat, engaged in internecine warfare with the Democratic Common Council in order to effect a nonpartisan police. The councilmen wanted to use the appointments to reward loyal party activists and to entrench themselves in office; some of the men they wanted to appoint belonged to strong arm political gangs. The mayor lost the fight, but he did not give up without a struggle. He frequently called the less than respectable policemen before him to give them advice, and on occasion, he dismissed policemen for failing to report for duty or for accepting bribes.[42]

After 1850, the concept of a personal mayoralty was not forgotten. In the mid-1850's, Mayor Fernando Wood established a citizens' complaint book for the listing of complaints which he would personally investigate. But Wood, by this time, was resurrecting a custom out of the remembered past rather than continuing a living tradition.[43] To follow the ongoing history of personal government, we must shift our attention to the lesser officials active in the wards, men such as aldermen and police justices.

Robert Taylor, a police (or special) justice dealt with many of the same kinds of cases Mayor Allen had dealt with a quarter century before, and his work also brought him into regular contact with petty thieves, gamblers, drunks, prostitutes, and unlicensed liquor dealers.

Taylor, unlike his Tammany Hall successors,[44] did not go easy on the accused. He curried no favors. Taylor was a middle class man who applied traditional standards, administering justice without regard to politics. In 1845, Taylor, a Whig, was the first man Democratic Mayor Havemeyer asked to serve as chief of police. The following year, he was offered the mayoral nomination by "reformers," nativists, and Whigs.

Accepting the Whig nomination, Taylor, nonetheless, remained aloof from the campaign, altering his normal daily routine not at all. (Taylor lost the election, but ran ahead of his ticket.)[45]

Taylor is of interest because his diary describes a work day which often differed markedly from that of a modern justice. Taylor actively pursued wrongdoers, functioning as a detective and a prosecutor as well as a judge.[46] He interrogated convicts in prison—at their request—and he routinely visited houses of prostitution. Both these activities increased his familiarity with the nether world.

Three times in the eighteen months he kept a diary, Taylor visited prisoners. On two of these occasions, he went as far afield as Sing Sing, the state institution at Ossining, New York, some thirty miles north of the city. Such a trip meant leaving at 7 or 8 o'clock in the morning and returning at 5 or 6 o'clock at night. Judging by his entries, none of the three interrogations—neither the two at Sing Sing nor the one in New York—produced startling admissions. In the case most fully described, the convict in the city prison asked to see Taylor "to make some disclosures," but none that he made interested the justice. Taylor told the prisoner that he had not consented to an interview out of compassion, and he reminded the prisoner that he "had little sympathy for rogues and would do as much to punish them as any one."[47]

Taylor did not always take such a hard line: he avidly sought to punish criminals, but he tolerated prostitutes. He recorded, clinically, with detachment, routine brothel visits, identifying the brothels by their addresses and by the madams who kept them.[48] In a single night, Taylor would visit—invariably with a companion—series of such houses in search of evidence. The following diary entry is typical:

> About 7 o'clock in the evening I met E. J. Cory, clerk of Police at Niblo's [a restaurant and public garden which contained a theater], according to appointment and with him went to Mrs. Dubos' 73 Wooster St.—a bawdy house—to endeavor to obtain information in relation to a divorce case, . . . from there we went to Mrs. Brewsters, 44 Broome St., and Mrs. Pratts 472 Broome—houses of the same character, and went there to obtain information in relation to an abortion said to have been caused at Mrs. Brewsters, and the mother of the child died in consequences in Sing Sing—Cory and I were together all the time, and staid [sic] but a short time in each place.[49]

Taylor, in the period covered by his diary, apparently never acted to close down the brothels. He either accepted them as an inevitable part of city life, or he consciously sought to use leniency as a carrot to gain the cooperation of the prostitutes and madams. In either case, Taylor's efforts could be successful. Once, for example, he tried to locate a shawl: a man had taken it from his wife and given it to a prostitute. (Taylor probably wanted the shawl as evidence for a divorce.) The madam Taylor approached was antagonistic. According to Taylor, she claimed "that She knew nothing about the Shawl and would not endeavor to get it"; but she did offer "that one of Mrs. Millers women would endeavor to get some information about it." The next day, Taylor learned, the shawl had been pawned.[50]

The justice, it appears, interpreted his responsibilities broadly. On one occasion, for example, the owner of a building in Greene Street asked Taylor to find out whether one of his tenants used her premises as a brothel. Taylor, honoring the request, went to the house in the company of another man; but Taylor entered the house alone, his companion waiting at the door. Taylor found no "proof" that the woman operated the house as a brothel, but he "suspected from what I saw and heard that improper persons visited there." He immediately reported his findings to the owner who awaited the justice at his home.[51]

Several months later, police clerk D. M. Frye asked Taylor to find his son Frederick who had mysteriously disappeared. Frederick had not been heard from since he had gone to the commencement ceremonies of Columbia College the previous day. So Taylor, the boy's father, E. T. Cory (another police clerk), a man by the name of Lyons, "and others" visited three brothels "to make enquiry and to search" for the missing youth. They found no clue as to his whereabouts, but Taylor seemed more relieved than distressed at this development. He had not expected to find Frederick in such a compromising situation, but he had sought him out in the brothels only because "we had certain statements which induced us to go to the places mentioned." Sure enough, the youth's father had no cause for alarm, for Frederick returned the next day from an excursion.[52]

Robert Taylor's behavior was not idiosyncratic. He made no secret of his brothel visits. To protect his reputation, he never went alone. On one occasion, he even served as tour guide to a fellow justice who had never visited "Bawdy Houses" officially. The two justices, accompanied by a police clerk, "went, officially, to Mrs. Stephens, Marion St., Mrs. Bakers Green Street, Mrs. Pratts, Broome St., and the house next door, Mrs. Lyons, and the house formerly kept by Julia Brown in Leonard St., Mrs. Millers, and Mrs. Berry's and Mrs. Williams in Duane St. . . . I omitted to mention that we also went to Mrs. Perry's in Grand St."[53] In one night, three men visited nine brothels. Ketchams, the justice new to this activity, accompanied Taylor the following month, when, together, they visited eight different houses trying to locate a particular prostitute.[54] Taylor also briefly alluded to a second justice making these brothel forays. On the night in question, he coincidentally met Justice William J. Roome at the house kept by Mrs. Stevens. Roome, like Taylor, was there with a police officer "on business."[55]

V

The activities of both Stephen Allen and Robert Taylor exemplify elite political behavior in a deferential and paternalistic society, but a society of this kind produced a leadership class that participated in private benevolence as well as in government. In the early nineteenth century, the qualities of humanitarianism and political leadership often combined in the same men. By the 1830s, however, gentlemen politicians were becoming increasingly rare, and the traditional politicians of the period, such as Judge Taylor, confined themselves to government. Other men administered the charitable institutions.[56]

NOTES

[1]Dumas Malone, *Jefferson and His Time*, vol. 4, *Jefferson the President: First Term, 1801-1805* (New York, 1970), pp. 29-31; Robert V. Remini, *The Election of Andrew Jackson*, Critical Periods of History (Philadelphia, 1963), p. 202, citing Margaret B. Smith, *The First Forty Years of Washington Society*, p. 283.

[2]Philip Hone, *The Diary of Philip Hone, 1828-1851*, ed. Allan Nevins, new and enl. ed. (New York, 1936), pp. 235-36 (January 3, 1837).

[3]Hone, *Diary*, p. 236 (January 3, 1837).

[4]George Templeton Strong, *The Diary of George Templeton Strong*, ed. Allen Nevins and Milton Halsey Thomas, vol. 1: *Young Man in New York, 1835-1849* (New York, 1952), pp. 63-64 (May 8, 1837).

[5]Lithograph, "The Would-Be Mayor Preparing to Quell a Riot" (New York, 1837), Print Division, New-York Historical Society. (Above, p. 148.)

[6]*New York Daily Express*, March 20, 1837; *Morning Courier and New York Enquirer*, March 18, 1837.

[7]*The Evening Post* (New York), March 28, 1937; see also April 11, 1837. On the illegalization of lotteries, see A. Franklin Ross, "History of Lotteries in New York" (Ph.D. Dissertation, New York University), reprinted in *The Magazine of History* (1907), p. 38. *New York Times*, April 13, 1837. For other comments of the Democratic press, see the *Plaindealer* (New York), April 8, 1837; *Sun* (New York), April 11, 1837.

[8]*The Evening Post*, April 12-13, 1837; *Sun*, April 11, 1837.

[9]New York (State), *Laws* (1835), c. 258.

[10]New York (State), Senate, *Report of the Select Committee on a Resolution Directing an Inquiry into the Propriety of Abolishing Public Executions*, Doc. 79, 58th sess., 1835.

[11]New Yorkers, in theory, did not recognize a separation of powers between the three branches of government as it applied to the city; and the physical location of the city's offices reflected this: government emanated from City Hall. After the bureaucracy outgrew the building, an attempt was made to continue the tradition. When a police court was established in the old Almshouse to the rear of City Hall, the old building was renamed "New City Hall." This suggests the belief that authority should be indivisible and maximized. *New-York As It Is, In 1834; and Citizens' Advertising Directory* (New York, 1834), p. 33.

[12]For a biographical sketch of Stanford, Raymond A. Mohl, *Poverty in New York; 1783-1825*, The Urban Life in America Series (New York, 1971), pp. 193-95, and passim.

[13]For accounts of the execution, see *New-York Commercial Advertiser*, November 19, 1825; *New-York Statesman*, November 21, 1825.

[14]Charles Chauncy, *The Horrid Nature, and Enormous Guilt of Murder. A Sermon Preached at the Thursday-Lecture in Boston, November 19th, 1754* (Boston, 1754), pp. 22-23; Moses Baldwin, *The Ungodly Condemned in Judgement. A Sermon Preached at Springfield, December 13th, 1770. On occasion of the Execution of William Shaw, for Murder* (New London [Conn.],1771), pp. 13-14; Aaron Bancroft, *The Importance of a Religious Education Illustrated and Enforced. A Sermon: Delivered at Worcester, October 31, 1793, Occasioned by the Execution of Samuel Frost, on That Day* (Worcester, Mass., 1793), pp. 20-22; Nathan Strong, *A Sermon Preached in Hartford, June 10th, 1797, at the Execution of Richard Doane* (Hartford, 1797), pp. 3-4, 11-12; Nathaniel Fisher, *A Sermon: Delivered at Salem, January 14, 1796, Occasioned by the Execution of Henry Blackbyrn, on That Day, for the Murder of George Williamson* (Boston, 1796), pp. 15-18; Elijah Waterman, *A Sermon, Preached at Windham, November 29th, 1803, Being the Day of the Execution of Caleb Adams, for the Murder of Oliver Woodworth. Also a Sketch of the Circumstances of the Birth, Education, and Manner of Caleb's Life; with Practical Reflections, Delivered at the Place of Execution,* by Moses C. Welch, *With an Appendix, Giving an Account of the Behavior of the Criminal at His Trial, during Confinement, and on the Day of Execution* (Windham, [Conn.], 1803), pp. 16-18, 23-25.

[15]Cited in *Commercial Advertiser,* January 2, 1833.

[16]*Commercial Advertiser,* December 7, 1833. For Canton's population, 1,500 at this time, see Warren Jenkins, *The Ohio Gazetteer and Traveller's Guide,* rev. ed. (Columbus, O., 1841), p. 99.

[17]*Commercial Advertiser,* April 2, 1824; *Evening Post,* April 2, 1824.

[18]*Commercial Advertiser,* May 7, 1829; January 10, 1834; *Courier and Enquirer,* May 8, 1829; *Evening Post,* May 7, 8, 1829.

[19]Negley K. Teeters and Jack H. Hedblom, *". . . Hang by the Neck . . .": The Legal Use of Scaffold, and Noose, Gibbbet, Stake, and Firing Squad from Colonial Times to the Present* (Springfield, Ill., 1967), pp. 152-53.

[20]Massachusetts, House of Representatives, *Report on the Abolition of Capital Punishment,* Doc. 4, 1837, p. 84.

[21]Ibid. Legislative reports from states other than Massachusetts could not be located.

[22]The state continued to support such practices as Bible reading in the schools.

[23]Edwin Scott Gaustud, *A Religious History of America* (New York, 1966), pp. 145, 148-53.

[24]Sam Bass Warner, Jr., *The Private City: Philadelphia in Three Periods of Its Growth* (Philadelphia, 1968), pp. 95-96, for Philadelphia's experience: in the mid 1850s, Philadelphia Mayor Richard Vaux, a gentleman democrat allied to the Irish bosses, prowled about his city's streets checking on its policemen.

[25]See Sidney I. Pomerantz, *New York: An American City, 1783-1803; A Study of Urban Life,* Studies in History, Economics, and Public Law, no. 442 (New York, 1938), pp. 36-37, 40, 241, and passim on the late eighteenth century mayor. For the early

nineteenth century, see Irene S. Fishbane, "The History of the Mayoralty of New York City, 1800 to 1834" (Master's thesis, New York University, 1949), pp. 11-23, and passim.

[26]Fishbane, "Mayoralty," p. 18.

[27]Ibid., p. 30.

[28]Daly, *Judicial Tribunals*, p. 65; *Commercial Advertiser*, May 28, 1828; October 1, 1834. *New-York As It Is, In 1834*, lists the officers of New York's philanthropic and cultural institutions, and the mayor's name (neither Lee [mayor until May] nor Lawrence) does not appear (pp. 41-86).

[29]New York (City), *By-Laws and Ordinances of the Mayor, Aldermen and Commonalty of the City of New York. Revised A.D. 1838-1839*, c. 53, title I. secs. 1 and 3. For other by-laws relating to licenses, see ibid., title II, sec. 1; c. 54, title I, secs. 1 and 10; c. 55, title I, secs . 1 and 4; c. 56, title I, sec. 1; c. 57, title I, sec. 1; title II, sec. 1; title III, sec. 1; c. 58, secs. 1-3; c. 59, sec. 1; c. 60, title I; sec. 4.

[30]Stephen Allen to Robert Wharton, June 1823, Letter book, Stephen Allen Papers, Manuscript Division, New-York Historical Society.

[31]Stephen Allen to Samuel S. Gardiner, March 20, 1823, Letter book, Allen Papers.

[32]John Morey v. John Latour, November 13-14, 1821, Court Minutes, 1821-22, Allen Papers.

[33]Peter Bridsall v. Peter Nodine, August 30, 1823, Court Minutes, 1822-23, Allen Papers.

[34]Henry Meade Mead v. Chris Teel, November 18, 1823, Court Minutes, 1822-23, Allen Papers.

[35]George L. Phillips, *England's Climbing-Boys: A History of the Long Struggle to Abolish Child Labor in Chimney-Sweeping*, The Kress Library of Business and Economics, publ. no. 5 (Soldiers Field, Boston, 1949), passim.

[36]Lewis George Phillips, *American Chimney Sweeps: An Historical Account of a Once Important Trade* (Trenton, N. J., 1957), passim.

[37]New York (City), *By-Laws, Revised A.D. 1838-1839*, c. 58.

[38]Andrew Marshal v. Henry Smith, November 20, 1821, Court Minutes, 1821-22, Allen Papers.

[39]James Simmons v. Henry Williams, March 30, 1821; complainant unnamed v. Henry Williams, August 4, 1821, Court Minutes, 1821-22, Allen Papers.

[40]John Orr v. John Charles Orr, May 29, 1821, Court Minutes, 1821-22, Allen Papers.

[41]For the mayor's continued involvement in license cases, see the *Commercial Advertiser*, January 10, 1839; May 234, August 2, 14, 1841. For a list of the marriage ceremonies performed by the city's mayors as a matter of course until August 1842, see Ray C. Sawyer, compiler and editor, "Marriages Performed by the Various Mayors and

Aldermen of the City of New York, As Well As Justices of the Peace, etc.: 1830-1854" Typescript, 1935, from the Original Books in the Office of the County Clerk for New York County, Hall of Records, New York City (New-York Historical Society).

[42]Howard B. Furer, *William Frederick Havemeyer: A Political Biography* (New York, [1965]), pp. 31-32, 66 .

[43]Samuel Augustus Pleasants, *Fernando Wood of New York*, Studies in History, Economics and Public Law, no. 536 (New York, 1948), p. 53. But note the following which indicates at least a continued partial involvement of the mayor:"Mary Elvend [?] of No. [illegible] called on me and complained that she paid Thomas Spink No. 114 Nassau Street Intelligence Office Fifty Cents on the 9th inst[ant] to get her a situation, & he agreed that in case he failed. . . to return her money, he now refuses to give her her money. I took her affidavit and gave it to Mr. Taylor the 1st Marshall, who notified Spink to appear before the Mayor tomorrow at 12 o"clock to answer the complaint." (William H. Bell MS Diary, January 21, 1851 [Bell was an inspector of second hand dealers and junk shops], Manuscript Division, New-York Historical Society.)

[44]Seymour J. Mandelbaum, *Boss Tweed's New York*, New Dimensions in History: Historical Cities (New York, 1965), pp. 107-108.

[45]Robert Taylor, MS. Diary, pp. 4-5, February 7, 10, 12, 16-18, March 14, 16, 18, April 2-4, 8, 14, 1846, Manuscripts and Archives Division, New York Public Library.

[46]For judicial duties prior to the development of the modern police department, see Oliver L. Barbow, *Magistrate's Criminal Law: A Practical Treatise on the Jurisdiction, Duty, and Authority of Justices of the Peace in the State of New York in Criminal Cases* (Albany, 1841), p. 479; Rayond Moley, *Tribunes of the People; the Past and Future of the New York Magistrates' Courts* (New Haven, Conn., 1932), p. 2.

[47]Ibid., March 17, April 7, 9, June 7, 1846. The June entry describes the visit to the city prison.

[48]Ibid., February 14, April 4, 5, 17, July 30, August 1, 16, 22, 29, October 16, November 17, 20, 21, December 5, 17, 1846; Januaray 6, 1847.

[49]Ibid., February 14, 1846. Most of Taylor's days as a police justice were spent "at the office all day."

[50]Ibid., November 21-23, 1846.

[51]Ibid., April 17, 1846.

[52]Ibid., July 30-31, 1846.

[53]Ibid., October 16, 1846.

[54]Ibid., November 20, 1846.

[55]Ibid., January 6, 1847.

[56]This chapter's theme is broadly compatible with Sam Bass Warner's thesis. In *The Private City*, Warner describes the progressive disappearance of a traditional elite in mid nineteenth century Philadelphia (chap. 5, "The Specialization of Leadership," pp. 79-98).

CHAPTER SEVEN

SOCIAL BENEVOLENCE

I

After 1805, philanthropic New Yorkers repeatedly resorted to ad hoc committees to relieve the needy. Within each ward, the city's well-to-do helped the poor living by their side. In more prosperous times, the municipal government took the lead in the field of poor relief,[1] with private benevolent societies concentrating on specifiic groups.[2] (The latter included such descriptively titled organizations as the "Association for the Relief of Respectable Aged Indigent Females" and "The Society for the Relief of Poor Widows with Small Children.") This arrangement, however, did not work in periods of economic hardship.

A first series of ad hoc ward committees spanned the years from 1805 to 1817, during which time New Yorkers intermittently collected donations, sought out the poor, and distributed alms.[3] After a ten year hiatus, a second series of committees operated from 1829 to 1838.[4] During the winters of 1829, 1831, and 1835, and during the late fall and winter of 1837-38, New Yorkers organized for the emergency relief of the poor. At these times and during the cholera epidemic in the summer of 1832, the press printed announcements of public meetings and often detailed reports of the subdivision of the wards into districts and the organization of small district committees to collect donations. In about half the wards, district collection committees had a dual function and also investigated the needs of the poor. In the remaining wards, the poor had personally to apply for relief to executive committees meeting regularly at specified locations. At its best, the ad hoc committees work was impressive—in many cases, 10 percent or more of a ward's residents received some help.[5]

Scattered figures, not directly comparable, nonetheless, are cumulatively impressive. In the eighth ward in 1829, approximately 3,500 (17 percent) of the ward's total population of 21,000 received aid. In 1831, the same ward provided about 1,600 persons per day with food from a soup kitchen. Elsewhere that year, 2,160 (9 percent) were aided in the ninth ward (total population 23,000): and 1,000 (8 percent) were aided in the fourth ward (total population 13,000). In 1838, allegedly 6,000 persons (32 percent) of the fifth ward's total population of 19,000 received relief—almsgiving stopped in mid February after the money ran out. In the seventh ward, 2,500 persons (11 percent) of a total population of 23,000 received relief. Typically, the second ward, in 1831, spent $1,033.93 to aid 359 persons; the sixth ward during the cholera epidemic (1832), $4,205 to aid 1,552 persons, and the seventh ward, in 1838, $3,200 to aid 2,500 individuals. In the three instances, $2.88, $2.71, and $1.28 were the per capita expenditures during crises of more than a month's duration.[6]

A laborer could at most times earn $2.88 in less than a week, but if a man could not find work, then this small sum—given in food, fuel, and clothing—was better than nothing. The monies raised for charity do not seem impressive but went far. Prices fluctuated, but $2.50 could usually buy one-half barrel of flour, enough to provide a family of five with bread for four weeks. It could buy, perhaps, 25 pounds of meat, an amount that could also be stretched far. Soup, doled out from a soup kitchen, probably cost less than 5 cents a bowl to prepare: $2.50 could buy more than fifty portions.[7]

The depression of 1837-43 ended this type of poor relief. The massive continual distress of the period defeated the system of recurrent aid in use since the early part of the century. Between 1839 and 1842, no ad hoc committees arose to aid the poor. Unemployment was too great a problem to be dealt with on a piecemeal basis.

Yet, at the end of the depression, the emerging organizational solution still embodied the concept of neighborhood assistance. In 1843, the newly founded New York Association for Improving the Condition of the Poor (abbreviation: A.I.C.P.), assumed most of the private responsibility for poor relief, but, in many ways, the Association resembled the earlier ad hoc committees. Its differences with them were fewer and less significant. Although the A.I.C.P. began the movement towards "professionalism" in social work,[8] in the 1840s this ground-breaking trend was barely discernible.[9]

The following section compares and contrasts the ad hoc ward committees of 1829 with the A.I.C.P. in 1845 and covers that half of the city where the needs of the poor in 1829 were determined by ad hoc committees going door to door.[10]

II

The most obvious difference between 1829 and 1845 was in the participation of the rich. In 1829, they belonged to door-to-door committees, in 1845, they did not. In the earlier year, as Table 6 indicates, 8.9 percent (22 of 247) of the visitors to the poor were men of great wealth. In 1845, the comparable figure was 1.2 percent (2 of 170). Significantly, the wealthy of 1829 did not come from just one part of the city—in fact, by an unexplained anomaly, none of them lived in the first ward, the section famous for its concentration of the rich.

Relatively subtle differences mark the two groups' occupational profiles. Partly, this reflects the shift in almsgiving from a broad-based community activity to an act of religious benevolence. The 1829 ad hoc committees were open to all, but the 1845 A.I.C.P. was a private association organized for a public purpose. In the latter year, government officials absented themselves and more clergymen participated.

TABLE 6

WEALTHY VISITORS TO THE POOR, 1829 and 1845

Ward	No. of Visitors		No. of Wealthy Visitors		Wealthy Visitors As a % of All Visitors	
	1829	1845	1829	1845	1829	1845
1	15	12	0	0	0	0
5	40	22	7	1	17.5	4.5
6	57	16	3	1	5.3	6.3
7	42	19	6	0	14.3	0
11[a]	37	35	0	0	0	0
13	20	20	2	0	10.0	0
14	36	14	4	0	11.1	0
Total	247	138	22	2	8.9	1.4

SOURCE: *Commercial Advertiser,* February 26, 27, 28, March 3, 10, 1829; Edward L. Pessen, "The Wealthiest New Yorkers of the Jacksonian Era: A New List, *"New York Historical Society Quarterly* 54 (April 1970): 145-72; New-York Association for the Improvement of the Condition of the Poor; *First Annual Report. . .for the Year, 1845, with the Constitution, Visitor's Manual and a List of Members* (New-York, 1845), pp. 5-7.

NOTE: The wealthy are defined as those belonging in the top one percent bracket of tax payers in 1828 and 1845. In the earlier year that meant having property assessed at a minimum of $25,000 and in the later year as having property assessed at a minimum of $45,000.

[a]The area comprising the eleventh ward in 1829 comprised the eleventh and seventeenth wards in 1845.

Yet charity relief was hardly the preserve of professional social workers or full-time religious reformers. The 1845 visitors were drawn from the same wide array of occupations as were the visitors of 1829. Visitors to the poor of both years included merchants, builders,

wholesalers, retailers, and (master?) craftsmen.   Merchants were a
plurality in the first and fifth wards, and retailers and craftsmen
predominated in the "workingmen's" eleventh and thirteenth wards, but
the other wards revealed no such polarity (see table 7). This conclusion
is not affected by the changes between 1829 and 1845 in the charity
workers' occupational profile. Representation from the building industry
increased and attorneys disappeared from the list altogether, but these
were modest changes.[11]

The ideology of relief and the method of distribution remained
the same.   Charity continued to foster "community"; and the
organizational structure of almsgiving remained non-bureaucratic.   In
1829, those serving on purchasing, distributing, interward, and executive
committees served also on the visiting committees.[12]

In 1845, although the A.I.C.P., in theory, was a highly structured
organization, it was not so in fact. Visitor to the poor, advisor, manager,
executive committee member, and executive officer were hierarchically
ordered positions which could be held in combination.   Five-man
advisory committees, in ward-wide districts, appointed the visitors, but 41
of the 80 advisors were themselves visitors.[13]   The advisors, when taken
together made up 80 of the 100 members on the Board of Managers; and
one member of each advisory committee belonged ex officio to the
executive committee.   Thus, 8 members of the 23 member executive
committee were visitors to the poor.[14]

The very top leadership of the association—the president, the
five   vice   presidents,   the   treasurer,   and   the   corresponding
secretary—remained aloof from day to day ward activities, except for
Joseph B. Collins, the recording secretary.   Collins simultaneously held
five different positions within the A.I.C.P. at five different levels of the
association's organizational structure.   In addition to being the recording
secretary, he was a visitor to the poor, a member of an advisory
committee, a member of the Board of Managers, and a member of the
executive committee.[15]   A number of the A.I.C.P.'s members held four
positions. Figures 3 and 4 describe the situation schematically. Figure 3
illustrates the association's formal structure. Figure 4 takes the numerous
involvements of many A.I.C.P. members into account and shows that the
men at the bottom were not far removed functionally—and by
implication personally—from the men at the top.

TABLE 7

OCCUPATIONS OF VISITORS TO THE POOR, 1829 AND 1845

Occupation	1829 Ward						1845 Ward					
	7 Wards[b] Combined		5th		11th[a]		8 Wards[b] Combined		5th		11th & 17th[a]	
	No.	%	No.	%	No.	%	No.	%	No.	%	No.	%
Merchants	29	11.7	9	22.5	0	0	18	13.0	4	18.2	4	11.4
Brokers, bankers, insurance co. executives	7	2.8	2	5.0	0	0	6	4.3	1	4.5	0	0
Wholesalers	10	4.0	2	5.0	1	2.7	7	5.1	2	9.1	2	5.7
Builders, shipbuilders, building and lumber yard owners	7	2.8	1	2.5	0	0	10	7.2	3	13.6	1	2.9
Manufacturers (esp. founders)[c]	9	3.6	0	0	0	0	3	2.2	0	0	2	5.7
Attorneys	10	4.0	4	10.0	0	0	1	0.7	0	0	0	0
Publishers & printers	0	0	0	0	0	0	5	3.6	2	9.1	2	5.7
Teachers & clergymen	2	0.8	0	0	0	0	7	5.1	3	13.6	1	2.9
Physicians	5	2.0	1	2.5	0	0	5	3.6	0	0	0	0
Accountants	0	0	0	0	0	0	1	0.7	0	0	1	2.9
Retail shopkeepers[d]	69	27.9	5	12.5	18	48.6	30	21.7	1	4.5	10	28.6

TABLE 7—Continued

Occupation	1829						1845					
	Ward						Ward					
	7 Wards[b] Combined		5th		11th[a]		8 Wards[b] Combined		5th		11th& 17th[a]	
	No.	%	No.	%	No.	%	No.	%	No.	%	No.	%
Craftsmen[e]	40	16.2	5	12.5	8	21.6	26	18.8	2	9.1	8	22.9
Public officials[f]	17	6.9	4	10.0	1	2.7	1	0.7	1	4.5	0	0
Subtotal	205	82.7	33	82.5	28	75.6	120	86.7	19	86.2	31	88.7
Unknown	42	17.0	7	17.5	9	24.3	18	13.0	3	13.6	4	11.4
TOTAL[g]	247	99.7	40	100.0	37	99.9	138	99.7	22	99.8	35	100.1

SOURCE: *Commercial Advertiser,* February 26, 27, 28, March 3, 10, 1829; for the A.I.C.P. visitors, see the note on sources to table 6; *Longworth's American Almanac, New-York Register, and City Directory,* 1827, 1828, 1829; *Doggett's New-York City Directory, for 1844 and 1845; for 1845 and 1846.*

[a]The area comprising the eleventh ward in 1829 comprised the eleventh and seventeenth wards in 1845.

[b]In 1829: wards 1, 5, 6, 7, 11, 13, 14; in 1845: wards 1, 5, 6, 7, 11, 13, 14, 17.

[c]Includes a distiller, a brewer, a brush manufacturer, etc.

[d]Includes bakers, butchers, clothiers, druggists, grocers, a bookseller, and a fishmonger; sellers of dry goods, and a seller or two each

TABLE 7–Continued

of carpeting, paints, and shoes; a tavern owner, and a livery stable keeper. Of these, grocers were by far the most numerous.

[e]Includes carpenters, chair makers, chandlers, hatters, masons, house and sign painters, boot and shoe makers, metal roofers, sash makers, shipwrights, smiths (of various kinds), tailors, and watchmakers; and also these—a cooper, a gold beater, a hat block maker, a hinge maker, a locksmith, a rope maker, and a wheelwright; and although not craftsmen at all, several cartmen.

[f]Includes one ship captain.

[g]Percentages do not in all cases total to 100 because they have been figured only to the nearest tenth of a percent.

FIGURE 3

THE ORGANIZATIONAL STRUCTURE OF THE A.I.C.P., 1845

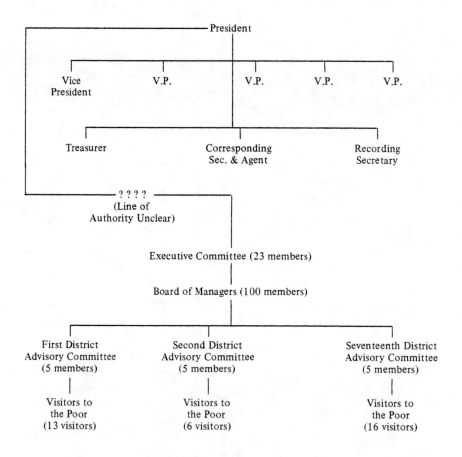

SOURCE: A.I.C.P., *First Annual Report*, pp. 4-12.

NOTE: The A.I.C.P. did not organize the semi-rural twelfth ward, in the northern part of the city. The association's districts were geographically the same as the city's wards.

FIGURE 4

PARTICIPATION OF A.I.C.P. MEMBERS IN OTHER UNITS OF THE ASSOCIATION, 1845[a]

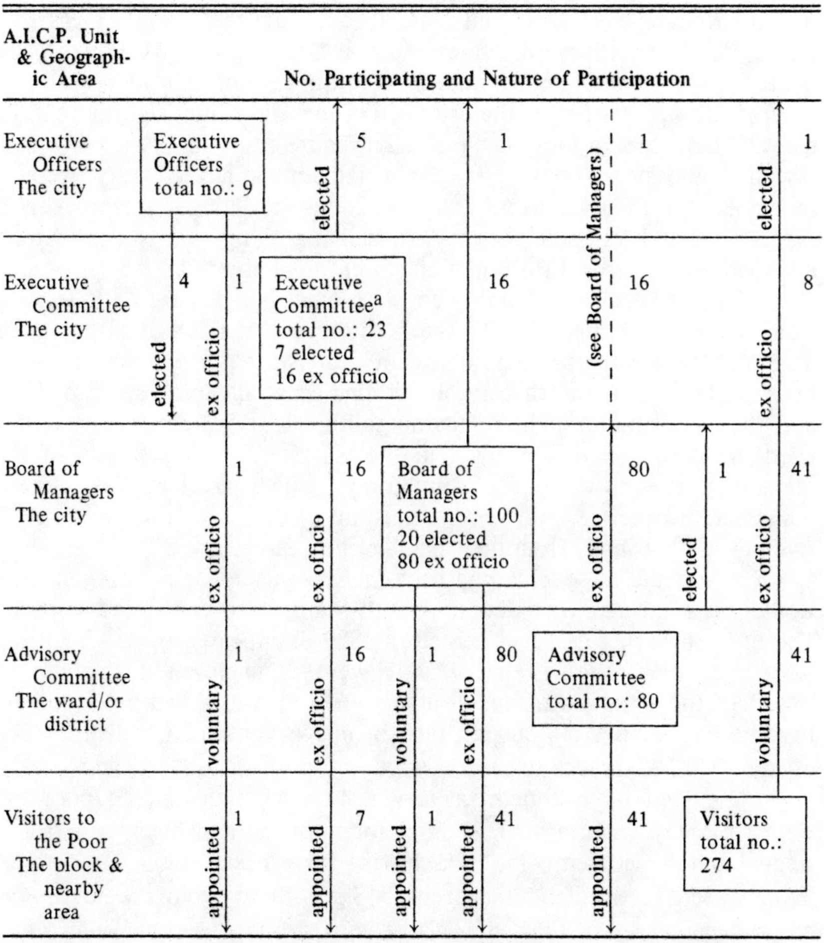

A.I.C.P. Unit & Geographic Area	No. Participating and Nature of Participation							

Executive Officers — The city
Box: Executive Officers total no.: 9
elected 5 | 1 | (see Board of Managers) 1 | elected 1

Executive Committee — The city
elected 4 | ex officio 1 | Box: Executive Committee[a] total no.: 23 / 7 elected / 16 ex officio | 16 | (see Board of Managers) 16 | ex officio 8

Board of Managers — The city
ex officio 1 | ex officio 16 | Box: Board of Managers total no.: 100 / 20 elected / 80 ex officio | ex officio 80 | elected 1 | ex officio 41

Advisory Committee — The ward/or district
voluntary 1 | ex officio 16 | voluntary 1 | ex officio 80 | Box: Advisory Committee total no.: 80 | voluntary 41

Visitors to the Poor — The block & nearby area
appointed 1 | appointed 7 | appointed 1 | appointed 41 | appointed 41 | Box: Visitors total no.: 274

SOURCE: A.I.C.P., First Annual Report, pp. 4-12

[a] e.g. Of the 23 members of the executive committee, 5 were executive officers and elected to their posts, and 16 were on the Board of Managers and served in that capacity by virtue of their executive committee membership.

III

"Community" was fostered not only by the relative absence of bureaucracy but also by residential patterns. Visitors to the poor almost invariably lived in the ward in which they volunteered their services, and many visitors did not live in exclusively middle class areas.[16] In 1829 particularly, some visitors lived close to even the city's worst areas (see figure 5). The sixth ward, for example, included the "Five Points," the United States's most famous nineteenth century slum. A saloon occupied each of the five corners of the intersection that gave the neighborhood its name, but visitors to the poor lived along more respectable thoroughfares just a few blocks away.   In the Chatham Square vicinity were a shoemaker, a thimblemaker, two dry goods dealers, a watchmaker, a silversmith, and an auctioneer. Visitors living along nearby Pearl Street included a hatter, a brush manufacturer, a clothier, and a physician.

In 1845, visitor distribution was somewhat different. It is clear from figure 6 that the A.I.C.P. visitors to the poor tended to cluster more than had the visitors in 1829. Most of the visitors for the seventh ward lived in the ward's north central portion, especially on East Broadway and the parallel thoroughfare to the south, Henry Street. In the fifth ward, most of the visitors lived in the ward's western section and the remaining few just west of Broadway, which marked the eastern boundary. In the eleventh ward, almost all of the visitors lived on or off Avenue C between Houston and Seventh streets.

Nonetheless, overemphasizing middle and upper class segregation would be a mistake. In the thirteenth ward, a reverse trend appears. The little clustering that had existed in 1829 disappeared by 1845. In the fourteenth ward, the visitors of 1845 were as unclustered as those of 1829. In the sixth ward, four visitors still lived within two blocks of the Five Points. Above all, enough men of means continued to live in each of the wards studied to make ward charity drives feasible.[17]

Judged by twentieth century residential patterns, the poor too were relatively unsegregated.[18] Both foreign-born and black Americans, singled out by contemporaries as having an especially low standard of living,[19] settled throughout the city. Since these groups were *in fact* economically poorer than the native-born whites,[20] ethnic integration reflected economic integration to at least some extent. The index numbers in table 8 show the percentage of the city's immigrant populations which would have had to relocate in other wards for each ward to have had the same proportion of the city's total immigrant population.

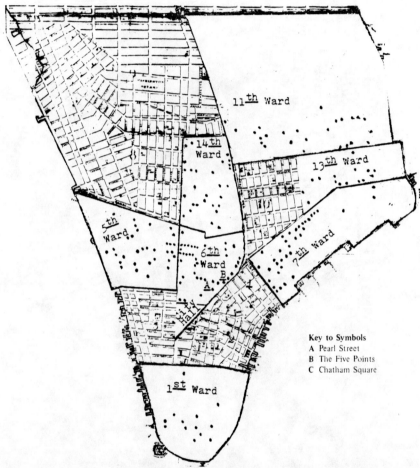

Fig. 5. Residences of visitors to the poor, ad hoc ward committees, 1829. The dots, which represent residences, indicate approximate locations. Shading shows areas of low population density.

Scale in Miles   (Five standard New York City blocks equal ¼ mile)

0   ¼   ½

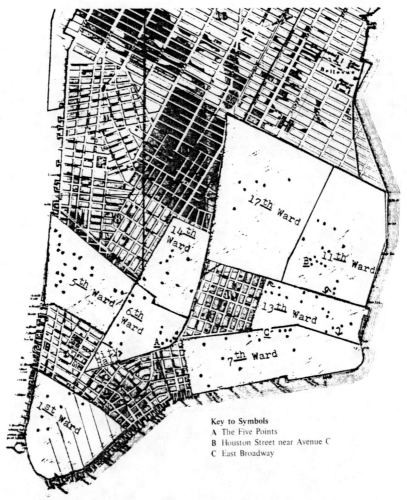

Fig. 6. Residences of visitors to the poor, A.I.C.P., 1845. The dots, which represent residences, indicate approximate locations. Shading shows areas of contiguous settlement (and has the opposite meaning of the shading in fig. 5). The lined area in the first ward was devoted mostly to business.

Scale in Miles ————————   (Five standard New York City blocks equal ¼ mile)
           0   ¼   ½

TABLE 8

INDEXES OF SEGREGATION FOR THE NATIVE AND FOREIGN-BORN POPULATIONS OF NEW YORK AND BOSTON, 1825-1865

| Year | Aliens | New York Immigrants | | | Boston |
		Total	Germans	Irish	
1825	23.9				
1830					28.6
1835	15.3				
1845	17.3	14.5	26.2		21.0
1850					24.4/18.8
1855	12.6	13.3	28.9	17.6	22.6
1865					14.8

SOURCE: Indexes for New York (State), Secretary of State, *Census of the State of New York for 1835; for 1845; for 1855;* James Hardie, The Description of the City of New York (New York, 1827), p. 154. For the Boston indexes, see Leo F. Schnore and Peter R. Knights, "Residence and Social Structure: Boston in the Ante-Bellum Period," in Stephan Thernstrom and Richard Sennett, eds., *Nineteenth Century Cities: Essays in the New Urban History,* Yale Studies of the City, No. 1 (New Haven, Connecticut, 1969), p. 254, table 6.

The most significant finding is that immigrant segregation lessened as the immigrant population increased. The 1845-55 decade witnessed the Irish potato famine, crop failures in Germany, and the collapse of the 1848 revolutions. Immigration from Europe to the United States began its century long surge upward. But the index of segregation in 1855 was almost half the index of thirty years earlier. At no time prior to the Civil War did a large ghetto isolate the foreign born from native Americans.

The raw data provides additional information. In 1825, relatively few immigrants settled in the northeast section of the city and in the area furthest south (the tenth, eleventh, thirteenth, and first wards in figure 5). In these areas, aliens made up only about 10 percent of the total population. They were most concentrated in the heart of the city, in the sixth ward. This ward contained a long established Irish neighborhood and about 50 to 60 percent of the inhabitants were foreign-born.[21] The immigrant population of the rest of the city fell in between these two extremes. Twenty years later, in 1845, a relatively large part of the population of each ward in the city consisted of immigrants, but still no ward excluded the native-born. The immigrant population was lowest in

TABLE 9

FOREIGN-BORN POPULATION OF NEW YORK, 1825 AND 1845

Ward	1825 Total Population	1825 (Male) Aliens Number	1825 Aliens Percent	1845 Total Population	1845 Aliens Number	1845 Aliens Percent	1845 Immigrants Number	1845 Immigrants Percent
1	9,929	428	4.3	12,230	2,209	18.1	5,954	48.7
2	9,315	763	8.2	6,962	1,343	19.3	2,746	39.4
3	10,801	1,001	9.3	11,900	2,524	21.2	4,342	36.5
4	12,240	1,688	13.8	21,000	4,955	23.6	10,778	51.3
5	15,093	1,748	11.6	20,362	3,041	14.9	7,820	35.9
6a	20,061	5,082	25.3	19,343	5,091	26.3	9,657	49.9
7	14,192	1,754	12.4	25,556	3,264	12.8	8,027	31.4
8b	24,285	2,049	8.4	30,900	2,452	7.9	8,269	26.8
9c	10,956	1,726	15.8	30,907	4,236	13.7	6,878	22.3
10d	23,332	1,183	5.1	20,993	2,531	12.1	5,812	27.8
11f	7,344	262	3.6	27,259	4,782	17.5	9,606	35.2
12e	7,938	1,142	14.4	13,378	2,579	19.3	4,989	37.3
13d	.	.	.	22,411	2,682	12.0	6,302	28.1
14ab	.	.	.	21,103	2,751	13.0	8,040	38.1
15c	.	.	.	19,422	1,627	8.4	5,194	26.7
16e	.	.	.	40,350	10,561	26.2	15,851	39.2
17f	.	.	.	27,147	4,318	15.9	8,697	32.0
Total	165,486	18,826	11.4	371,223	60,946	16.4	128,462	34.6

TABLE 9–Continued

SOURCE: James Hardie, *The Description of the City of New York* (New York, 1827), p. 154; New York (State), Secretary of State, *Census of the State of New York for 1845.*

[a]In 1825, includes part of the later fourteenth ward.

[b]In 1825, includes part of the later fourteenth ward.

[c]The area comprising the tenth ward in 1825 comprised the ninth and fifteenth wards in 1845.

[d]The area comprising the tenth ward in 1825 comprised the tenth and thirteenth wards in 1845.

[e]The area comprising the twelfth ward in 1825 comprised the twelfth and sixteenth wards in 1845. The sixteenth was the ward further south.

[f]The area comprising the eleventh ward in 1825 comprised the eleventh and seventeenth wards in 1845.

the northwest with the ninth ward having a population 22.3 percent foreign-born; and it was greatest in the fourth ward where the percentage of foreign-born was 51.3.

In the case of the blacks, segregation began in the ante-bellum period, but it is inappropriate to talk of a black ghetto. In 1845, the index of segregation was 29.5—29.5 percent of the city's Negroes would have had to relocate in different wards for each of the wards to house the same proportion of the black population. In the ensuing ten years, the index rose to 42.5, lower than is usual in most cities in the twentieth century. In 1910, an average for ten northern cities was 54.1, and in 1920, after large scale migration began from the South, the index for these cities rose to 60.2.[22] While no two cities or the same city at different

TABLE 10

INDEXES OF SEGREGATION FOR NEGROES IN NEW YORK, BOSTON AND PHILADELPHIA, 1830-1860

Year	New York	Boston	Philadelphia
1830	18.0	44.1	
1835	23.0		
1840		52.4	
1845	29.5		
1850		59.1	
1855	42.5		
1860		62.3	47.3

SOURCE: New York (State), Secretary of State, *Census of the State of New York for 1835; for 1845; for 1855;*Schnore and Knights, "Residence and Social Structure," p. 252, table 4. Sam Bass Warner, *The Private City; Philadelphia in Three Periods of Its Growth* (Philadelphia, 1968).

NOTE: The figures in this table are not directly comparable because the wards from which they are computed vary in population and size. Nevertheless, the Boston statistics, and the single index for Philadelphia, are compatible with the findings of this study for New York.

points in time are strictly comparable because of different ward or other unit boundaries, the differences in the indexes between the nineteenth and twentieth centuries seem so great as to be incontrovertible. A ghetto separating blacks and whites did not exist in New York in the ante-bellum years.[23]

The raw data again provides us with additional information. In 1830, blacks lived in all sections of the city. At one end of the spectrum, they constituted 4.3 and 4.4 percent of the population in the seventh and ninth wards respectively; and at the other end, 11.8 and 13.8 percent in the fifth and sixth wards respectively. By 1845, in certain sections of the city, Negroes were almost a rarity. Taking the extreme case, they made up only 0.9 percent of the fourth ward's population. On the other hand, they were most numerous in the contiguous fifth and eighth wards. But still, while the fifth ward's population was 11.9 percent black, the ward, in its western section, continued to house some of New York's wealthiest citizens. As figure 6 shows, West Broadway (where the Negroes lived) skirted this area, and paralleling West Broadway two blocks to the east was fashionable Broadway.

The poor dwelt apart from the rich only in the shanty-towns constructed on the city's outskirts. In 1829, such districts existed in the twelfth ward, which included all of Manhattan Island north of Fourteenth Street, and along the river front in the northeastern section of the city (in the eastern sections of the seventh and thirteenth wards).[24] By 1845, the outlying ward's southern boundary had moved north to Fortieth Street.[25] At both dates, however, the wards encompassing these extensive slum districts also included the suburban homes of prosperous New Yorkers.[26]

Ward-centered charity relief worked as well as it did because the street and the neighborhood played a far greater role in the lives of most people than they do today. Even as the city grew, localism was encouraged. Inadequately developed systems made intra-urban transportation difficult.[27] The charity workers are a case in point. In 1829, 44.2 percent of the volunteers in the seven analyzed wards lived and worked in the same area (defined as a three block radius). In 1845, the corresponding percentage for the A.I.C.P. volunteers was 47.6.[28] Although of a selected group, these percentages appear, pending further research, not much different than the percentage for the population at large. As late as the 1840s—despite horse drawn omnibuses and commuter railroads—New York remained a walking city. The 12 1/2 cent fare was too high for the workingman earning $1.00 or $1.50 per day,[29] and the pattern of uptown residence and downtown business still applied only to the relatively few merchants, attorneys, agents, corporation executives, wholesalers, and assorted businessmen who scaled the economic ladder. The middle class held to tradition: retail storeowners and craftsmen continued to live above their shops or close by; and others walking to work included many teachers, wholesalers, coal dealers, doctors, and even some manufacturers and attorneys.[30]

TABLE 11

NEGRO POPULATION OF NEW YORK, 1830 AND 1845

Ward	1830			1845		
	Total Population	Negroes		Total Population	Negroes	
		Number	Percent		Number	Percent
1	11,327	804	7.1	12,230	192	1.6
2	8,202	426	5.2	6,962	277	4.0
3	8,649	631	6.5	11,900	530	4.5
4	12,705	609	4.8	21,000	190	0.9
5	17,722	2,098	11.8	20,362	2,433	11.9
6	13,596	1,878	13.8	19,343	1,073	5.5
7	15,868	682	4.3	25,556	368	1.4
8	20,921	1,819	8.7	30,900	1,841	6.0
9[a]	22,752	991	4.4	30,907	367	1.2
10	16,438	1,040	6.3	20,993	445	2.1
11[b]	14,901	641	4.3	27,259	540	2.0
12[c]	11,901	999	8.4	13,378	559	4.2
13	12,655	565	4.5	22,411	667	3.0
14	14,370	899	6.3	21,103	1,243	5.9
15[a]	. . . .			19,422	712	3.7
16[c]	. . . .			40,350	1,079	2.7
17[b]	. . . .			27,147	397	1.5
Total	203,007	14,082	6.9	371,223	24,416	3.5

SOURCE: U.S., Department of State, *Fifth Census, or Enumeration of the United States, 1830;* New York (State), Secretary of State, *Census of the State of New York for 1845.*

[a]The area comprising the ninth ward in 1830 comprised the ninth and fifteenth wards in 1845.

[b]The area comprising the eleventh ward in 1830 comprised the eleventh and seventeenth wards in 1845.

[c]The area comprising the twelfth ward in 1830 comprised the twelfth and sixteenth wards in 1845. The sixteenth was the ward further south.

IV

The published diary of Michael Floy Jr. describes charity work during this period. During the winters of 1835 and 1836 Floy worked on behalf of a private society unassociated with the ward committees, but operating on the same neighborhood principle. Single and in his twenties, Floy operated a nursery with his father and lived with his family over the shop. He was an active Methodist who belonged to a Bible society and taught Sunday school; he favored the abolitionists and voted Democratic.[31]

The family lived at Broadway and Twelfth Street, along the eastern edge of well-to-do Greenwich Village. Yet, the poor were visible there, too, and some even lived down the block.

The young man considered charity work as a learning experience as well as a social service, and his entries (commenting on fourteen visits in 1835 and twelve in 1836)[32] reflect both curiosity and emotional involvement. One case, for example, "proved to be as great an object of charity as ever I saw." A couple had both sickened from the strain of caring for their epileptic child. "Sensible and well-in-formed," the parents had "seen better days." Floy believed that anyone looking at the boy "and not feeling some emotion arising in his breast, cannot have a very feeling heart."[33] Another "very interesting case" involved "a venerable old man and his wife—very poor and in need." Their "room was neat and in order." Floy thought that he was "well paid for the visit."[34]

Charity was hard work, even if it did make the charity worker feel self-satisfied. On one occasion, Floy wrote, he " had to go thro[ugh] storm and mud to get there."[35] At another time, bringing a widow and her children "a bag of potatoes on my shoulders . . .brought on my fever again."[36] For one woman who appealed to him on a Friday, Floy "ran about and got enough to keep her warm in the night," which was all he could do by himself over the weekend. He had to wait until Monday before introducing the woman to the managers and having her properly clothed.[37] After one particularly punishing day spent visiting the poor, he wrote that he had "nearly perished in so doing."[38]

In one instance, Floy's contact with a poor family carried over from one winter into the next.[39] He first met the objects of relief the day before the head of the household died of tuberculosis. Following the man's death, he visited the widow and provided her and her two daughters with shoes and stockings. Floy also attended the funeral. When the woman thanked him for his help, he begged off humbly, claiming that "a rich man can say no more than that he is a steward." Floy visited the widow again several days later, and on this occasion he first met the dead husband's mother. The old woman had now lost the last of thirteen children and had no recourse but the almshouse. She "appeared quite disconsolate," but nevertheless thanked God that "I have a resting place in the Almshouse, and I shall soon have a better place than that to rest in." Several weeks later, Floy saw the family for the last time that winter—ostensibly to bring them provisions. The meeting was charged with emotion. The widow gave Floy a small strop which had belonged to her husband, and Floy wrote that he would keep it "to remember her by." When the two shook hands to say goodbye, Floy "saw a smile on her pale cheeks" which made him think he had "never felt happier in my life."

This poor and bereft family did not exit from the young man's life. The following winter, tragedy struck again, and in January 1836 he was again visiting the family, now as the eldest daughter lay dying of tuberculosis. It was the same fate that had befallen her father the year before. Floy brought along a bag of potatoes as "an offering" and prayed with the unfortunate girl. Although, at first, he felt averse to praying, "she made lazy Mike perform that duty for her, and as is always the case, he felt much blessed."

It is dangerous to generalize from a single account. In the instance of Floy, we need to be especially wary of his youthfulness and of the generally good character of his neighborhood. Yet taking this into consideration, it remains true that the experiences and responses of this one visitor to the poor do not differ substantially from those of other visitors as they were recounted in the pre-1837 annual reports of New York's charitable societies. Sentiment, to the contrary, did exist, but the charitable generally equated the poor with the aged, the sick, and the widowed. European poverty was said not to exist in the United States. As the Protestant Episcopal City Mission Society stated it, the poor did not form a class in the United States: "individuals alone are poor;. . .with them poverty is but a transient evil. . .save paupers and vagabonds. . .all else form one common class of citizens;. . .all with individual exceptions, going on, by industry and economy, to acquire it."[40]

V

From the 1840s, the reality of a poor class could not be avoided: but while special efforts went into the emerging tenement house and public health reform movements, there was a corresponding unwillingness among the charitable to seek out and help the poor directly. In the most interesting parallel to previous efforts, the attempt to organize ad hoc committees in the winter of 1854-55 (in the midst of a depression and for the first time in nearly twenty years) was opposed by the A.I.C.P., which charged that it could meet the emergency and that ad hoc committees were unnecessary. In addition, these broadly based efforts were only partially successful. In only twelve of the twenty-two wards were poor relief committees created, and some of the wards received contributions only to have them distributed by the A.I.C.P.[41]

When New York underwent its next economic crisis in the winter of 1857-58, no ad hoc committees were formed. The A.I.C.P. could not dampen agitation, and the unemployed asked that they be given work on public projects. The city government became alarmed, and the mayor guarded City Hall with two hundred policemen, and the United States Assistant Treasurer telegraphed Washington for troops to protect the subtreasury building in Wall Street. The cement that held the old social fabric together had crumbled.[42]

NOTES

[1]Raymond A. Mohl, *Poverty in New York: 1783-1825,* The Urban Life in America Series (New York, 1971), pp. 3-118, passim; Sidney I. Pomerantz, *New-York: An American City, 1783-1803: A Study of Urban Life,* Studies in History, Economics and Public Law, no. 442 (New York, 1938), pp. 327-38; David M. Schneider, *The History of Public Welfare in New York State, 1609-1865,* Social Service Monographs (Chicago, 1938), I, passim.

[2]*New-York As It Is; Containing a General Description of the City of New-York* (New York, 1840), pp. 75-108; *The Picture of New-York, and Stranger's Guide through the Commercial Emporium of the United States* (New York, 1818), pp. 176-89.

[3]Mohl, *Poverty in New York,* pp. 110, 142-43.

[4]Fuel funds were common throughout the period: *New York Commercial Advertiser,* January 26, 27, 29, 31, February 8, 20, 21, March 3, 1821. A fund was instituted by the Society for the Prevention of Pauperism (see ibid., February 6, 22 April 3, 13, 17, May 5, 9, June 1, September 12, 28, 1821). See also Mohl, *Poverty in New York,* pp. 250-52; for references to other funds, see *Commercial Advertiser,* February 1, 1823; April 21, May 8, 28, 1827, January 15, 1828; February 8, 14, 27, March 3, 13, 1832; February 5, 1834. See also *Minutes of the Common Council of the City of New York: 1784-1831,* XI, 452 (January 22, 1821).

[5]See *Commercial Advertiser,* February-March, 1829; passim; January-March, 1831, passim; January-February, 1835, passim; November-December, 1837, passim; July-September, 1832, passim.

[6]*Commercial Advertiser,* March 10, 1829; January 24, 27, February 28, March 16, 1831; September 14, 1832; January 16, February 19, April 2, 1838. (See Smith, Walter Buckingham, and Arthur Harrison Cole, *Fluctuations in American Business, 1790-1860* [Cambridge, Mass., 1935], pp. 60, 94, 154 for the equivalence of price between the 1830s and the 1850s.)

[7]George Rogers Taylor, *The Transportation Revolution: 1815-1860* (New York, 1951), p. 296.

[8]*Frontiers in Human Welfare: The Story of a Hundred Years of Service to the Community of New York, 1848-1948* ([New York], 1948); Roy Lubove, *The Professional Altruist: The Emergence of Social Work as a Career, 1880-1930* (Cambridge, Mass., 1965), pp. 2-3; Frank Dekker Watson, *The Charity Organization Movement in the United States: A Study in American Philanthropy* (New York, 1922), pp. 79-85. For the A.I.C.P.'s own statement of its goals and methods, see *Address to the Public; Constitution and By-Laws; and Visitor's Manual, of the New York Association for the Improvement of the Condition of the Poor* (New-York, 1844). In 1939, the A.I.C.P. merged with the Charity Organization Society of the City of New York to form the Community Service Society of New York.

[9]The A.I.C.P. was founded in 1843 as an outgrowth of the New York City Tract Society. The tract society, during the depression, had found its visitors having to mix

relief with religion. Carroll Smith Rosenberg, *Religion and the Rise of the American City: The New York City Mission Movement, 1812-1870* (Ithaca, N. Y., 1971), pp. 93-94, 245-48.

[10]In 1829, wards 1, 5, 6, 7, 11, 13, 14; in 1845, wards 1, 5, 6, 7, 11, 13, 14, 17.

[11]In the case of the builders and building owners, the growth of the city may be responsible; in the case of the attorneys, it was owing to their withdrawal from public affairs in general. Edward Pessen, "Who Governed the Nation's Cities in the 'Era of the Common Man'?" *Political Science Quarterly* 87 (December 1972): 596, 599.

[12]For reports on the activities of the ad hoc committees, see the *Commercial Advertiser,* February 26-28, March 2-6, 10, 13, 16, 24, 26, 1829.

[13]New-York Association for the Improvement of the Condition of the Poor, *First Annual Report. . .for the Year 1845, with the Constitution, Visitor's Manual, and a List of Members* (New-York, 1845), pp. 4-7.

[14]Ibid.

[15]Ibid., pp. 4-6.

[16]See New-York Association for the Improvement of the Condition of the Poor, *The Directory of the New-York Association of the Condition of the Poor* (New-York, 1844) for the name and residence of each visitor and his assigned section.

[17]According to I. N. Phelp Stokes, genteel families lived on the following streets, scattered throughout much of the city: "State--street, fronting the Battery, Bridge--street, Bowling Green, Greenwich--street, from the Battery to Cortlandt--street, Broadway from the Battery to Rector--street, and facing the Park; also north of Anthony--street, Bond--street, the streets around Hudson Square, Hudson--street, Park Place, Chambers--street, Liberty and Cortlandt--streets west of Broadway, Dey--street, Vesey--street, opposite St. Paul's church-yard, Barclay--street, Murray--street, Warren--street, Bleeker--street, Prince--street, the streets around Washington Square, La Fayette Place, Broome--street, Spring--street, and Grand--street, Franklin, White and Walker streets." ("Chronology," *The Iconography of Manhattan Island, 1498-1909, Compiled from Original Sources and Illustrated by Photo-Intaglio Reproduction of Important Maps, Plans, Views and Documents in Public and Private Collections,* 6 vols. New York, [1915-28], 2: 1673.)

[18]Sam Bass Warner, Jr., *The Urban Wilderness: A History of the American City* (New York, 1972), pp. 30-34. The degree of residential segregation for west European immigrants remained low throughout the great era of immigration, from the 1840s to the 1920s. The new immigrants, those from eastern and southern Europe, were more isolated. Either west Europeans integrated themselves easily into American urban society because they were west Europeans, or in the twentieth century assimilation has been difficult. In any case, the effect is the same: increased segregation in the twentieth century.

[19]Stokes, "Historical Summary," *Iconography,* 3: 526-27, 650-51; "Chronology," ibid., October 13, 1823, V. 1633; Robert Ernst, *Immigrant Life in New York City 1825-1863,*

Empire State Historical Publications, 37 (New York, 1949; reprint ed., Port Washington, N. Y., 1965), pp. 102-105.

[20]Mohl, *Poverty in New York*, pp. 24-25; Ernst, *Immigrant Life in New York,*, table 20, p. 201; George E. Haynes, *The Negro at Work in New York City; a Study in Economic Progress*, Studies in History, Economics and Public Law, vol. 49, no. 3 (New York, 1912), pp. 67-68.

[21]For the most recent study of the sixth ward, see Carol Groneman Pernicone, "The 'Bloody Ould Sixth': A Social Analysis of a New York City Working-Class Community in the Mid-Nineteenth Century" (Ph.D. dissertation, University of Rochester, 1973). See also Isaac James Quillen, "A History of 'The Five Points,' New York City, to 1890" (Master's thesis, New York University, 1932).

[22]Karl E. Taeuber and Alma F. Taeuber, *Negroes in Cities; Residential Segregation and Neighborhood Change* (Chicago, 1965), p. 54.

[23]Slavery disappeared in New York State during the first quarter of the nineteenth century. For all practical purposes it ceased to exist in 1827. In its immediate aftermath, many of the city's blacks lived near the whites for whom they worked, and this explains the low level of segregation existing in 1830.

New York grew racially more segregated as its black population declined. From 18,061 or 5.7 percent of the population in 1835, the city's blacks dropped to 11,840 or 1.9 percent in 1855. It is possible that this decline reflected, in a measurable way, increased segregationist pressures.

[24]For the city's neglect of the outlying wards, see a petition to the Common Council: "Inhabitants of the Seventh and Tenth Wards petition the common council that the law regarding swine be so amended that they may run at large in that district. The bell-carts do not come often into that section, which makes it necessary that the swine should eat the garbage thrown into the streets." New York (City), *Minutes of the Common Council*, 1784-1831, June 24, 1822, 12: 447, cited by Stokes, "Chronology," *Iconograpahy*, 5: 1623. The petition was granted [*Minutes of the Common Council*, 12: 460-61]).

[25]Contiguous settlement extended only as far as Thirtieth street (see *Walker's New Map of New York City, 1846*).

[26]As indicated in figures 5 and 6 and by the visitors to the poor for the twelfth ward in 1829 (*Commercial Advertiser*, March 10, 1829).

[27]Seymour J. Mandelbaum's description of New York in the sixties applies also to the ante-bellum period (see his *Boss Tweed's New York*, New Dimensions in History: Historical Cities [New York, 1965], pp. 12-15). His estimate of 135 trips on public transportation lines per person annually indicates how seldom New Yorkers ventured forth from their homes. Routes ran north-south. In 1840, there were four stage lines: from Wall Street to (a) Fourteenth Street and the Hudson River, (b) Tenth Street and the East River, (c) Fourteenth Street and Broadway; and on the Bowery to Fourteenth Street. *New-York As It Is* (New York, 1840), p. 208. (In 1975, New Yorkers averaged about 225 fares annually, but this figure excludes populations and transit

systems in the larger metropolitan area and does not take the automobile into account [average daily fares were provided by the Metropolitan Transit Authority for August 1975].)

[28]Computed from sources for table 7.

[29]*New-York As It Is,* p. 208; On the walking city, see David Ward, *Cities and Immigrants: A Geography of Change in Nineteenth-Century America* (New York, 1971), pp. 106-107.

[30]Brian J. Danforth, "The Influence of Socioeconomic Factors Upon Political Behavior: A Qualitative Look at New York City Merchants, 1828-1844" (Ph.D. dissertation, New York University, 1974), p. 44. Ward, *Cities and Immigrants,* pp. 87, 105-106, 120, 130-31, discusses mid nineteenth century urban geography with its upper class suburbs and middle and lower class cities. A nonsystematic scanning of the business directories appears to confirm Ward's conclusions for New York City. The occupations mentioned are used as examples only.

[31]Michael Floy, Jr., *The Diary of Michael Floy, Jr.: Bowery Village 1833-1837,* ed. Richard A. E. Brooks (New Haven, Conn., 1941), passim.

[32]Ibid., January 17, 25, 26, 29; February 1, 4, 5, 8, 10, 11, 12, 14, 28; March 2, 1835; January 12, 15, 16, 29; February 5, 6, 7, 9, 12, 16, 23; March 1, 1836.

[33]Ibid., February 4, 1835.

[34]Ibid., January 2, 1835.

[35]Ibid., January 25, 1835.

[36]Ibid., January 12, 1836.

[37]Ibid., January 29, 1836.

[38]Ibid., February 5, 1836.

[39]Ibid., February 10, 11, 12, 14, 28, 1835; January 12, 16, 1836.

[40]Protestant Episcopal City Mission Society, *Sixth Annual Report,* pp. 15-16, cited by Carroll Smith Rosenberg, *Religion and the Rise of the American City: The New York City Mission Movement, 1812-1870* (Ithaca, N. Y., 1971), p. 156. On the concept of the worthy poor, see Rosenberg,*Religion,* pp. 28-29, 36-37, 91, 94-95, 155-57, 178-79. Mohl,*Poverty in New York,* pp. 159-70 and passim, argues that poverty was widespread in New York and intractable to traditional charity by the 1820s—well before the depression following the Panic of 1837. There is no right interpretation of the extensiveness of poverty; "extensiveness" is a subjective measure. But the 1840s saw economic as well as social changes to an extent not true of the 1820s.

[41]Schneider, *History of Public Welfare,* 1: 270-71.

[42]Ibid., pp. 272-75.

EPILOGUE

I

About 1840, rioting of a new kind appeared. Social changes were occurring which were to manifest themselves nationally, politically, in the Know-Nothingism of the 1850s. Gangs of youths, tied to fire company volunteers and political party factions began stalking the streets. Native-born Americans, more than immigrant Americans, were the personae involved.

Youthful disorderliness had once been mischievous and innocent. Such behavior—frolics—ranged, in the 1820s, from breaches of the Sunday laws to minor vandalism (for example, removing street signs), to prizefighting, to false fire alarms, to parading the streets on New Year's Eve, to Fourth of July celebrations (overdrinking, overeating, and the exploding of firecrackers), to drunkenness, to bull-baiting, to horse racing, to kite flying, to brawling, to cock fighting, to parades, to nude bathing, to stagecoach racing.[1]

Sometimes, large crowds would gather. In City Hall Park, on Sundays, 1,000 to 1,500 youths engaged in noisy sport and "ran riot." At the Horse Market, at Sixth Avenue and Greenwich Lane, 200 to 300 lower class whites and blacks gathered every Wednesday and Saturday nights, disturbing the peace by their drinking, betting, boxing, and racing. One hundred to 200 boys in the Corlaer's Hook slum neighborhood had behaved mischievously, fighting with stones "for a long time past."[2]

Organized gang violence was seldom reported. In 1827, a gang called the "Hell Fire Club" would "bully and abuse every person they meet." Some unwary persons would be beaten. "Females passing by have been black-guarded and insulted." In 1829, a gang called the "Forty Thieves," or "Highbinders," attacked two young bakers out of "mere wantonness."

The "Chicester Gang" was the first gang of which we know that was not evanescent. The gang rioted for several hours in March 1836. The incident was one the press thought "originated altogether from a mere spirit of insubordination and love of mischief,"[3] but temporarily, it caught the fancy of New Yorkers, and reportage of other organized gangs of youths increased.[4]

In 1840, gang violence arrived on the scene permanently. Mike Walsh brought his "Spartan Band" into Tammany Hall and added organized violence to Democratic party politics. Walsh first made the news during the November 1840 election (a year after he arrived in New York as a twenty-nine year old lithographer).[5] The *Commercial*

Advertiser, in its first report on the "Spartan Band," compared it to the "Chicester Gang" of four years before. Forty or fifty strong, its members paraded the streets, short clubs in hand, appearing in the midst of election day disorders. The Band, in one instance, were in the mob that invaded a Whig campaign headquarters, pulling down handbills and posters, assaulting the dozen Whigs in the room, and taking over the bar.[6]

During the election of the following November, the "Spartan Band" had 300 members and the Band effectively disrupted a Democratic ratification meeting. It succeeded in having Walsh's name substituted for that chosen by the nominating committee which ordinarily would have been confirmed without opposition.[7]

In April 1842, the "Spartan Band," taking up the cause of nativism, spearheaded a mob contesting the right of Catholics to share in educational funds and policy making. The mob attacked the regular Democratic headquarters in Dunn's hotel, smashing windows and destroying the hotel's barroom furniture. The mob also attacked the house of New York's Catholic bishop, John Joseph Hughes, damaging it considerably. The police and the militia finally had to restore order.[8]

II

In antebellum New York, the volunteer fire department was a social club as well as a civil service. Membership represented status and underage youths hung about the different companies as unofficial "volunteers" to bask in the reflected glory. The youths helped drag the engines to fires and, in the engine houses, cleaned the equipment.[9] A fire company would vie to be the first to reach a fire, but competition could be counterproductive. The cry of fire might be falsely and deliberately raised. One report had hundreds of boys gathering regularly in the evening in Fireman's Hall yard and shouting "fire" to such an extent that it had "become a perfect nuisance." Some years later, a Common Council investigation found that "boys and young men, too, obtained very ready access to the fire engines, and made it a matter of amusement to raise an alarm of fire as an excuse or cover to get the engines out and have a run."[10]

In the theater, several incidents were fictionalized. One had its origin in the competition in the late 1830s between engine companies 15 and 40. The two companies, allegedly, crossed paths frequently in Chatham Street. On one particular Sunday, a brawl sucked in 1,000 men and boys, firemen and non-firemen alike. Some details, oft described, may be fiction (hand to hand combat?), but it was the most disgraceful riot in a long time according to one contemporary reporter. The fight which lasted thirty minutes was led by Mose Humphreys for Company 40 and Hen Chanfrau for Company 15. The stage version gave both men, but especially Humphreys, legendary stature.[11]

On New Year's Eve, December 31, 1839, firemen were involved in a deadly ruckus. About fifty firemen forced their way into a German tavern, broke a number of bottles, splintered a table, and then were ejected; when they returned with reenforcements one fireman was killed by gunshot as he sought to break down the door. Other shots followed, as the Germans sought to protect themselves, and rumors circulated that the incident resulted in an additional number wounded.[12]

The authorities' silence on the behavior of the firemen and the underage "volunteers" lasted only until January 1840. The resolution that the mayor and the Common Council passed stated that "a great excitement prevails in this community, in consequence of frequent breaches of the peace, alleged to have been committed by a large number of dissolute and profligate young men, usually attending fire engines in the dress of Firemen, and under the assumed name of 'volunteers.'" The resolution required the fire company foremen to report "the names, ages, condition, and place of abode" of those youths "running" with the fire companies and whether the youthful "volunteers" used the engine houses to congregate. The Council wanted to know also how firemen were selected.[13] The "committee of public safety" that was created following this resolution described the character of the youthful "volunteers" as unreliable.[14]

The Common Council's Special Committee on Fire and Water echoed the same theme, and in April 1841, urged the rigid enforcement of the existing ordinances and the adoption of measures "to check the riotous and disorderly spirit which is making such inroads among a certain portion of the Fire Department."[15] In the summer of 1841, Chief Engineer Cornelius W. Anderson, in his annual report, raised the issue again. He too urged taking strong disciplinary measures: an improved department would result from "strict subordination and discipline" and the punishment of violators by the Common Council. Fire company officers should be held responsible for the men's conduct and they should be required to point out the offenders in cases of riot. As the firemen could not "keep constant watch over" the youthful volunteers, he saw "some salutary law on the subject" as the only remedy.[16]

III

Mike Walsh died in 1859, an outsider within the Democratic party. Mose Humphreys became an eight foot legend and disappeared from public sight. While these men added color to the New York scene, they never attained to positions of real power or respectability, and the onset of mass immigration a few years afterwards obliterated whatever prominence these men had achieved as "pure-blooded Americans." Today, ironically, the collective violence of antebellum nativists is often ascribed to (Irish Catholic) immigrants.[17]

In fact, both the decline of deference and mass immigration were developments largely of the years after 1837. The response to the 1830s' rioting, seen from an historical perspective, was little affected by modern-day class and ethnic consciousness.

NOTES

[1] All the following references are from the *New-York Commercial Advertiser*, except where noted. On violation of the Sunday laws, see February 8, 1823, June 21, 1826, December 29, 1828, April 7, July 2-3, 1829. On vandalism, see the *Evening Post* (New York), September 3, 1819; *Commercial Advertiser*, May 25, 1822, April 1, 1824, December 27, 1827. (The press indicated that much vandalism was tolerated, if not approved.) On prizefighting, see May 10, 1821, July 11, 1823, October 15, 1824, February 4, 1835; on false fire alarms, April 9, 1822, February 9, 1824, September 11, 13, 1826, July 24, 1832, January 17, 1834; on New Year's Eve parading, January 3, 1828, December 30, 1828. On July 4th celebrating, see the editorials advocating the banning of public booths selling food and drink in City Hall Park. The editorials appeared between May and July each year from 1826 onwards. Firecrackers were banned in 1833. Reports of drunkenness were frequent, but note the use of the term "drunken frolic," May 20, 1823. On bull-baiting, see July 1, 1823, September 1, 3, 1827; on horse racing, July 2, 1823, June 9, 1831. On kite flying, see April 10, July 29, 1824, March 10, 1825, March 22, 1827. On minor brawling, see June 25, 1825, June 21, 1826, February 1, March 28, October 1, 1827 (in the first two instances, the brawls were called frolics). On cock fighting, see December 29, 1825, April 1, 7, 1829; on parades, June 28, 1832, June 24, 1829; on nude bathing, July 24, 1829; on stage coach racing, July 14, 1831.

A spate of reports about street crowds appeared in 1826 (March 7, 11, May 17, August 24, September 11, 13). The year before, one judge on passing sentence in a case of street violence felt impelled to state that "we. . .do not consider ourselves at liberty to close our eyes upon the fact that we reside in an immense and growing city, comprising a mixed population; . . .containing a multitude of vicious spirits, . . .Riotous assemblages. . .are, from the sudden combination of strength which they can readily acquire, peculiarly calculated to break down the safeguards in the law, and to lay the community open to lawless violence." (July 2, 1825.)

[2] *Commercial Advertiser*, July 2, 1821; March 7, 1826; March 28, 1827.

[3] Ibid., February 1, 1827, March 5, 1836; on the arrest of Chicester, see ibid., April 6, 1836.

[4] *Commercial Advertiser*, October 26, December 28, 1836; January 6, 1837. The "Chicester Gang" perhaps harbingered the 1850s. Its members were mostly butchers (even as were the members of the 1827 "Hell Fire Club"), and, in the Know-Nothing violence of the 1850s, it was a butcher—Bill "the Butcher" Poole—who led the nativists. And even more intriguing, if only grounds for conjecture, Chicester's arrest occurred at 44 Bowery, near to 40 Bowery, the drinking headquarters of the "Bowery Boys" in the 1850s. The "Bowery Boys" was probably the most famous of the nativist gangs.

[5] Arthur M. Schlesinger, Jr., *The Age of Jackson* (Boston, 1945), pp. 348, 408, 409, 508; Frank C. Rogers, Jr., "Mike Walsh: A Voice of Protest" (Master's thesis, Columbia University, 1950), p. 5 and passim.

[6] *Commercial Advertiser*, November 2, 1840; Robert Hone, MS Diary, November 2, 1840, Manuscript Division, New-York Historical Society.

[7]Rogers, "Mike Walsh," pp. 16-20.

[8]Ibid., p. 23; Robert Hone, MS Diary, April 13, 1842.

[9]Among the most recent studies of the fire department is that of Stephen F. Ginsberg, "History of Fire Protection in New York City, 1800-1842" (Ph.D. dissertation, New York University, 1968). Of the older studies, Augustine E. Costello's semiofficial *Our Firemen. A History of the New York Fire Department. Volunteer and Paid* (New York, 1887) is the most thorough. George W. Sheldon, *The Story of the Volunteer Fire Department of the City of New York* (New York, 1882), is also useful; but other histories, while containing a great deal of lore, are factually inaccurate. On the volunteers, see Ginsberg, "Fire Protection," pp. 239-42.

[10]*Commercial Advertiser*, April 9, 1822; Costello, *Our Firemen*, p. 95.

[11]Costello, *Our Firemen*, pp. 178-80; *Sun* (New York), September 30, 1839. *A Glance at New York* [New York, 1848] by Benjamin A. Baker was first presented in New York City February 15, 1848.

[12]Leo Hershkowitz, "New York City, 1834 to 1840, A Study in Local Politics" (Ph.D. dissertation, New York University), 1975, pp. 431-32; *Commercial Advertiser*, January 2, 1840. For other instances of departmental rowdiness, see Costello, *Our Firemen*, pp. 175-81 and passim; Ginsberg, "Fire Protection," pp. 294-314, passim; Henry A. Patterson, MS Diary, August 28, 1838, Manuscript Division, New-York Historical Society.

[13]New York (City), Board of Aldermen, Preambles and Resolutions, Doc. No. 41, Vol. VI (1840).

[14]New York (City), Committee of Safety: Appointed by the Public Meeting of Citizens, on the Subject of Fires, *Report of the Committee of the Subject of Paid Fire Department* (New York, [1840]), p. 21.

[15]New York (City), Board of Aldermen, *Report of the Special Committee on Fire and Water*, Doc. No. 86, Vol. VII (1841).

[16]Idem, *Annual Report of the Chief Engineer*, Doc. No. 16, Vol. VIII (1841).

[17]Schlesinger, *Age of Jackson*, pp. 408-409, describes Walsh as "a tough Irish rabble-rouser," "the particular hero of the 'Bowery b'hoys;'" Jerome Mushkat, *Tammany: The Evolution of a Political Machine 1789-1865* (Syracuse, N. Y., 1971), pp. 208, 210. But Walsh, though born in Country Cork, Ireland, was ardently anti-Catholic. When he died, the funeral ceremony was conducted by an Episcopalian clergyman (Rogers, "Mike Walsh," pp. 1, 121). On Moses "Old Moses" Humphreys as Irish born, see Lowell M. Limpus, *History of the New York Fire Department* (New York, 1940), p. 169; Humphreys "led a tough bunch of Irish followers, generally called the Bowery Boys."

"Blackguards" acquired the name of "soap locks" after the hair style popular from about 1838 to the mid 1850s. At first the slang connoted only native Americans, but by the 1850s it was used as a synonym for rowdies generally. For example, "the hostility between the Yankee *soap locks* and the Dutch musicians, in regard to the

Ellsler serenade, has come to a happy termination." *Daily Pennant* (St. Louis), September 12, 1840, cited by Richard H. Thornton, *American Glossary; Being An Attempt to Illustrate Certain Americanisms upon Historical Principles,* expanded 3 vol. ed. (New York, 1962), 2:825. On the other hand, Mitford M. Mathews, ed., *Dictionary of Americanisms,* 2 vols. (Chicago, 1951), 2:1587-88, citing the *Spirit of the Times* (New York), January 23, 1858, uses this example: "In the case of Ezra White, he was the chief of a gang of 'soap locks,' *vice* 'Dead Rabbits,' an Irish gang." See also *Commercial Advertiser,* April 28, 1840.

APPENDIX

APPENDIX

TABLE 12

COMPLAINTS AGAINST NEW YORK CITY LICENSE HOLDERS
HEARD BY THE MAYOR, MARCH 20, 1821-JULY 6, 1822
AND NOVEMBER 22, 1822-NOVEMBER 19, 1823

Date	Licensee(s)	Complaint	Mayor's Action
3/20-21/1821	marshal	failed to turn over money collected from executing a warrant	dismissed case [ordered money to be turned over?]
3/24/1821	hand cartman	collected reward money under false pretenses	reduced reward money
3/30, 6/2/1821	sweepmaster	ill treated his servant	reprimanded master and servant; advised servant he had recourse to the mayor if he was "cruelly used"
3/31/1821	marshal	failed to appear in court	dismissed case
3/3/1821 [4/3/1821]	marshal	conspired to execute a warrant illegally	dismissed case—complainants failed to appear
4/6/1821	2 cartmen	engaged in a fray and altered a license number	suspended both licenses one week
4/6/1821	cartman	reported falsely that he lived in the city	suspended license until cartman moved his family to the city

TABLE 12—Continued

Date	Licensee(s)	Complaint	Mayor's Action
4/6/1821	cartman	frequented houses of ill fame while leaving his horse unfed	warned cartman that a second complaint would result in the loss of his license
4/10, 14/1821	cartman	expressed his opposition to republican institutions; was intemperate and a single man	refused request for license; granted license upon representation of a character reference
5/9/1821	cartman	ran over a child	returned license to licensee
5/22/1821	marshal	failed to supply a bill of sale for attached property	directed marshal to supply a bill of sale
5/22/1821	cartman	fathered an illegitimate child— (was also an alien)	refused request for license
5/29/1821	sweepmaster	ill used and inadequately clothed his servant	reprimanded servant; advised master to correct servant with judgement or to bring him before the mayor if he committed another fault
6/1/1821	cartman	overcharged for services	suspended license; returned license at the request of complainant
6/2, 12/1821	3 cartmen	monopolized the purchase of firewood	suspended cart owner's license, returned it subsequently; withdrew drivers' licenses on their failing to prove ownership of carts

TABLE 12–Continued

Date	Licensee(s)	Complaint	Mayor's Action
6/4/1821	————	requested the release of a prostitute from the penitentiary for her return to Stonington, Connecticut	granted request
6/10, 29/1821	sweepmaster	swept a chimney that subsequently caught fire	suspended license; restored license after sweepmaster made "ample satisfaction" to complainant
6/27/1821	2 cartmen	refused to follow wood inspector's direction for loading; used abusive language	warned cartmen that a second complaint would result in the loss of their licenses
6/29/1821	2 hack drivers	committed a riot; used improper language	withdrew licenses
7/7/1821	hack driver	disturbed the peace (second complaint)	withdrew license
6/30, 7/2/1821	cartman	interfered with a regiment parade	withdrew license; returned license after complainant testified to cartman's "contrition"
7/7/1821	————	operated a dance house and kept a shuffle board	dismissed case
7/12, 20/1821	cartman	drove recklessly	suspended license for eight days

TABLE 12—Continued

Date	Licensee(s)	Complaint	Mayor's Action
7/13/1821	marshal	failed to turn over all money collected	abrogated commission
8/4/1821	sweepmaster	beat servant	withdrew license
not stated	hack driver	used abusive language	not stated
8/14/1821	cartman	watchman detained cartman after cartman had charged a prostitute with stealing his money and running off	withdrew license
9/7, 24/1821	hack driver	drove recklessly	withdrew license; returned license at the request of the complainants
10/16/1821	2 marshals	issued an execution improperly	warned marshals to discontinue the practise under penalty of losing their office
11/3/1821	cartman	refused to cart an article	dismissed case; warned cartman that a second complaint would result in the loss of his license
11/13-14/1821	cartman	beat his horse	restored license after cartman promised not to commit the offense again

TABLE 12—Continued

Date	Licensee(s)	Complaint	Mayor's Action
11/13-14/1821	cartman	used abusive language	dismissed case—insufficient evidence; cartman warned that a second complaint would result in the loss of his license
11/20/1821	sweepmaster	employed a boy under eleven years of age	withdrew license
11/29/1821	cartman	drove a cart that he did not own	withdrew license
12/27, 28/1821	marshal	failed to turn over money collected	surrendered warrant
1/2/1822	cartman	drove a cart and horse which he did not own	dismissed case
not stated	marshal	failed to turn over money collected	not stated
1/22/1822	marshal	used abusive language; was intemperate	not stated
2/7/1822	tavern keeper	sold liquor which resulted in death	withdrew license
2/9, 19/1822	cartman	used abusive language	suspended license; returned license after complainant "forgave" cartman and the latter promised "to conduct himself as a good citizen ought to do"

TABLE 12–Continued

Date	Licensee(s)	Complaint	Mayor's Action
2/16/1822	marshal	was drunk in court; was a noted gambler	suspended commission for three months
3/3, 6, 19/1822	cartman	was intoxicated; used abusive language	annulled license; returned license at the request of complainant
3/25/1822	cartman	frequented a house of ill fame	warned cartman not to do the like again "on his peral [sic]"
3/29/1822	marshal	requested a bribe from a prostitute	suspended warrant
4/1, 2, 11/1822	cartman	drove without a license	refused request for a license; granted license eventually at the request of the Common Council
4/8, 9/1822	sweepmaster	beat his apprentice in the street	warned sweepmaster that a second complaint would result in the loss of his license
4/17/1822	cartman	submitted information attempting to prove his residency in the city	not stated
4/26, 5/10/1822	cartman	was habitually drunk	withdrew license
not stated	cartman	did not live in the city	dismissed case

TABLE 12–Continued

Date	Licensee(s)	Complaint	Mayor's Action
5/31/1822	cartman	used abusive language	dismissed case
6/13/1822	cartman	used abusive language	withdrew license
6/15/1822	cartman	drove too fast; used abusive language	acknowledgement by cartman of his fault; warned that a second complaint would result in the loss of his license
6/17, 25 and 7/9/1822	2 cartmen	treated his horse brutally	suspended licenses; returned licenses "on petition & proper acknowledgments"
6/18/1822	cartman	committed assault and battery	not stated
6/18/1822	cartman	used abusive language; malice	dismissed case
6/20-21/1822	cartman	attempted to prevent the police from rounding up stray hogs; used abusive language	suspended license; returned license after cartman made satisfactory acknowledgements
6/21/1822	tavern keeper	sold liquor on Sunday; kept a disorderly house	annulled license
7/6/1822	cartman	ran over child; used abusive language	suspended license

TABLE 12—Continued

Date	Licensee(s)	Complaint	Mayor's Action
11/22/1822	cartman	engaged in a dispute over fees; used abusive language	returned license with complainant's consent after cartman "acknowledged that if he said any thing improper he was sorry for it"
11/26/1822	6 hack owners and drivers	disturbed the peace	dismissed case after licensees promised that no further complaints would be heard
11/28-29 and 12/3-4/1822	2 cartmen	refused to cart as they had arranged; used abusive language	suspended licenses; reinstated licenses at the request of complainant after he had received apologies
1/16/1823	cartman	ran over a child without stopping	suspended license; reinstated license upon request of citizens
1/25/1823	cartman	drove recklessly	cartman made "necessary and proper acknowledgments" to the satisfaction of complainant
1/27/1823	cartman	engaged in argument	dismissed complaint—unsatisfactory evidence
1/27/1823	intelligence office keeper	made improper advances to a chambermaid	not stated
not stated	hack driver	used abusive language	claimed he lacked the authority to act

TABLE 12—Continued

Date	Licensee(s)	Complaint	Mayor's Action
3/12, 17/1823	tavern keeper	kept a disorderly house "and a nuisance to the neighbourhood"	deprived of license; restored license
not stated	tavern keeper	not stated	not stated
not stated	cartman	drove too fast	not stated
July 1823	hack driver	refused to move his carriage; "used very indecent language"	not stated
7/19/1823	marshal	failed to perform duty	withdrew license effective 7/29/1823
8/30/1823	cartman	used abusive language	reprimanded cartman
9/1/1823	cartman	drove too fast	dismissed case—complainant did not appear
11/18/1823	cartman	drove too fast; used abusive language	withdrew license
11/19/1823	cartman	refused to move his cart; used abusive language	complaint withdrawn; cartman "had acknowledged his fault and he [complainant] forgave him

SOURCE: Court Minutes, 1821-22; Court Minutes, 1822-23, Stephen Allen Papers, New-York Historical Society.

NOTE: It is not clear whether the records summarized in this table represent the sum total of cases heard by the mayor or

TABLE 12—Continued

whether the mayor heard all complaints lodged against licenses. Specifically, the Stephen Allen papers at the New York Historical Society contain a book entitled Tavern Complaints, April 1822 (not used in the dissertation) which is thumb indexed. A
total of 110 complaints are listed for letters "A" through "P". (Letters "R" through "Z" have been cut out of the book.) An
entry consists of the name of the tavern keeper and the nature of the complaint, although there is no indication what action, if
any, was taken in each case.

It is not clear from the court records whether "suspended license," "withdrawn license," and "annulled license" are
interchangeable terms or whether they were distinct penalties.

A NOTE ON SOURCES

This dissertation, because of the broad subject matter it covers over a period of a quarter-century, has involved the use of distinctly different kinds of sources for each of its several chapters. The contemporary press, however, has been relied upon throughout the work. The newspapers, in addition to providing information, also disseminated the views of editors who themselves were public figures. The press is important for this reason as well.

The *Commercial Advertiser* generally reported local events most completely. A reading of the file for the 1820s and 1830s provided a continuum of the era's social history as well as information on a number of little known riots. In the mid 1830s, the *Sun, Transcript*, and *Herald*, all versions of the new cheap press, reported local news with greater interest than was common among elite oriented press of earlier years. Notations on the usefulness of newspapers as a research tool are contained in the body of the dissertation. Chapter two contains biographical sketches of the editors; chapter three, a review of their attitudes towards violence; and chapter four, an analysis of the role of the press in shaping public opinion.

Public addresses were used extensively in two instances—in chapter four, for attitudes towards political demagoguery; and in chapter six, for ministerial attitudes towards public executions. In the first instance, the addresses—mostly fourth of July orations—served to confirm editorial opinion; in the second, they established the rationale for executing men ceremonially.

Public documents, in chapter five, trace the legislative history of a proposed reorganization of the police. They were important also in chapter one, for information on the election riot of 1834. But documents—reports and statistics—relating to the city were not compiled before the early 1830s (census returns were the one exception), and their usefulness for this dissertation was somewhat restricted. The city's bylaws and ordinances, periodically updated throughout the years under study, were needed compendia, but, for rioting itself, proved of limited value.

Manuscript collections were generally not used, but there were important exceptions. Much of chapter six is based upon Robert Taylor's diary and the Stephen Allen court papers. The latter are especially important because official proceedings of testimony for criminal courts in New York City are extant for only several isolated months prior to 1846. Other essential manuscript collections included: (1) the Verplanck correspondence on the mayoral election (chapter one);

and (2) the Cornelius Lawrence file on the anti-abolitionist rioting (chapter two). The latter provides a command post's view of rioting and rumors of rioting.

A search was made for relevant diaries, and the two used, aside from Taylor's, were Michael Floy's, for his account of helping the poor (chapter seven), and the often used Philip Hone's, for his comments on many aspects of the city's life. Hone, mayor of the city in the 1820s, remained a socially and politically aware citizen through the 1840s. Resort was frequently made to the manuscript diary because the edited published version concentrates on Hone's political entries.

Many secondary sources do bear directly upon this study, but those of the late nineteenth century usually reflect the concern with labor and order common to that period. For example, 1834 as the "Year of the Riots," repeated in source after source, first appears in print in 1872 as an eye-catching opening sentence to a chapter ("The year 1834* [sic] may with propriety be called the Year of Riots."). The phrase was not to be found in any of the sources printed in the 1830s. More recent secondary sources are marred because they uncritically use these earlier histories.

BIBLIOGRAPHY

A.   Newspapers

1.   New York City

Emancipator, and Journal of Public Morals, 1834.

Evening Post, 1816-1837.

Evening Star, 1833-1837.

Man, 1834-1835.

Mercantile Advertiser and New-York Advocate, 1821; 1834-1836.

Morning Courier, 1828.

Morning Courier and New-York Enquirer, 1828-1837.

Morning Herald, 1835-1837.

National Advocate, 1821; 1823.

New Era 1837.

New-York American, 1819-1837.

New-York American Advocate, 1831.

New-York Commercial Advertiser, 1816-1841.

New-York Daily Advertiser, 1817-1834.

New-York Daily Express, 1837.

New-York Enquirer, 1828.

New York Evangelist, 1834-1835.

New-York Evening Journal, and Patron of Industry, 1821.

New-York Gazette and General Advertiser, 1816-1837.

New York Journal of Commerce, 1831-1837.

New-York National Advocate, 1825.

New-York Observer, 1834.

New York Standard, 1831-1832; 1834.

New-York Statesman, 1822; 1824-1825.

New York Times, 1834-1837.

New York Transcript, 1834-1836.

New-Yorker, 1834.

Plaindealer, 1837.

Spirit of '76, 1835.

Sun, 1833-1839.

Truth Teller, 1834; 1836.

    2.   Other

Niles's Weekly Register (Baltimore), 1835.

B.   **Government Documents**

    1.   New York City

       a)   Common Council

Board of Aldermen. *Documents.* 1834-1845.

_____. *Proceedings.* 1833-1840.

Board of Assistant Aldermen. *Documents.* 1834-1845.

_____. *Proceedings.* 1833-1839.

Boards of Aldermen and Assistant Aldermen. *Proceedings Approved by the Mayor.* 1831-1839.

Common Council. *Minutes of the Common Council of New York, 1784-1831.* 19 vols. New York: Published by the City of New York, 1917.

      i)   Documents of Special Interest

Board of Aldermen. *Communication from the Mayor Transmitting with Approval the Plan of Reorganization Drawn Up by Mr. Justice O. M. Lownds.* Doc. No. 25. Vol. III (1836-1837).

_____. *Report of the Joint Select Committee on the Subject of the Reorganization of the Police Department.* Doc. No. 88. Vol. III (1836-1837).

Board of Assistant Aldermen. *Communication from His Honor, the Mayor, Relative to the Late Riots, Etc., Accompanied with Two Proclamations, Issued by the Mayor, on the 11th and 12th of July, 1834.* Doc. No. 11, Vol. I (1834).

b) Ordinances

Laws and Ordinances, Made and Established by the Mayor, Aldermen & Commonalty of the City of New-York, in Common Council Convened, A.D. 1827.

A Digest of all the Laws and Ordinances, Made and Established by the Mayor, Aldermen & Commonalty, of the City of New-York, in Common Council Convened, Up to the First of January, 1830 (By a Student at Law).

Laws and Ordinances, Made and Established by the Mayor, Aldermen and Commonalty of the City of New-York, in Common Council Convened, A.D. 1833-1834.

By-Laws and Ordinances of the Mayor, Aldermen and Commonalty of the City of New York. Revised A.D. 1838-1839.

c) Court Records

Court of General Sessions. MS Minutes of the Proceedings, May 1819, July 1820, March 1821. Kept by Peter August Jay, Recorder of the City of New York. (New York Public Library.)

_____. MS Minutes of the Proceedings, April 1825. Kept by Alderman John Webb. (New York Public Library.)

New-York City Hall Recorder. 1816-1822.

Sawyer, Ray C., comp. and ed. Marriages Performed by the Various Mayors and Aldermen of the City of New York, As Well As Justices of the Peace, etc.: 1830-1854 (Typewritten, 1935, from the Original Books in the Office of the County Clerk [New-York Historical Society].)

Police Department File. (Museum of the City of New York.)

2. New York State

Assembly. *Journal.* 1835-1836.

_____. *Report of the Commissary-General to the Committee on the Militia and the Public Defence, in Relation to the Arsenal in the City of New-York.* Doc. 389, 57th sess., 1834.

Senate. *Journal.* 1836.

_____. *Report of the Select Committee on a Resolution Directing an Inquiry into the Propriety of Abolishing Public Executions.* Doc. 79, 58th sess. 1835.

Laws (1834-1839).

Laws of the State of New York, Relating Particularly to the City of New York (1833).

Secretary of State. *Census of the State of New York, for 1835; Containing an Enumeration of the Inhabitants of the State, with Other Statistical Information.* Albany: Printed by Croswell, Vanbenthuysen & Burt, 1836.

_____. *Census of the State of New York, for 1845. Containing an Enumeration of the Inhabitants of the State, with Other Statistical Information.* Albany: Carroll & Cook, Printers to the Legislature, 1846.

_____. *Census of the State of New York, for 1855.* Prepared from the original returns, under the direction of Hon. Joel T. Headley, Secretary of State, by Franklin B. Hough, Superintendent of the Census. Albany: Printed by C. Vanbenthuysen, 1857.

Twenty-seventh Regiment Artillery. Fourth Company. MS Orderly Book, 1828-1839. (New-York Historical Society.)

Twenty-seventh Regiment Artillery. Second Company. MS Minute Book, 1826-1839. (New-York Historical Society.)

3.   Outside New York State

Massachusetts. House of Representatives. *Report on the Abolition of Capital Punishment.* Doc. 4, 1837.

Purrington, Tobias. *Report on Capital Punishment Made to the Maine Legislature in 1836.* Boston: J. Wilson & Son, 1852.

U.S. Congress. *The Congressional Globe.* 23rd-24th Cong., 1833-1835.

U.S. Department of State. *Fifth Census: or Enumeration of the Inhabitants of the United States, 1830.* 2 vols. Washington, [D.C.]: Printed by D. Green, 1832.

C.   Diaries

1.   Published

Floy, Michael, Jr. *The Diary of Michael Floy, Jr., Bowery Village 1833-1837.* Edited by Richard A. E. Brooks. New Haven: Yale University Press, 1941.

Hone, Philip. *The Diary of Philip Hone, 1828-1851.* Edited by Allan Nevins. New and enl. ed. New York: Dodd, Mead & Co., 1936.

Strong, George Templeton. *The Diary of George Templeton Strong.* Vol. I: *Young Man in New York, 1835-1849.* Edited by Allan Nevins and Milton Halsey Thomas. New York: Macmillan, 1952.

2. Manuscript

William H. Bell Diary. (New-York Historical Society.)

Philip Hone Diary. (New-York Historical Society.)

Robert Hone Diary. (New-York Historical Society.)

Henry A. Patterson Diary. (New-York Historical Society.)

Robert Taylor Diary. (New-York Historical Society.)

D.   Memoirs and Reminiscences

Finney, Charles G. *Memoirs of Rev. Charles G. Finney.* New York: A. S. Barnes & Co., 1876.

Greeley, Horace. *Recollections of a Busy Life.* New ed. New York: n.p., 1873.

Haswell, Charles H. *Reminiscences of an Octogenarian of the City of New York (1816 to 1860).* New York: Harper & Bros., 1896

Kernan, J. Frank. *Reminiscences of the Old Fire Ladders and Volunteer Fire Departments of New York and Brooklyn. Together with a Complete History of the Paid Departments of Both Cities.* New York: M. Crane, 1885.

Sturtevant, John J. "Recollections of a Resident of New York City from 1835 to 1905." (Typewritten transcript, New York Public Library.)

Reminiscense of the Flour Riot in 1837. By one of the veterans. New York: n.p., n.d.

Spring, Gardiner. *Personal Reminiscences of the Life and Times of Gardiner Spring.* 2 vols. New York: C. Scribner & Co., 1866.

[Taylor, Asher.] *Recollections of the Early Days of the National Guard Comprising the Prominent Events in the History of the Famous Seventh Regiment, New York Militia, by an Ex-Orderly Sergeant.* New York: Bradstreet, 1868.

E.   Manuscript Collections

1. New York. New-York Historical Society

Stephen Allen Papers.

James W. Harper Letter File.

Miscellaneous MSS. Cornelius Lawrence Papers Pertaining to the July 1834 Riots.

Miscellaneous MSS. New York City Box 20. Letter, M. H. Mott, July 19, 1834.

Miscellaneous MSS V.   Gulian C. Verplanck to R. H. Wilde, March 24, 1834. Gulian C. Verplanck Papers.

        2.   Washington, D.C.   U.S. Library of Congress

Joshua Leavitt Papers.   Letter, Joshua Leavitt to his Parents, July 12, 1834.

Benjamin Tappan Papers.   Letter, Lewis Tappan to Benjamin Tappan, August 28, 1834.

Manuscript collections also listed under categories B., C., D., H., and I.

F.   **Public Addresses**

Baldwin, Moses. *The Ungodly Condemned in Judgment. A Sermon Preached at Springfield, December 13th 1770. On occasion of the Execution of William Shaw, for Murder.* New London, Conn.: Printed by T. Green, 1771.

Bancroft, Aaron. *The Importance of a Religious Education Illustrated and Enforced. A Sermon: Delivered at Worcester, October 31, 1793, Occasioned by the Execution of Samuel Frost, on That Day, for the Murder of Captain Elisha Allen, of Princeton, on the 16th Day of July, 1793.* Worcester, Mass.: Printed by Isaiah Thomas, 1793.

Bethune, George W[ashington]. *Our Liberties: Their Danger, and the Means of Preserving Them.* A Discourse. Philadelphia: George W. Mentz & Son; John C. Clark, Printer, 1835.

Broom, Jacob. *Oration Delivered on the 4th July, 1835, before the Union Literary and Debating Society. Washington, [D.C.]:* Printed by William Thompson, 1835.

Chauncy, Charles. *The Horrid Nature, and Enormous Guilt of MURDER. A SERMON Preached at the Thursday-Lecture in Boston, November 19th, 1754. The Day of the Execution of William Wieer, for the MURDER of William Onism.* Boston: Printed by Thomas Fleet, 1754.

Cunningham, A. F. *An Oration Delivered before the Trades Union of the District of Columbia, in the City of Washington, in the Baptist Church, on the Fourth of July, 1835.* Washington, [D.C.]: Printed by J. D. Learned & Co., 1835.

Fisher, Nathaniel. *A Sermon: Delivered at Salem, January 14, 1796, Occasioned by the Execution of Henry Blackbyrn, on that Day, for the Murder of George Williamson.* Boston: Printed by S. Hall for J. Dabney, 1796.

Goodrich, Samuel G[riswold]. *The Benefits of Industry: An Address Delivered before the Inhabitants of Jamaica Plain, July 4, 1835.* Boston: William D. Ticknor, 1835.

Hillard, George S[tillman]. *An Oration Pronounced before the Inhabitants of Boston, July the Fourth, 1835, in Commemoration of American Independence.* Boston: Press of John H. Eastburn, City Printer, 1835.

Hubbell, Levi. *Oration Delivered before the Young Men's Association of the City of Albany, at the First Presbyterian Church, July 4, 1835.* Albany: Printed by Hoffman & White, 1835.

Livingston, Edward. *Remarks on the Expediency of Abolishing the Punishment of Death.* Philadelphia: n.p., 1831.

Moses, Myer. *Oration, Delivered at Tammany Hall, on the Twelfth May, 1831, Being the Forty-Second Anniversary, of the Tammany Hall, or, Columbian Order.* New-York: P. Van Pelt, Printer, 1831.

Parson, Theophilus. *An Address Delivered before Phi Beta Kappa Society of Harvard University, 27 August 1835. On the Duties of Educated Men in a Republic.* Boston: n.p., 1835.

Remarks on Capital Punishment; to Which Are Added, Letters of Morris N. B. Hull, &c. Utica: Printed by William Williams, 1821.

Smith, J[erome] V[an] C[rowningshield]. *An Oration Delivered before the Inhabitants of South Boston, on Saturday, July 4, 1835, the Fifty-Ninth Anniversary of American Independence.* Boston: Russell, Odiorne & Co., D. Clapp, Jr., Printer, 1835.

Stevens, Thaddeus. *An Address Delivered on the Fourth of July, 1835, at an Anti-Masonic Celebration of the Anniversary of American Independence, Composed of About 2000 Substantial Citizens of Pennsylvania, in Pursuance of Invitations Given by Citizens of Pittsburgh, &c.* [Pitsburgh: n.p., 1835.]

Strong, Nathan. *A Sermon Preached in Hartford, June 10, 1797, at the Execution of Richard Doane, To Which is Added, a Short Account of His Life, As Given by Himself: Also of the State of His Mind During the Time of His Confinement , and His Death.* Hartford, Conn.: Printed by Elisha Babcock, 1797.

Thatcher, Thomas. *The Danger of Despising the Divine Counsel: Exhibited in a Discourse, Delivered at Dedham, Third Precinct, September 13, 1801, the Lord's Day after the Execution of Jason Fairbanks.* Dedham, Mass.: Printed by Hyman Mann, 1802.

Waterman, Elijah. *A Sermon, Preached at Windham, November 29th, 1803, Being the Day of the Execution of Caleb Adams, for the Murder of Oliver Woodworth. Also a Sketch of the Cicumstances of the Birth, Education, and Manner of Caleb's Life; with Practical Reflections, Delivered at the Place of Execution by Moses C. Welch. With an Appendix, Giving an Account of the Behavior of the Criminal at His Trial, during Confinement, and on the Day of Execution.* Windham, Conn.: Printed by John Byrne, 1803.

Williams, Joseph R. *An Oration Delivered before the Citizens of the Town of New Bedford, on the Fourth of July, 1835.* New Bedford, Mass.: J. G. W. Pope, 1835.

G. Directories, Guidebooks, Etc.

Doggett's New-York City Directory, 1844-1846.

[Greene, Asa.] *A Glance at New York: Embracing the City Government, Theatres, Hotels, Churches, Mobs, Monopolies, Learned Professions, Newspapers, Rogues, Dandies, Fires and Firemen, Water and Other Liquids, Etc., Etc. . . .* New York: A. Greene, 1837.

Hardie, James. *The Description of the City of New-York.* New-York: S. Marks, 1827.

Knapp, Samuel L[orenzo]. The Great American Metropolis, or Remarks Statistical, Historical, and Critical, upon the City of New-York. *New-York: A. Neal & Co., 1837.*

Longworth's American Almanac, New-York Register, and City Directory, 1827-1829; 1831-1833; 1836-1837.

New-York As It Is, in 1834; and Citizen's Advertising Directory. Containing a General Description of the City and Environs, Lists of Officers, Public Institutions, and Other Useful Information; for the Convenience of Citizens, as a Book of Reference, and a Guide to Strangers. New York: J. Disturnell, 1834.

New-York As It Is, in 1835; Containing a General Description of the City and Environs, List of Officers, Public Institutions, and Other Useful Information; for the Convenience of Citizens, As a Book of Reference, and a Guide to Strangers. New-York: J. Disturnell, 1835.

New-York As It Is, in 1837; Containing a General Description of the City of New-York, List of Officers, Public Institutions, and Other Useful Information. Including the Public Officers, &c. of the City of Brooklyn. New York: J. Disturnell, 1837.

New-York As It Is; Containing a General Description of the City of New-York, List of Officers, Public Institutions, and Other Useful Information: Including the Public Officers, &c. of the City of Brooklyn. New York: T. R. Tanner, 1840.

New-York Association for the Improvememt of the Condition of the Poor. *The Directory of the New-York Association for the Improvement of the Condition of the Poor.* New-York: John S. Taylor & Co., 1844.

The Picture of New-York, and Stranger's Guide through the Commercial Emporium of the United States. New York: Printed for and Published by A. T. Goodrich & Co., 1818.

H.   Other Writings of Contemporaries

1.   Reports of Private Organizations

American Anti-Slavery Society. *Annual Report.* New York: American Anti-Slavery Society, 1834.

American Anti-Slavery Society. *Second Annual Report.* New York: American Anti-Slavery Society, 1835.

Colonization Society of the City of New-York. *Fifth Annual Report with the Constitution of the Society.* New York: Mercein & Post's Press, 1837.

New-York Association for the Improvement of the Condition of the Poor. *Address to the Public; Constitution and By-Laws; and Visitor's Manual.* New-York: John S. Taylor & Co., 1844.

New-York Association for the Improvement of the Condition of the Poor. *First Annual Report for the Year 1845, with the Constitution, Visitor's Manual, and a List of Members.* New York: Printed by John F. Trow & Co., 1845.

New-York Anti-Slavery Society. *Address of the New-York City Anti-Slavery Society to the People of the City of New York.* New York: Printed by West & Trow, 1833.

New-York Young Men's Anti-Slavery Society. *Address of the New-York Young Men's Anti-Slavery Society, to Their Fellow Citizens.* New-York: W. T. Coollidge & Co., 1834.

    2.   Miscellaneous

Abdy, Edward Strutt. *Journal of a Residence and Tour in the United States of North America, from April, 1833, to October, 1834.* 3 vols. London: John Murray, 1835.

Baker, Benjamin A. *A Glance at New York.* [New York]: n.p., [ca. 1848].

Brothers, Thomas. *The United States of North America As They Are; Not As They Are Generally Described: Being a Cure for Radicalism.* London: Longman, 1840.

Byrdsall, Fitzwilliam. *The History of the Loco-foco, or Equal Rights Party, Its Movements, Conventions and Proceedings.* New York: Clement & Packard, 1842.

Daly, Charles P. *Historical Sketch of the Judicial Tribunals of New York from 1623 to 1846.* New York: J. W. Amerman, 1855.

Furman, Gabriel. "The Customs, Amusements, Style of Living and Manners of the People of the United States, from the First Settlement to the Present Time ca. 1844." (Manuscript. New-York Historical Society.)

Furman, Gabriel. "How New York City Used to Celebrate Independence Day: Gabriel Furman's Account, 1845." *New-York Historical Society Quarterly* 21 (July 1937): 93-96.

Furman, Gabriel. "Winter Amusements in New York in the Early Nineteenth Century, Written about 1830 by Gabriel Furman (1800-1854) of Brooklyn." *New-York Historical Society Quarterly* 23 (January 1939): 3-18.

New York (City). Committee of Safety: Apointed by the Public Meeting of Citizens, on the Subject of Fires. *Report of the Committee on the Subject of a Paid Fire Department.* In *Reports of Sub-Committees: Presented to the Committee of, Safety, February 15th, 1840.* [New York: n.p., 1840.]

Orangeism Exposed, with a Refutation of the Charges, &c. &c. Brought Against the Irish Nation, by Lawyer David Graham, of New-York, in his Defence of the Orangemen, Tried in This City, on the 13th and 14th Days of September, 1824, for Assault and Battery on a Poor Irishman by an Unbiased Irishman. New York: By the Author, 1824.

I. Biographical Sources

Bannan, Phyllis Mary. "Arthur and Lewis Tappan: A Study in New York Religious and Reform Movements." Ph.D. dissertation, Columbia University, 1950.

Crouthamel, James. *James Watson Webb: A Biography.* Middletown, Conn.: Wesleyan University Press, 1969.

Dictionary of American Biography. S. v. "Bennett, James Gordon," "Cox, Samuel Hanson," "Hale, David," "Hallock, Gerard," "Wilde, Richard Henry."

Dictionary of National Biography. S. v. "Edmund Kean."

[Fisher, William Logan. *An Account of the Fisher and Logan Families.* Wakefield, Penn.: n.p., 1839.]

Furer, Howard B. *William Frederick Havemeyer: A Political Biography.* New York: American Press, [1965].

Goldberg, Isaac. *Major Noah: American-Jewish Pioneer.* New York: Alfred A. Knopf, 1937.

Historical Records Survey. *Inventory of the Church Archives of New York City. Presbyterian Church in the United States of America.* New York: Historical Records Survey, 1940.

Hanyan, Craig, R. "De Witt Clinton and Partisanship: The Development of Clintonianism from 1811 to 1820." *New-York Historical Society Quarterly* 56 (April 1972): 109-31.

July, Robert W. *The Essential New Yorker: Gulian Crommelian Verplanck.* Durham, N. C.: Duke University Press, 1951.

Monaghan, Jay. *The Great Rascal: The Life and Adventures of Ned Buntline.* Boston: Little, Brown & Co., 1952.

O'Brien, Frank. *The Story of the Sun, New York: 1833-1928.* New. ed. New York: Greenwood Press, 1928.

Perkins, A[lice] J. G., and Wolfson, Theresa. *Frances Wright, Free Enquirer. The Study of a Temperament.* New York: Harper & Bros., 1939.

Pessen, Edward. "The Wealthiest New Yorkers of the Jacksonian Era: A New List." *New-York Historical Society Quarterly* 54 (April 1970): 145-72.

Pessen, Edward. "Who Governed the Nation's Cities in the 'Era of the Common Man?'" *Political Science Quarterly* 87 (December 1972): 591-614.

Rogers, Frank C., Jr. "Mike Walsh: A Voice of Protest." Master's thesis, Columbia University, 1950.

Roper, Donald M. "The Elite of the New York Bar as Seen from the Bench: James Kent's Necrologies." *New-York Historical Society Quarterly* 56 (July 1972): 199-237.

Simpson, Henry. "Redwood Fisher" in *The Lives of Eminent Philadelphians, Now Deceased. Collected from Original and Authentic Sources,* pp. 362-64. Philadelphia: William Brotherhood, 1859.

Stone, William L. *The Life and Times of Red Jacket, or Sa-Go-Ye-Wat-Ha, by the Late William L. Stone with a Memoir of the Author by His Son.* Albany: J. Munsell, 1866.

Daniel Ullman Papers. R[edwood] Fisher to Daniel Ullman, January 24, 1849. (New-York Historical Society.)

[Tappan, Lewis.] *The Life of Arthur Tappan.* New York: Hurd and Houghton, 1870.

Willis, Edmund P. "Social Origins of Political Leadership in New York City from the Revolution to 1815." Ph.D. dissertation, University of California, Berkeley, 1967.

Wyatt-Brown, Bertram. *Lewis Tappan and the Evangelical War against Slavery.* Cleveland: Press of Case Western Reserve University, 1969.

For biographical sources, see also category J.

J.   Other Secondary Sources

Alexander, S[amuel] D[avies]. *The Presbytery of New York, 1738-1888.* New York: A. D. F. Randolph & Co., 1887.

Allbee, Charles Allen. "The Abolition Movement in New York City, 1830-40." Master's thesis, New York University, 1961.

Asbury, Herbert. *All Around the Town.* New York: A. A. Knopf, 1934.

Asbury, Herbert. *The Gangs of New York: An Informal History of the Underworld.* New York: Alfred A. Knopf, 1937.

Asbury, Herbert. *Ye Olde Fire Laddies.* New York: A. A. Knopf, 1930.

Bailyn, Bernard. *The Origins of American Politics.* The Charles K. Colver Lecutres, Brown University, 1965. New York: Knopf, 1968.

Bartlett, John Russell. *Dictionary of Americanisms. A Glossary of Words and Phrases, Usually Regarded as Peculiar to the United States.* New York: Bartlett & Welford, 1848.

Billington, Ray Allen. *The Protestant Crusade, 1800-1860: A Study of the Origins of American Nativism.* New York: Macmillan Company, 1938; reprint ed., Chicago: Quadrangle Paperbacks, 1964.

Brown, T. Allston. *A History of the New York Stage: From the First Performance in 1732 to 1901.* 3 vols. New York: Dodd, Mead & Co., 1903.

Clark, Emmons. *History of the Second Company of the Seventh Regiment (National Guard) N. Y. S. Militia.* 1 vol. (vol. 2 not published). New York: J. G. Gregory, 1864.

Clark, Emmons. *History of the Seventh Regiment of New York 1806-1889.* 2 vols. New York: Seventh Regiment, 1890.

Clark, Emmons. "The New York Military." In *The Memorial History of the City of New-York: From Its First Settlement to the Year 1892,* vol. 4, chap. 9. Edited by James Grant Wilson. 4 vols. [New York]: New-York History Co., 1892-1893.

Cole, Arthur Harrison. *Wholesale Commodity Prices in the United States 1700-1861. Statistical Supplement: Actual Wholesale Prices of Various Commodities.* Cambridge: Harvard University Press, 1938.

Commons, John R.; Andrews, John B.; Hoagland, H. E.; Mittelman, E[dward] S.; Pearlman, Selig; Saposs, David J.; Sumner, Helen L. *History of Labor in the United States.* 4 vols. New York: Macmillan Company, 1921-1935.

[Costello, Augustine E.] *Our Firemen. A History of the New York Fire Departments. Volunteer and Paid.* New York: Knickerbocker Book Pub. Co., 1888.

Costello, Augustine E. *Our Police Protectors. History of the New York Police from the Earliest Period to the Present Time. Published for the Benefit of the Police Pension Fund.* [New York: C. F. Roper & Co.], 1885.

Danforth, Brian J. "The Influence of Socioeconomic Factors upon Political Behavior: A Qualitative Look at New York City Merchants, 1828-1844." Ph.D. dissertation, New York University, 1974.

Davis, David Brion. *Homicide in American Fiction, 1789-1860: A Study in Social Values.* Ithaca, N. Y.: Cornell University Press, 1957.

Dayton, Abram C. *Last Days of Knickerbocker Life in New York.* New York: G. P. Putnam's Sons, 1897.

Ernst, Robert. *Immigrant Life in New York City: 1825-1863.* Empire State Historical Publications, 37. New York: King's Crown Press, Columbia University, 1949; reprint ed., Port Washington, N. Y.: Ira J. Friedman, Inc., 1965.

Filler, Louis. *The Crusade against Slavery: 1830-1860.* The New American Nation Series. New York: Harper & Bros., 1960; reprint ed., New York: Harper Torchbooks, 1963.

Fishbane, Irene S. "The History of the Mayoralty of New York City, 1800-1834." Master's thesis, New York University, 1949.

Fischer, David Hackett. *The Revolution in American Conservatism: The Federalist Party in the Era of Jeffersonian Democracy*. Harper Torchbook ed. New York: Harper & Row, 1965.

Frontiers in Human Welfare: The Story of a Hundred Years of Service to the Community of New York, 1848-1948. [New York]: Community Service Society of New York, 1948.

Geffen, Elizabeth M. "Violence in Philadelphia in the 1840's and 1850's." *Pennsylvania History* 36 (October 1969): 381-410.

Gilchrist, David T., ed. *The Growth of the Seaport Cities, 1790-1825*. Proceedings of a Conference Sponsored by the Eleutherian Mills--Hagley Foundation, March 17-19, 1966. Charlottesville, Va.: The University Press of Virginia, 1967.

Ginsberg, Stephen A. "The History of Fire Protection in New York City, 1800-1842." Ph.D. dissertation. New York University, 1968.

Grimsted, David. *Melodrama Unveiled: American Theater and Culture 1800-1850*. Chicago: University of Chicago Press, 1968.

Grimsted, David. "Rioting in Its Jacksonian Setting." *American Historical Review* 77 (April 1972): 361-97.

Hammett, Theodore M. "Two Mobs of Jacksonian Boston: Ideology and Interest." *Journal of American History* 62 (March 1976): 845-68.

Harlow, Alvin F. *Old Bowery Days: The Chronicles of a Famous Street*. New York: Appleton and Co., 1931.

Headley, Joel T. *The Great Riots of New York, 1712 to 1873*. New York: E. B. Treat, 1873.

Heale, M. J. "From City Fathers to Social Critics: Humanitarianism and Government in New York, 1790-1860." *Journal of American History* 63 (June 1976): 21-41.

Hershkowitz, Leo. "The Loco-Foco Party of New York: Its Origins and Career, 1835-1837." *New-York Historical Society Quarterly* 56 (July 1962): 305-29.

Hershkowitz, Leo. "The Native American Democratic Association in New York City, 1835-1836." *New-York Historical Society Quarterly* 46 (January 1962): 41-60.

Hershkowitz, Leo. "New York City, 1834 to 1840; A Study in Local Politics." Ph.D. dissertation, New York University, 1960.

Hicks, Hattie G. "The Beginnings of American Urban Life: New York in 1822." Master's thesis, University of Wisconsin, 1923.

Hofstadter, Richard. *The Idea of a Party System: The Rise of Legitimate Opposition in the United States, 1780-1840*. Jefferson Memorial Lectures. Berkeley, Cal.: University of California Press, 1970.

Hofstadter, Richard and Wallace, Michael, eds. *American Violence: A Documentary History.* New York: A. A. Knopf, 1970.

Hugins, Walter. *Jacksonian Democracy and the Working Class: A Study of the New York Workingmen's Movement, 1829-1837.* Stanford Studies in History, Economics, and Political Science, 19. Stanford, Cal.: Stanford University Press, 1960.

Kerber, Linda K. "Abolitionists and Amalgamators: The New York City Race Riots of 1834." *New York History* 48 (January 1967): 28-40.

Leonard, Ira M. "New York City Politics, 1841 to 1844: Nativism and Reform." Ph.D. dissertation, New York University, 1965.

Leonard, Ira M. "The Rise and Fall of the American Republican Party in New York City, 1843-1845." *New-York Historical Society Quarterly* 50 (April 1966): 151-92.

Limpus, Lowell M. *History of the New York Fire Department.* New York: E. P. Dutton & Co., Inc., 1940.

Lossing, Benson J. *History of New York City Embracing an Outline Sketch of Events from 1609 to 1830, and a Full Account of its Development from 1830 to 1884.* 2 vols New York: Perime Engraving & Publishing Co., [1884].

Lubove, Roy. "The New York Association for Improving the Condition of the Poor: The Formative Years." *New-York Historical Society Quarterly* 43 (July 1959): 307-27.

Lubove, Roy. *The Professional Altruist. The Emergence of Social Work As a Career. 1880-1930.* Cambridge: Harvard University Press, 1965.

McCormick, Richard P. *The Second American Party System: Party Formation in the Jacksonian Era.* Chapel Hill: University of North Carolina Press, 1966.

Maier, Pauline. "Popular Uprising and Civil Authority in Eighteenth-Century America." *William and Mary Quarterly* 3rd series, 27 (January 1970): 3-35.

Marshall, Lynn L. "The Strange Stillbirth of the Whig Party." *American Historical Review* 72 (January 1967): 445-68.

Mathews, Mitford M., ed. *Dictionary of Americanisms.* 2 vols. Chicago: University of Chicago Press, 1951.

Mohl, Raymond A. *Poverty in New York: 1783-1825.* The Urban Life in America Series. New York: Oxford University Press, 1971.

Moss, Frank. *The American Metropolis From Knickerbocker Days to the Present Time: New York City Life in All Its Phases.* 3 vols. New York: P. F. Collier, 1897.

Murray, Andrew E. *Presbyterians and the Negro—A History.* Philadelphia: Pesbyterian Historical Society, 1966.

Mushkat, Jerome. *Tammany: The Evolution of a Political Machine 1789-1865.* Syracuse, N. Y.: Syracuse University Press, 1971.

Myers, Gustavus. *The History of Tammany Hall.* 2nd ed. rev. and enl. New York: Boni & Liveright, Inc., 1917.

Odell, George C. D. *Annals of the New York Stage.* 15 vols. New York: Columbia University Press, 1927-1949.

Pessen, Edward. "Jacksonian America: Society, Personality, and Politics. *Homewood, Ill.: Dorsey Press, 1969.*

Phillips, George Lewis. *American Chimney Sweeps: An Historical Account of a Once Important Trade.* Trenton, N. J.: The Past Time Press, 1957.

Pocock, J. G. A. "The Classical Theory of Deference." *American Historical Review* 81 (June 1976): 516-23.

Pomerantz, Sidney I. *New York: An American City, 1783-1803: A Study of Urban Life.* Studies in History, Economics and Public Law, no. 442. New York: Columbia University Press, 1938.

Quillen, Isaac James. "A History of 'The Five Points,' New York City, to 1890." Master's thesis, Yale University, 1932.

Ratner, Lorman. "Northern Concern for Social Order as Cause for Rejecting Anti-Slavery, 1831-1840." *Historian* 28 (November 1965): 1-18.

Rayback, Joseph G. *A History of American Labor.* Expanded and updated ed. New York: The Free Press, 1966.

Richards, Leonard L. *"Gentlemen of Property and Standing:" Anti-Abolition Riots in Jacksonian America.* New York: Oxford University Press, 1970.

Richardson, James F. *The New York Police: Colonial Times to 1901.* The Urban Life in America Series. New York: Oxford University Press, 1970.

Rock, Howard B. "The Independent Mechanic: The Tradesmen of New York City in Labor and Politics during the Jeffersonian Era." Ph.D. dissertation, New York University, 1974.

Rosenburg, Carroll Smith. *Religion and the Rise of the American City: The New York City Mission Movement, 1812-1870.* Ithaca, N. Y.: Cornell University Press, 1971.

Rosenwaike, Ira. *Population History of New York City.* [Syracuse, N.Y.]: Syracuse University Press, 1972.

Schlesinger, Arthur M., Jr. *The Age of Jackson.* Boston: Little, Brown, 1945.

Schnieder, David M. *The History of Public Welfare in New York State, 1609-1866.* Chicago: University of Chicago Press, 1938.

Schnieder, John Charles. "Mob Violence and Public Order in the American City, 1830-1865." Ph.D. dissertation, University of Minnesota, 1971.

Scisco, Louis Dow. *Political Nativism in New York State.* Studies in History, Economics and Public Law, vol. 13, no. 2. New York: The Columbia University Press, 1901.

Sheldon, George W. *The Story of the Volunteer Fire Department of the City of New York.* New York: Harper & Bros., 1882.

Still, Bayrd. "Patterns of Mid-Nineteenth Century Urbanization in the Middle West." *Mississippi Valley Historical Review* 28 (September 1941): 187-206.

Stokes, I. N. Phelps. *The Iconography of Manhattan Island, 1498-1909, Compiled from Original Sources and Illustrated by Photo-Intaglio Reproductions of Important Maps, Plans, Views and Documents in Public and Private Collections.* 6 vols. New York: Robert H. Dodd, 1915-1928.

Stone, William L. *History of New York City from the Discovery to the Present Day.* New York: Virtue & Yorston, 1872.

Tabachnik, Leonard. "Irish and German Immigrant Settlement in New York City, 1815-28." Master's thesis, Columbia University, 1960.

Taylor, George Rogers. *The Transportation Revolution: 1815-1860.* New York: Holt, Rinehart & Winston, 1951.

Teeters, Negley K., and Hedblom, Jack H. ". . .*Hang by the Neck. . .:" The Legal Use of Scaffold, and Noose, Gibbett, Stake, and Firing Squad from Colonial Times to the Present.* Springfield, Ill.: Charles C. Thomas, 1967.

Thornton, Richard H. *American Glossary; Being an Attempt to Illustrate Certain Americanisms upon Historical Principles.* Expanded 3 vol. ed. New York: Frederick Ungar Publishing Co., 1962.

Tilly, Charles, and Rule, James. *Measuring Political Upheaval.* Center of International Studies, Princeton University, research monograph no. 19. Princeton: Center of International Studies, Woodrow Wilson School of Public and International Affairs, Princeton University, 1965.

Wall, Alexander, J., Jr. "The Great Fire of 1835." *New-York Historical Society Quarterly* 20 (January 1936): 3-22.

Wallace, Michael. "Changing Concepts of Party in the United States: New York, 1815-1828." *American Historical Review* 73 (December 1968): 453-91.

Wallace, Michael. "The Ideology of Party in the Age of Jackson." Ph.D. dissertation, Columbia University, 1973.

Ward, David. *Cities and Immigrants: A Geography of Change in Nineteenth-Century America.* New York: Oxford University Press, 1971.

Watson, Frank Dekker. *The Charity Organization Movement in the United States: A Study in American Philanthropy.* New York: Macmillan Co., 1922.

Young, Alfred. "The Mechanics and the Jeffersonians, 1789-1801." *Labor History* 5 (Fall 1964): 247-76.

INDEX